PRAISE FOR *DO BIGGER THINGS*

"*Do Bigger Things* inspires us to dream bigger, think broader, and pursue audacious opportunities. If you're a big-picture visionary thinker seeking a more powerful approach to innovation, this is the book you've been waiting for."

—**BARRY O'REILLY,** *New York Times* best-selling author of *Unlearn*

"Resistance pushes us to do small work. Perhaps it's time to realize just how much agency we have and to commit to work worth doing instead."

—**SETH GODIN,** author of *The Practice*

"Required reading for anyone who wants to claim disruptive opportunities or shape powerful solutions."

—**MARK JOHNSON,** cofounder of Innosight and author of *Lead from the Future*

"What do launching a dynamic company, responding to a Himalayan disaster, and putting together a community-based musical have in common? They all require ecosystem innovation. Dan McClure and Jennifer Wilde provide the practical and inspiring playbook for mobilizing this powerful form of innovation to build a better future."

—**RICHARD FLORIDA,** author of *The Rise of the Creative Class*

"I loved the book—it made me want to do bigger things! For those who know that the change they want to see in the world requires a whole new ecosystem change, *Do Bigger Things* gives you the essential tools to bring it all together and succeed."

—**KASSIA ECHAVARRI-QUEEN,** director of community investment at the Wikimedia Foundation

DO BIGGER THINGS

DAN MCCLURE
AND JENNIFER WILDE

DO BIGGER THINGS

A Practical Guide to Powerful Innovation in a Changing World

FAST
COMPANY
Press

This publication is designed to provide accurate and authoritative information in regard to the subject matter covered. It is sold with the understanding that the publisher and author are not engaged in rendering legal, accounting, or other professional services. Nothing herein shall create an attorney-client relationship, and nothing herein shall constitute legal advice or a solicitation to offer legal advice. If legal advice or other expert assistance is required, the services of a competent professional should be sought.

Fast Company Press
New York, New York
www.fastcompanypress.com

Distributed by Greenleaf Book Group

For ordering information or special discounts for bulk purchases, please contact Greenleaf Book Group at PO Box 91869, Austin, TX 78709, 512.891.6100.

Design and composition by Greenleaf Book Group
Cover design by Greenleaf Book Group

Publisher's Cataloging-in-Publication data is available.

Print ISBN: 978-1-63908-069-4

eBook ISBN: 978-1-63908-070-0

To offset the number of trees consumed in the printing of our books, Greenleaf donates a portion of the proceeds from each printing to the Arbor Day Foundation. Greenleaf Book Group has replaced over 50,000 trees since 2007.

Printed in the United States of America on acid-free paper

24 25 26 27 28 29 30 31 10 9 8 7 6 5 4 3 2 1

First Edition

CONTENTS

List of Figures and Tables ix

Foreword by Jim Highsmith xi

Introduction 1

Part I: The Possibilities 13

1 Taking on Big Challenges 15

2 What Is Ecosystem Innovation? 31

3 The Five Sources of Power 45

4 The Innovation Practice Space 63

Part II: The People 81

5 The Choreographers 83

6 What It Takes to Be Successful 103

Part III: The Practice 117

7 Set an Ambitious Goal 121

8 Understand the Challenges and Opportunities 139

9 Design the Future 161

10 Plan to Implement the Future 185

11 Build the Future 209

Conclusion: Rising to the Challenge 227

Notes 233

About the Authors 249

FIGURES AND TABLES

FIGURES

I.1. The amazing creative ecosystem behind a small-town musical . . . 3
1.1. Piecemeal solutions to a complex challenge . . . 17
1.2. The Aravind Eye Care treatment ecosystem . . . 19
1.3. Gillette and Schick's retail-based ecosystem . . . 21
1.4. Dollar Shave Club's disruptive ecosystem . . . 23
1.5. Solar Sister's ecosystem, enabling electricity access and women's entrepreneurship . . . 27
2.1. The diverse parts of a bakery's ecosystem . . . 32
3.1. Five sources of power in ecosystem innovation . . . 45
3.2. Connecting technology like Legos in an ecosystem . . . 50
3.3. Airbnb's ecosystem, built from diverse blocks . . . 53
3.4. Positive feedback loops naturally drive growth in the Airbnb travel ecosystem . . . 58
4.1. Agile pilots and products—quickly exploring new spaces . . . 67
4.2. Reductionist innovation—tightly planned waterfall project delivery . . . 72
4.3. Incremental optimization—measure and test new ideas . . . 77
4.4. A variety of approaches to innovation—different tools for different jobs . . . 79
5.1. Creative roles emerge with each new innovation practice . . . 87
6.1. Having most of an ecosystem isn't enough—you can't leave pieces out . . . 107
III.1. The ecosystem innovation journey . . . 118

7.1. Freedom without direction leads to energetic but unaligned action . . . 125
7.2. Goals and guardrails work together to define the playing field for the innovation . . . 132
8.1. The ecosystem for international vaccine delivery has many parts . . . 140
8.2. Starting an ecosystem map . . . 151
8.3. Expanding the ecosystem surrounding childhood nutrition . . . 153
9.1. Fragmented innovations seldom lead to big solutions . . . 164
9.2. Current versus future ecosystem . . . 165
9.3. An initial future ecosystem for electric vehicles . . . 169
9.4. Making the future ecosystem of EVs more complete . . . 171
9.5. Future ecosystem for EV-based transportation . . . 175
9.6. Reimaging the EV future ecosystem by adding self-driving cars . . . 179
9.7. Feedback loop: more production drives cheaper EV cars, which drives more sales . . . 180
10.1. Future ecosystem for Irina's international tutoring innovation . . . 192
10.2. A thin slice to test ideas . . . 196
10.3. Evolving the future ecosystem with a series of thin slices . . . 202
11.1. The act-learn-adapt cycle manages risk in messy environments . . . 214
11.2. You can adapt everything from small details to the future ecosystem design . . . 217

TABLES

10.1. Irina's Tutoring: major thin slices . . . 204
11.1. The three types of ecosystem building measurement . . . 224

FOREWORD

Six decades ago, transistors were the size of a pencil eraser, and today, five billion fit on a microchip. Computing power that automated routine accounting functions in early years can now drive your car in a rainstorm. New technologies seem to emerge daily, such as the one that enabled Pfizer and Moderna to rapidly develop a vaccine for COVID-19.

It's easy to be fascinated by these bright and shiny inventions, but what about transformations in thinking about innovation itself? Over the years, the practice of innovation has been reimagined multiple times.

One of those revolutions came from software engineers—specifically seventeen individuals (including me) who gathered at the Snowbird Ski Resort in Utah in February 2001. From this meeting emerged "The Manifesto for Agile Software Development," a document that helped change how people thought about creating the future. We challenged the prescriptive belief that teams and executives could forecast the details of every challenge, that they could "plan the work and work the plan," and that any deviations from the plans were mistakes.

This agile practice was widely embraced by technologists and innovators around the world, but it required an entirely different mindset—one that was scary to traditionists. Detailed plans were replaced by short, iterative work cycles that could change as reality dictated. We freed ourselves to innovate differently.

Today, as the world becomes more complex, as events cascade into each other faster and faster, and as uncertainty about the future increases, how we think about innovation must continue to evolve. Wicked problems confront both our organizations and our world—climate change, pandemic aftermath, social inequality, and disruptions in almost every industry demand ambitious new innovations.

In this book, Dan McClure and Jennifer Wilde usher in another timely revolution in innovation thinking. They lay out how to use the method of ecosystem innovation to assemble people, organizations, and technology into systems that tackle hard challenges and claim big opportunities. "Ecosystem innovation is simply about assembling Lego blocks drawn from the world around us," Dan and Jennifer tell us when explaining this practical approach. "Essentially, you are building an ecosystem that works in the real world."

Do Bigger Things is written in such an easygoing, conversational, story-enhanced style, it is easy to get caught up in the narrative, but at some point, you are likely stop and reflect on what you have read and think, "Wow, this is really important stuff!"

Whether you are looking to respond to a disruptive business competitor, make an impact on big social issues, or build a startup that draws on the talents of global collaborators, you will find in this book an engaging and realistic approach for addressing these exciting challenges.

Jim Highsmith
Agile manifesto signatory, author, and storyteller

INTRODUCTION

> Make no little plans; they have no magic to stir men's blood and probably themselves will not be realized. Make big plans; aim high in hope and work.
>
> **—Daniel Burnham**[1]

Do you want to do big things that matter, claim ambitious challenges and new opportunities, save the business, create incredible innovations, or build something new that changes the game? In today's world of fast-moving change, we see and work with energized people who are taking on and succeeding with these bigger challenges. There are many different journeys to this work, but those who are delivering some of today's most impactful ideas in business and the world are practicing a powerful, but perhaps unfamiliar, approach to innovation and change. It's called *ecosystem innovation*, and in the chapters that follow, we explore the concepts of this powerful approach to doing bigger things and how you can take advantage of it.

But first, to see how we got here, let's rewind the clock forty years and meet Dan McClure. He was a six-foot-three, gangly teenager weighing under 175 pounds when he walked into the backstage of a theater for the first time. For the next three months, he'd spend his afternoons there as part of an annual effort to stage a small-town musical. Of course, there are countless stories and films about this creative rite of passage—the challenge of mastering parts, overcoming stage fright, and the chance to discover hidden talents. But for Dan, this was a different kind of revelation. He saw how big things could be created, seemingly out of nothing. It showed him a way of creating that would ultimately be repeated over and over in his lifelong profession as a different kind of innovator.

Forget for a moment all the drama class stories you've heard and instead step back to think about what an amazing thing a working stage production is. There are actors who each learn individual parts and then for two hours weave their paths across the stage. But they aren't alone. In the orchestra pit musicians perform from different parts of a score, led by a conductor whose job is to blend those performances together. And unseen—on catwalks suspended high above the stage—are the lighting crew who apply technology to the performance.

In the days leading up to the show, costumers sew clothing, and set designers build a wood-and-canvas city of backdrops, while outside the theater, staff promote the performance and sell tickets. In an unseen office, someone is paying the bills and handling the red tape. None of these people are professionals in theater; they all come together just this one time each year. And yet, in just a few short weeks, ushers are welcoming in a new crowd of participants, an audience of a thousand people a night.

Finally, rather miraculously, the show goes on. Stagehands move props and furniture on and off the stage in a choreographed dance while scenes are performed. And then afterward, volunteers help clean up and set the stage for the next night (as shown in Figure I.1).

All this happened in a Midwest factory town, inside a commonplace high school auditorium. And yet the amazingly complex web of different talents, tasks, and resources was seamlessly woven together to create an exciting performance.

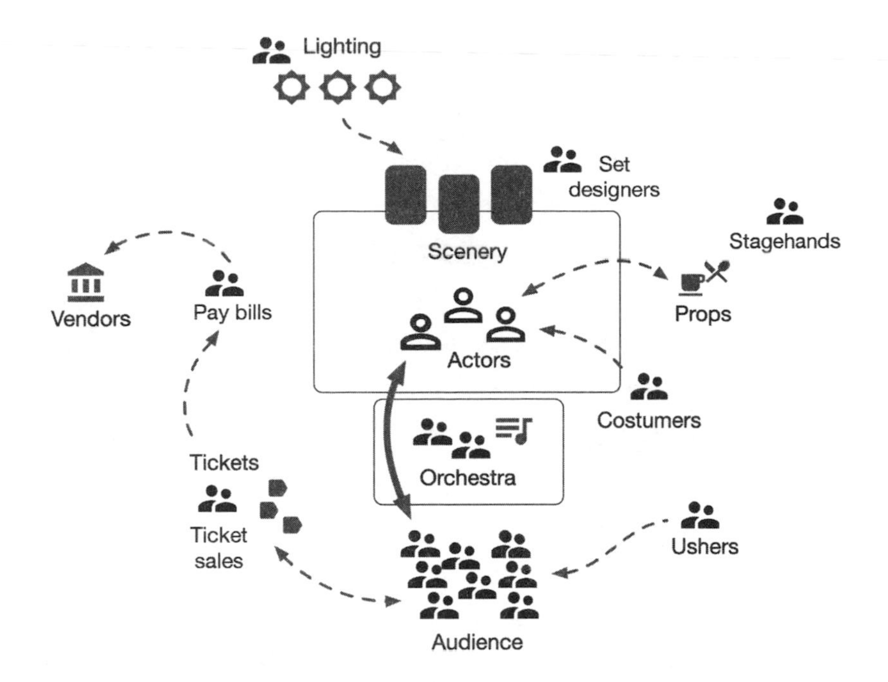

Figure I.1. The amazing creative ecosystem behind a small-town musical

Dan was gobsmacked, struck by the fact that in under a dozen weeks so many varied talents were applied and somehow everything came together on stage. In the beginning nothing was there, and then the pieces were suddenly connected in a collaboration that was enthusiastically applauded by the audience every single night.

How was it possible for a small town in the midwestern United States to do something that popped and strutted with such energy, when so many other things that need doing in life seem so hard? What was it that enabled so many individuals—each with different skills and different passions—to merge their efforts to deliver a shared, complex result in such a short period of time?

This experience laid the foundation for a decades-long career helping people embrace big challenges. Dan partnered with global companies who wanted to thrive in the disruption of a changing world, and supported entrepreneurs pursuing bold ideas to succeed. He's even been a successful entrepreneur himself, the founder of a fast-growing company that made public sector organizations more nimble. Surprisingly, at the heart of all these opportunities were the same principles that made it possible to weave together a high school musical.

Decades later, on the other side of the world, Jenny Wilde was applying the same concepts, doing big things in a critically demanding and life-threatening situation. On April 25, 2015, a few minutes before noon, a 7.8 magnitude earthquake struck Nepal, with an epicenter about fifty miles northwest of the country's capital of Kathmandu. The words *devastating* and *tragic* fail to capture the tremendously destructive effects of this earthquake and the hundreds of aftershocks that followed. All told, approximately 9,000 people died, 23,000 were injured, more than 500,000 homes were destroyed, and another 270,000 were damaged. The earthquake was so powerful that it pushed Mt. Everest three centimeters to the southwest.[2]

Jenny's job was to lead crisis response teams for an international aid organization, supporting communities in devastated cities and towns, as they worked to respond to the urgent challenges of the crisis and then to rebuild their lives. Every response in the aftermath of a natural disaster is different and difficult. In Nepal the damage wasn't limited only to the major cities. The earthquake also affected remote villages deep in the Himalayas, which could be five or ten, or even more, days on foot from the nearest road.

Some of the areas hit disappeared under rockslides, while others sustained losses of houses, buildings, water systems, electric power generation, health clinics, and so much more. These were big, messy challenges with few straightforward solutions. Any effective action required lots of people, organizations, and resources to come together—even as the challenges were unfolding and changing in real time.

Jenny saw this as a place where impactful innovations could make a real difference in people's lives. New solutions could matter, but they would have to be developed quickly and genuinely address the complex challenges people faced. What wasn't needed was another cool mobile app, or other throwaway innovation, adding to what one senior aid leader disdainfully described as digital litter.

Working with other similarly minded colleagues, Jenny's team found funding for what would be known as the Nepal Innovation Lab. The lab was set up in Kathmandu, where challenges of the crisis were right outside their front door. It was conceived as a place where people with diverse talent and knowledge could come together to deal with the crisis in Nepal. This included heads of United Nations (UN) agencies and local innovators, those affected by the earthquake, mixed with Harvard graduates and specialists from organizations from around the world—all working together on hard, messy challenges.

Out of the lab came multiple innovations that grew to global scale. For example, an innovative way of rebuilding infrastructure moved into seventeen countries and over $1 billion (USD) worth of projects in just a few years.

While the lab's work could hardly be more different from putting together a high school musical, there was at its heart a shared view of what it takes to make big things happen. Both those putting on the high school musical and those working on humanitarian challenges in the lab needed to move quickly, creating innovation and change that had many parts, and intentionally bringing together diverse people, ideas, and resources.

Later that year, we (Jenny and Dan) met for the first time at a UN conference on innovation hosted at the University of California, Berkeley. By then Dan had moved beyond being part of a lighting crew in a community musical to holding the position of innovation lead for a large global innovation and technology consultancy. It didn't take long before we found a corner table in a coffee shop and started sketching out a vision for Response Innovation Labs, affectionately known as RIL, a global system of labs that could extend the impact of what was happening in Nepal.

Jenny then took these ideas, using the big vision to garner support from organizations around the world. In just a few months, she was able to assemble a formal collaboration with international aid organizations, including Save the Children, Oxfam, and World Vision. While other innovation lab initiatives—including some high-profile programs with big, top-down support—stumbled and failed, RIL quickly grew. In its first two years, RIL programs were set up in five countries and supported by thirteen global funders. From Somalia to Iraq, RIL has intentionally taken on messy challenges by stepping back and seeing a big picture view of problems and then assembling innovative collaborations that matter to real people's lives.

THE POWER OF ECOSYSTEM INNOVATION

> It's my vision against chaos. Why let chaos win?
>
> **—Twyla Tharp**[3]

It might not seem that a midwestern high school musical and a Nepalese community in the middle of a natural disaster should have much in common. And yet, in each case, there was an opportunity to do something new in a different way—a way that assembled ideas, resources, and capabilities to take on a messy challenge. This is the heart of *ecosystem innovation*, a practice that builds an ecosystem of different actors and resources that all work together to achieve a goal. It's a lot like putting together Lego blocks, but where the world around you provides the Lego pieces you need to create powerful new innovations. This is what many leaders today are doing to thrive in a changing world.

You might be asking yourself, "Is this innovation?" For many people, innovation is about invention, such as when Thomas Edison methodically tested thousands of lightbulbs in his Menlo Park lab. Or if you've recently taken an innovation course, you might think of innovation as agile, user-centered product design, Silicon Valley's way of developing better apps. It's true that many innovators work this way, but unfortunately, neither of these approaches is particularly good at dealing with the messy challenges many of us face in the world today.

We live in an amazing moment of human history full of big challenges and opportunities. It's obvious that problems like climate change or persistent poverty aren't going to be addressed with just another new mobile app, or by fine-tuning the operation of the status quo. Likewise, individual companies face ever-faster and deeper disruption in their industries. If organizational leaders simply try to incrementally improve performance, slowly optimizing products and operations, they won't deliver the level of change and reinvention that's needed for success. A grim end is the most likely outcome.

Today, the world is filled with problems and opportunities that need ambitious solutions and fast action. Is there a time where you have seen the power of a system? One that can radically change the status quo? Have you ever wanted to tap the power of a good system? Or imagined new ways of working that break from the status quo?

If you're going to step up to these kinds of challenges, you need a way to intentionally take on complex and messy problems in a rapidly changing world. This is what ecosystem innovation does best. It provides tools and practices that make it possible for you to be among those who embrace real-world creative challenges and do bigger things.

So often we meet people who are stuck, perhaps in a business losing market share, or one that just can't seem to make the leap into new opportunities. People who are not sure what to do next, not sure why projects haven't seemed to work. They are lost in the gray areas of hard challenges. The concepts and practices in this book allow you to confidently chart a new, more sophisticated direction. You can pursue game-changing ideas and more strategic moves forward that get you out of that gray area. If you aspire to do more than incremental change or follow someone else's instruction manual of best practices, the ideas in this book can open the door to ambitious opportunities, doing bigger things where others get stuck.

Ecosystem innovation has this power because it allows you to leverage the complexity and messiness of our world today. Whether it is technology shifts, shifts in the market, or just trying to solve problems, these tools help see the bigger picture of what's going on. They allow you to work in a fast-changing world and see new opportunities. Rather than just playing the part you have been given, or nibbling around the edges of change, you get to change the rules of the game, dodge barriers and bureaucracy, and create new ways for the world to work.

THE OPPORTUNITY TO DO BIGGER THINGS

> As the economist Paul Romer has said, the big advances in standards of living—not to mention the big competitive advantages in the marketplace—have always come from "better recipes, not just more cooking."
>
> **—Richard Florida**[4]

Unfortunately, to date, much of the writing about ecosystem innovation has been academic or abstract, making it difficult to take the ideas from the page and put them into practice. Our goal is for this book to be anything but that.

The practices we detail in the pages you are about to read have grown up piece by piece from hands-on ecosystem innovation work done within big companies, government agencies, nonprofits, family businesses, and startups—all organizations we have worked for, consulted with, and coached. In this book, we capture these experiences and put them into a clear set of practices that you can use on real problems.

Ideally, this book will serve as an accessible guide for both the thinking and the practice of ecosystem innovation. To help you along the way, we've organized the book into three parts:

- *Part I: The Possibilities.* How can you thrive in an ever-changing, complex world? Here you'll explore the new role of innovation and how ecosystem innovation's powerful tools take on important challenges and make it possible to do bigger things.
- *Part II: The People.* This powerful approach creates the need for a new role, the *choreographer*, who applies big-picture thinking, builds connections, and does some rule-breaking in the service of tackling important challenges.
- *Part III: The Practice.* Here we present a practical, step-by-step method to change the way the world works by innovating ecosystems. This method works equally well whether it's used for reimagining a small business, reinventing an industry, or responding to a global challenge.

There are really no limits on the kinds of problems and opportunities you can address with the ideas in this book. As you'll soon see, we haven't limited ourselves to just one business domain. The ideas in this book come from strategic challenges in fields as diverse as manufacturing, international aid, retail, education, medicine, energy, agriculture, and hospitality. The common thread is a different approach to innovation—one that can change initiatives you're working on, drive new strategies for your organization, and even affect who you choose to hire for your team.

THE COOL THINGS YOU GET TO DO

When you take on important challenges with ecosystem innovation, you get opportunities to do really exciting work and deliver meaningful impact. We can tell you from our own experience that this is an amazing job. Consider the wide range of projects we've had the chance to dive into over the last couple of years:

- *Succeeding on hard problems.* Design innovative new collaborations between government, local organizations, and businesses to address tough problems like preparing for hurricanes in the Caribbean and getting reliable health information out to everyone across Mongolia—challenges that no one organization could tackle alone.
- *Untangling big enterprises.* Help Fortune 10 company executives put their arms around the multibillion-dollar challenges in their core operations.
- *Thriving in disruption.* Work with venerable organizations whose long-term success is threatened by new competitors, helping their leaders transform their organizations and claim a new place in their industry.
- *Rising to global challenges.* Support sophisticated efforts to target climate change investments that shift how energy, transportation, and agriculture systems work in huge economies like India, China, and the United States.
- *Supporting next-generation innovators.* In organizations ranging from international law enforcement to global aid, set up next-generation enterprise innovation programs that use new techniques to foster bold, high-impact ideas and people.
- *Enabling high-impact startups.* Support ambitious startup innovators who work on urgent challenges, such as delivering job opportunities to teens, improving the operation of refugee camps, and bringing solar energy to communities across the globe.

YOU SHOULD BE BUILDING THE FUTURE

> Every company today harbors people who view their job as their life's work. . . . Solutions occupy their waking and sleeping moments.
>
> **—Jim Taylor and Watts Wacker**[5]

This is a time where it makes sense to feel excitement and fear at the same moment. Humans have never been able to do more. Our ability to imagine incredible things and act on ideas is unprecedented. But to address the challenges we all face, you must *act boldly*. The cost of failing to act—whether it's a small business, a global enterprise, or an entire country—is also unprecedented. Big opportunities come with big risks for those who choose not to rise to the challenge.

We are not asking you to be a naïve idealist. Quite the opposite. At the heart of rising to urgent challenges is being a well-grounded realist and understanding the problems and opportunities you face. Ecosystem innovation is really about empowering *you* to act on your dreams in a world filled with ever-changing opportunities. The rags-to-riches stories of entrepreneurs who reinvent industries or solve global challenges are not magic. They are people who set big goals and then work hard with the right kinds of practices and methods to shape the world they imagine.

Our own big goal is to change the world by creating world-changers. We wrote this book for you, because we know how powerful ecosystem innovation is. We're challenging you to go out and deliver on *your* big dreams. It doesn't matter if your "stage" is a startup, the business where you work, your local community, or a global challenge. Regardless of where you are and where you are headed, we want you to take the brilliant ideas that are swirling around in your head and create a new way for the world to work. As Lao Tzu is famously believed to have said, "The journey of a thousand miles starts with one step."

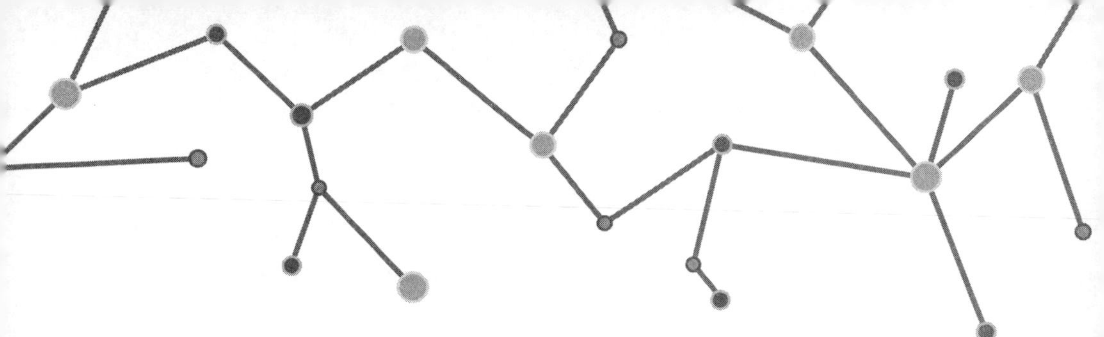

PART I

THE POSSIBILITIES

What better way to illustrate the exciting possibilities of ecosystem innovation than to introduce you to innovators who are already doing big things, making an enormous impact on the world around them? In Chapter 1, we do just that, moving the idea of ecosystem innovation from abstract to concrete.

Next, we delve further into exactly what ecosystem innovation is, its power to solve complex real-world problems, and where this power comes from. We explore how innovators who see their solutions as ecosystems are better able to scale their ideas and keep their solutions relevant in a changing world.

Later in Part I, we look at how other innovators commonly approach problems and how their simplifying assumptions put unavoidable limitations on their practices. These are the very limitations that ecosystem innovators have the power to work around.

But, first, let's start this creative adventure by looking at three stories that show exactly how people are doing some very big things in the world today.

1

TAKING ON BIG CHALLENGES

You never change things by fighting the existing reality. To change something, build a new model that makes the existing model obsolete.

—Buckminster Fuller[1]

Globally, about 34 million people are blind, in great part because they don't have access to adequate eye care. Approximately 45 percent of this group goes blind because of cataracts—a progressive clouding of the eye's lens—which requires surgery to correct.[2] In India, 12 million people are blind, which is a little more than one-third of the world total! In a sprawling country with a diverse mix of urban and rural areas and where families have access to widely varying levels of economic resources, helping those who need treatment to prevent or cure their blindness is a difficult problem.[3]

In India, as in many other parts of the world, a persistent challenge is that advances in medical care are often available only to more affluent members of society. Those most in need of medical care often lack access to well-established medical procedures that could change their lives for the better.

This kind of challenge is often seen as a problem of money. The thinking goes that if the government or some big nonprofit would simply provide more funding, the problem could be solved. It seems like a simple and direct solution. However, choosing to throw more money at the challenge doesn't actually address all the other parts of the problem that need to be considered to deliver care in a sustainable way. We see this over and over again in organizations where allocating more money to a problem is seen as the solution. Unfortunately, for the hard challenges that matter most, money alone won't help, unless many other pieces are changed.

For eye hospital chain Aravind, there was an ongoing need for trained professionals—doctors and nurses—and for better access to critical medical supplies in the form of inexpensive acrylic or silicone replacement lenses. And then there's the issue of accessibility. Simply providing transportation to treatment facilities—often traditionally located in urban centers—is a difficult proposition in such a large country where many people live in rural areas. And finally, there is the sheer scale of the problem. Millions of people need to be served, making this an exceptionally difficult challenge to address successfully.

As you can see in Figure 1.1, simply funding a solution to one part of this problem or addressing the problem one piece at a time isn't enough to deliver the quality medical care required to prevent blindness in a large population. More money won't create the staff out of thin air, it won't get people to clinics, and it won't provide the needed supplies. Parts of a solution are not enough.

Does this mean that some problems are so big, so complex, so persistent that they just can't be solved? As it turns out, this is not the case at all.

The mission of Aravind Eye Care is as simple and direct as it can be: eliminate needless blindness.[4] Instead of nibbling around the edges of India's blindness problem by just throwing more money at it, or hiring more doctors, or sourcing more lenses, Aravind created an entire

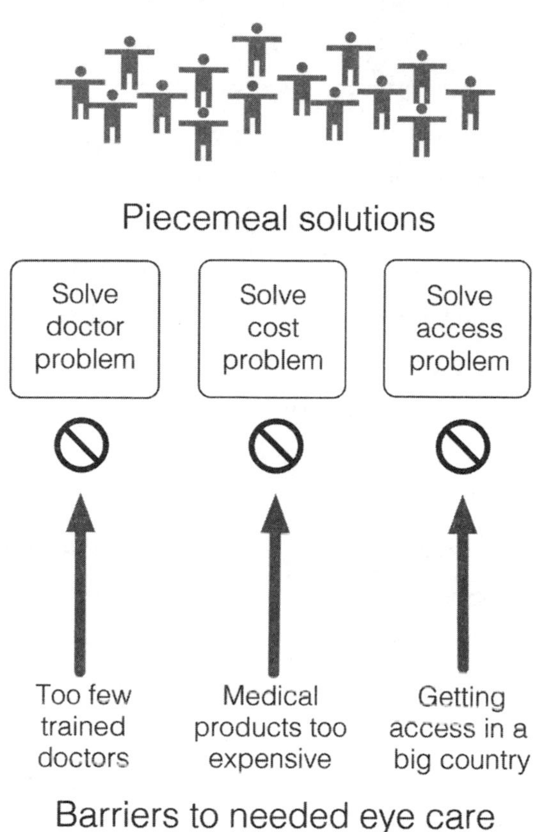

Figure 1.1. Piecemeal solutions to a complex challenge

working ecosystem specifically designed to solve this intractable problem. This approach was inspired by the vision that fighting blindness should be at a price anyone could afford. Aravind's founder, Dr. Govindappa Venkataswamy, asked, "If Coca-Cola can sell billions of sodas and McDonald's can sell billions of burgers, why can't Aravind sell millions of sight-restoring operations?"[5]

So how did they do it?

Aravind developed a complete, sustainable solution—an ecosystem that addresses all the interlocking parts of the challenge while ensuring that the treatments can be implemented at scale across one of the largest and most densely populated countries in the world. At the heart of Aravind's ecosystem is the way it weaves together doctors and nurses. Nurses are assigned most of the nonsurgical tasks: taking vitals, conducting eye tests, and prepping patients for surgery. The doctors then swoop into the operating rooms—doing the cataract surgeries, one after another.

Large groups of patients arrive at Aravind's eye hospitals each day. Seated in a line, one by one, their vitals are taken, their eyes tested, and then they are examined by a doctor. If they are found to be candidates for surgery, they are put on the next day's schedule. When their time comes, patients are prepped for surgery by nurses and then led into the operating room—each with a minimum of two operating tables. Nurses complete the final preparation and administer anesthesia. A doctor arrives and completes the surgical procedure on the first patient in the operating room and then turns around and gets started on the next patient.

In this way, doctors can complete six to eight surgeries an hour versus the standard single surgery an hour.[6] According to Aravind, half of its patients pay little or nothing for these services, and the organization has performed almost eight million eye surgeries since its founding, saving millions from a life of blindness.[7]

This isn't the end of the innovation, though. Figure 1.2 shows what happened next. The Aravind team looked across the rest of the cataract treatment ecosystem for other opportunities to improve. This led them to invest in the low-cost local production of lenses, which then enabled the organization to strengthen its supply chain and create jobs while avoiding high-cost imports. Inexpensive care hasn't meant low-quality care for Aravind. Their surgical outcomes are consistently equal to, or better than, those of the UK's National Health Service—at one-thousandth of the cost.[8]

Aravind replicated this entire cataract care ecosystem many times over using local treatment spaces in different parts of the country. The

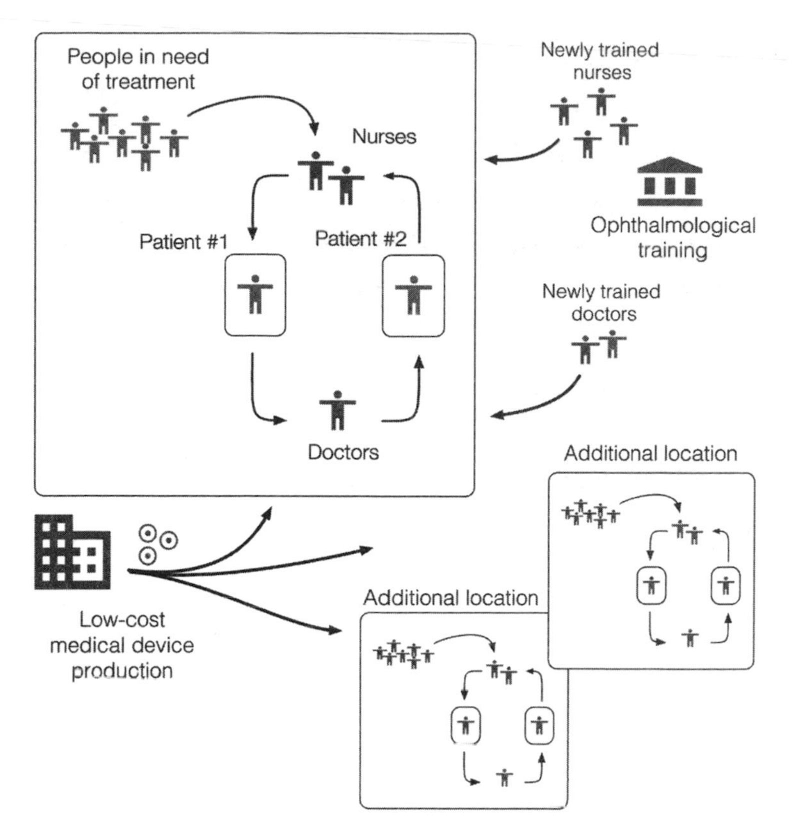

Figure 1.2. The Aravind Eye Care treatment ecosystem

organization continues to expand from its base in southern India into the rest of the country and Bangladesh. It's a concrete example of how bringing all the pieces of a working ecosystem together—local doctors and nurses, training, low-cost medical devices and their production, accessible locations for people in need—can solve a really complex problem.

Aravind is an ecosystem innovator. They have been able to solve a big problem and scale the solution, because they imagined and implemented an entirely new ecosystem. This ecosystem has diverse parts that work together to deliver a set of services in a challenging environment. And they did this by embracing a bigger view of what needed to be done, building on the following approach:

- *Look at the whole solution.* They saw that the different parts of the problem were interconnected and addressed them together.
- *Circumvent barriers.* They used the creative flexibility of a new ecosystem to go around existing barriers and limitations of the status quo.
- *Use diverse parts.* They creatively built their solution out of widely different "Lego blocks"—training, technology, manufacturing, process design, and existing facilities.

ECOSYSTEM DISRUPTORS

> No industry will be left unscathed, no supply chain left unscrambled, no strategic plan left unraveled.
>
> **—Larry Downes and Paul Nunes[9]**

Aravind is an example of an innovator that created an ecosystem to solve a big intractable problem. That's an amazing thing to do, but other ecosystem innovators have different goals in mind, like disrupting and reinventing happily stable industries led by overly comfortable entrenched players. When those entrenched players have a century of experience, deep pockets, and an iron grip on distribution channels, revolutionary change might seem to be something only a powerful well-funded competitor could pull off.

Yet, time and again, disruptive reinvention doesn't turn on battles between establishment dinosaurs. Instead, an innovator suddenly emerges to change the rules of the game and claim an exceptional opportunity. Just ask the folks at Gillette.

As evidenced by prehistoric cave drawings of shark's teeth, flint blades, and other tools used for shaving, razors in one form or another have been removing hair from human faces, heads, and bodies for tens of thousands of years. However, it wasn't until the 1880s that single-edged safety razors were introduced, incorporating a steel guard to reduce the chance of nicks and cuts. In 1895, King Camp Gillette took this innovation another step forward with the use of low-cost and convenient disposable blades. Although fewer than three hundred of Gillette's razors and blades were sold in 1903—his first year in business—the very next year, that number rocketed to more than two hundred thousand.[10]

King Camp Gillette became wealthy from his invention, and the company that bore his name dominated the retail-based shaving universe (shown in Figure 1.3) for more than one hundred years. Sure, other companies sold razors and blades, including Schick (which claimed the number two spot for decades), BIC, American Safety Razor, and others. Still, at the turn of the twenty-first century, Gillette held a 70 percent share of the US market—attracting the attention of consumer goods giant Procter & Gamble, which acquired Gillette in 2005 for the astronomical sum of $57 billion.[11] This market dominance, however, was soon to change.

Disruption—"in which an industry is shaken up and previously successful incumbents stumble"[12]—is happening faster than ever, even for deeply entrenched companies whose executives and shareholders never

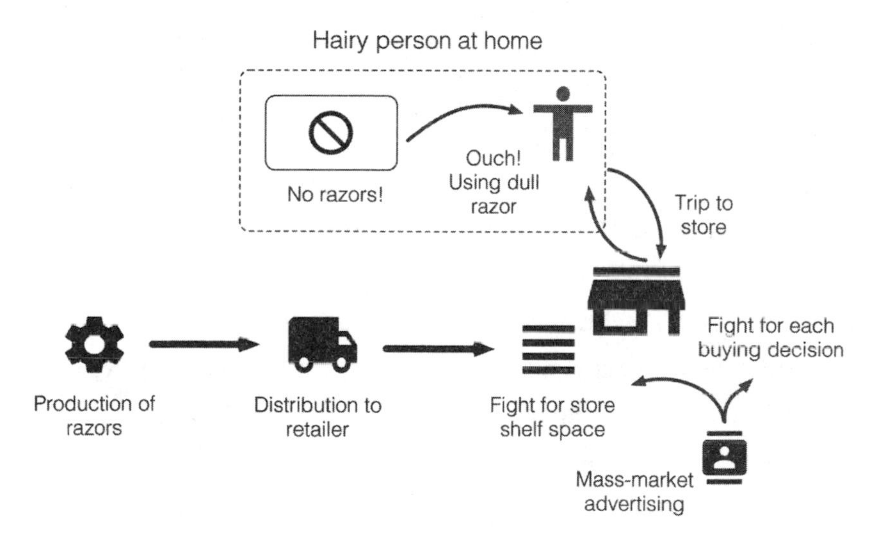

Figure 1.3. Gillette and Schick's retail-based ecosystem

imagined they would be challenged by a new competitor. Instead, building on long experience with familiar markets and players, they see the most credible threats coming from other businesses that look like them and compete according to the rules they know.

They don't anticipate the competitor who changes the rules. For example, the taxi industry didn't see Uber coming. The hotel industry didn't see Airbnb coming. The video rental industry didn't see Netflix coming. Brick-and-mortar bookstores didn't see Amazon coming.

And Gillette didn't see Dollar Shave Club coming.

In 2010, the year before improv comedian Michael Dubin founded Dollar Shave Club, a family friend had a problem. He had purchased 250,000 razors from a manufacturer in South Korea and desperately needed to sell them—*fast*.[13]

Dubin thought about the possibilities, and he came up with a unique idea. What if instead of selling the razors through retailers—the ecosystem of grocery stores, pharmacies, convenience stores, and all the rest of the major distribution channels that Gillette had a lock on—consumers could buy a monthly subscription for his razors at just one dollar apiece? And what if, instead of having to remember to periodically schlep to the store in the middle of the night to buy razors, the razors would be delivered directly to their homes?

This new ecosystem was the genesis of Dollar Shave Club. And while Dubin's innovative direct-to-consumer distribution approach was a good one, it took more than just that to make Dollar Shave Club great. What the company did was break the status quo by using irreverent online viral marketing aimed right at the target audience,[14] and then as sales grew, contracting out their production. They built a network of different elements that allowed them to compete on a different basis. In short, Dollar Shave Club created a new ecosystem that played by different rules (see Figure 1.4).

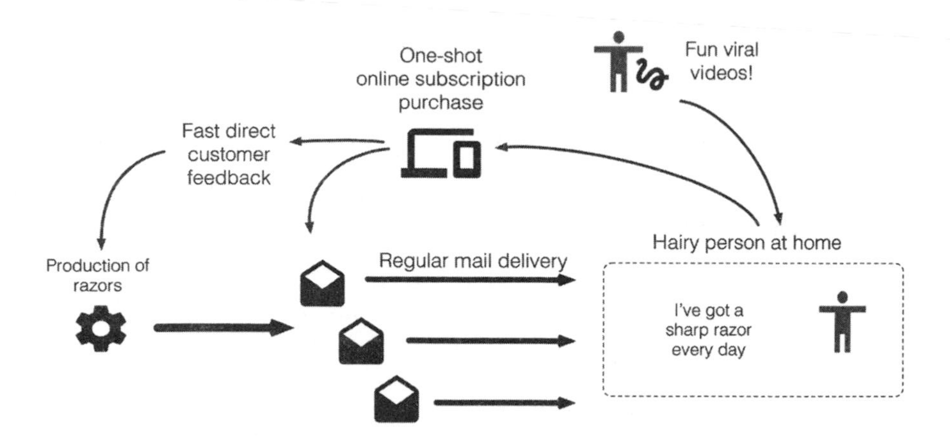

Figure 1.4. Dollar Shave Club's disruptive ecosystem

In 2016, the company was acquired by Unilever for $1 billion, and by 2019, it had captured almost 7 percent of the US non-disposable-razor market.[15] But Dollar Shave Club wasn't the only disruptive threat to Gillette's market dominance. In 2012, another razor startup—a company by the name of Harry's—was founded by Andy Katz-Mayfield and Jeff Raider.[16] (Raider was also a cofounder of another disruptive ecosystem innovator, the online eyewear company, Warby Parker.) Borrowing the subscription direct-sales model pioneered by Dollar Shave Club, Harry's quickly attracted customers—and funding. By the end of 2014, the company raised almost $300 million in various funding rounds, enabling Harry's to acquire Feintechnik, its own razor blade manufacturing company in Germany.[17]

Like Dollar Shave Club, Harry's built its own original ecosystem, quickly moving into a market still dominated by Gillette and further disrupting it. The founders of Harry's attribute much of their success to what they call virtual or v-commerce—owning the entire ecosystem, including sales, manufacturing, R&D, and more. Their goal was not twentieth-century supply chain efficiencies, but rather the ability to get feedback from customers and incorporate those insights everywhere from product design through distribution to make a better service and company.

It's an ecosystem for adaptive creativity. Katz-Mayfield says, "It creates this virtuous circle that makes for really happy customers, and then they become our best advocates."[18] In 2019, Edgewell Personal Care (owner of Schick, Wilkinson Sword, and numerous other consumer brands) announced plans to acquire Harry's for $1.37 billion,[19] but the FTC sued to block the deal and it was dropped.

And what about Gillette? Its US market share plunged from 70 percent in 2010 to less than 50 percent in 2017.[20] Gillette didn't lose this market share because it was beaten by a better-quality product or even because they were undercut on price. They lost because the new ecosystems developed by the market disruptors worked under different rules. By putting together product design, production, sales, and distribution in new ways, companies a fraction of Gillette's size stepped around the barriers of traditional retail distribution manufacturing that Gillette took advantage of for so long.

Ecosystem disruptors are at play in every industry, breaking apart "business as usual" and changing how the game is played in their sector. These innovators don't need revolutionary new inventions or exceptional size. They explode on the scene by taking advantage of a collection of strategic tenets:

- *Don't compete head-on.* Ecosystem innovators like Dollar Shave Club and Harry's didn't compete with Gillette on its own terms. They created a new set of rules where they had the advantage.
- *Assemble solutions.* They didn't try to build everything from scratch. Instead, they used Legos that already existed in the world to create their new ecosystem.
- *Move fast.* And because they assembled their own ecosystem, they were able to quickly create a disruptive play that could be put into markets and scale.

Existing market leaders may try to follow fast when disruptive ecosystem innovators strike, only to discover that new ecosystems are hard to copy inside organizations designed to support old, familiar ways of work. While Gillette quickly saw the writing on the wall and started its own online subscription razor service in 2014, Gillette Shave Club, it couldn't move as fast or scale as large. Consequently, the company still relies on its traditional retail distribution model for the vast majority of its sales.

SOLAR SISTER: MAKING GOOD IDEAS WORK

> Every single day in recent years, another 325,000 people got their first access to electricity. Each day more than 200,000 got piped water for the first time. And some 650,000 went online for the first time.
>
> **—Nicholas Kristof[21]**

People often talk about the need for more creativity, but the happy truth is, the world doesn't lack for amazing new inventions or original ideas. Every day new ideas appear that can make a real difference at a small or big scale. Unfortunately, far too many of these promising inventions, pilots, and prototypes fail to move beyond their early success.

What sets apart the innovators who are able to really make their ideas work? Consider the success of Solar Sister, an organization that works in Sub-Saharan Africa where more than 600 million people live without access to electricity.[22]

Providing "affordable, reliable, sustainable, modern energy for all" is one of the UN's Sustainable Development Goals for improving life across the globe.[23] Fortunately, this is a field where there has been a huge amount of technical innovation. And yet, even though technology innovations exist, putting power in the hands of people living in remote villages has proven to require more than simply producing a personal solar device and sticking it in a box. The last mile that separates that box from the actual use in people's lives is quite daunting.

Solar Sister, however, figured out how to solve this challenge by embracing yet another difficult problem. Sub-Saharan Africa is an area where, although women make up just over 50 percent of the population, there can be significant gaps to social or economic empowerment.[24] The organization's founders saw an opportunity to take on both challenges at once with a strategy that "provides women with economic opportunity, training, technology, and support to distribute clean energy to underserved communities in Africa."[25]

They looked beyond technology alone, setting up a complete ecosystem to enable new sustainable energy markets in their villages. Solar Sister provides solar-powered products—including lights, radios, fans, and mobile phone chargers—to Solar Sister entrepreneurs. These women, in turn, sell these key technologies to family, friends, and neighbors who live off the grid and lack conventional sources of electricity, or simply cannot afford it. Being able to charge your cell phone or to have reliable, quality light in your home at night might sound like a small thing. But small things like this can make a huge leap in the opportunities someone can access.

As illustrated in Figure 1.5, Solar Sister recognized that creating successful entrepreneurs required more than just giving them access to solar power products. In addition to providing products to sell, Solar Sisters provides training in entrepreneurship and ways to build the connections the women need to get their ventures off the ground.

Consider how these interconnected parts of the ecosystem have been used by Hilaria—a farmer, basket weaver, and Solar Sister entrepreneur from the Manyara region of northern Tanzania. Hilaria first heard about Solar Sister through the African Wildlife Foundation, and in 2013, she became one of the very first Solar Sister entrepreneurs.

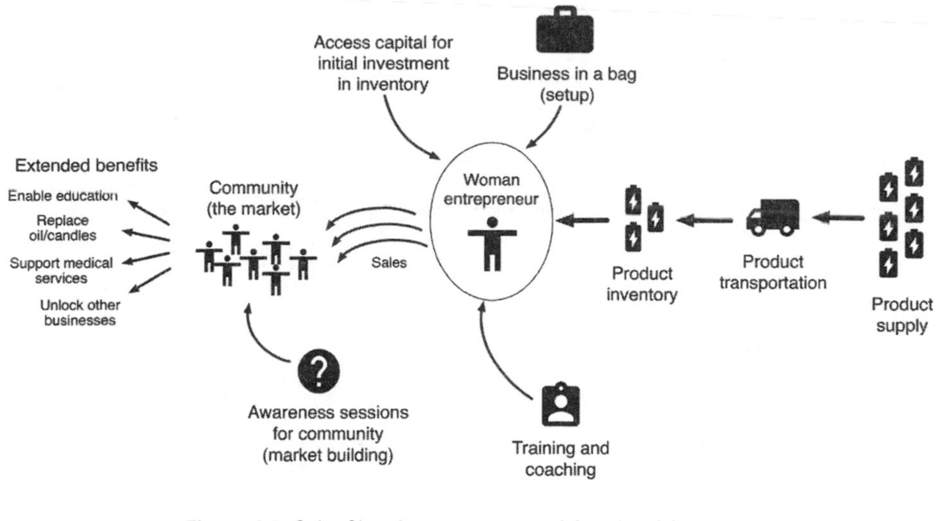

Figure 1.5. Solar Sister's ecosystem, enabling electricity access and women's entrepreneurship

Hilaria says, "I decided to become an entrepreneur because there is no electricity in this area or in neighboring villages. I learned about Solar Sister and then got training from them. And my husband helped me start with some capital."[26]

Before she decided to sign on as a Solar Sister entrepreneur, Hilaria first bought one of the organization's lights to try out for herself. Pleased with the results, Hilaria bought twelve more lights—including some with built-in phone-charging capability—and within a month, she had sold her first twenty-five Solar Sister products. Since then, Hilaria has sold more than four hundred products, improving the lives of more than two thousand people, including herself and her family.

To succeed, it was not enough for Hilaria to show up at a prospective customer's door with a bag full of technology. She needed to enable an entirely new market, providing instruction and support to her customers. Hilaria adds, "Solar Sister training helped me increase my income. They taught me about customer care, how to save, and the importance of building trust."[27]

Hilaria's work is woven into the broader community, shifting the economic prospects and well-being of her family and neighbors. The simple ability to have some light in the evening really changes things. Medical personnel are better able to deliver quality health services. Children can study better at night, providing for better educational outcomes. Adults can work after dark, increasing income and job prospects. People don't have to rely on candles, flashlights, or unhealthy, expensive-to-fuel, and dangerous kerosene lanterns for their indoor lighting needs.

Although Solar Sister's individual women entrepreneurs operate on a very small scale, the ecosystem that enables these businesses to be set up and sustained can be replicated over and over again, providing positive health, educational, and income benefits. According to Solar Sister, in the years since its founding, the organization has kickstarted more than 7,400 entrepreneurs, and these entrepreneurs have distributed more than 718,000 clean energy products, including solar energy and clean cookstoves. In fact, it has been so successful, Solar Sister entrepreneurs have reached more than 3.4 million people, including family, friends, neighbors, and other members of their communities.[28]

What's important to note is Solar Sister didn't simply deliver technology to communities that needed it. Instead, they created a working new ecosystem that did much more. This powerful ecosystem offered:

- *Complete solutions.* Solar Sister brought together technology, services, and learning that a woman entrepreneur needed to take on a new role in her community.
- *Enabled other outcomes.* Each product sold by Solar Systems entrepreneurs enabled other outcomes in the community, improving health, education, and livelihoods.
- *Scalable impact.* By creating ecosystems that can be replicated, impact can be scaled without having a centralized government or organization directing decisions and work.

PEOPLE TAKING ON BIG CHALLENGES

> The chief worth of civilization is just that it makes the means of living more complex; that it calls for great and combined intellectual efforts, instead of simple uncoordinated ones.
>
> **—Oliver Wendell Holmes Jr.[29]**

Each of these stories is different. Aravind's ecosystem solved a seemingly intractable problem and restored sight to millions. Dollar Shave Club and Harry's took on a century-old market leader and reshaped an industry. Solar Sister took new technology and put it in the hands of thousands of women entrepreneurs living in remote communities.

And yet there are common threads. While they each worked on different challenges and operated at very different scales—one creating a nationwide health practice while another focused on individual entrepreneurs in remote villages—they all embraced innovations that built on many interconnected parts, people, organizations, and technology. They were part of a growing tribe of ecosystem innovators creating huge value and impact from "messy" challenges and opportunities in the real world.

The potential of these opportunities is exciting, but before you can learn how to become an ecosystem innovator—changing the world, or at least your part of it—you'll first need to know more about what ecosystem innovation is and why it's so powerful in the world today. And those topics just happen to be what we explore in the next chapter.

2

WHAT IS ECOSYSTEM INNOVATION?

Seizing white space is hard. It requires looking at markets and customers in new ways. It requires an openness to experimentation and uncertainty. It requires a willingness to challenge and change those well-honed systems and models that made your enterprise successful in the first place.

—Mark Johnson[1]

In the previous chapter, we tell you three stories of bold innovation that tackled problems or opportunities that were both important and challenging. In each of these examples, ecosystem innovation creatively joined people, organizations, technologies, and resources in a real-world system that was able to address big problems and pursue bold opportunities.

Most of us were introduced to the concept of ecosystems in grade school science class. We learned how in nature a host of different plants, animals, and other organisms fit within their environment to create a sustainable relationship where all the parts work together—an ecosystem. This same idea is everywhere around us, not just out in some woodland. We live among different ecosystems of people, organizations, technology, and resources that come together to support our lives, businesses, and communities.

For example, do you have a favorite bakery where you love to buy fresh sourdough loaves, croissants, or cupcakes? Even if it's a small, mom-and-pop business, that bakery is a real-world example of an ecosystem where different people, institutions, and technology all come together for everyone's benefit.

In this scenario you've got a bakery owner who employs a couple of bakers, who order flour, eggs, butter, yeast, baking pans, and other items from a few favorite suppliers. There are hungry customers—some who buy the bakery's products in person, and others who buy them online for delivery or pickup—and then we have the delivery truck driver and cashiers and other bakery staff. There's also the building owner, who rents space to the bakery, as well as the electric and gas company, the health department, the local tax authorities, and others who all play a role in supporting this business.

This ecosystem (shown in Figure 2.1) combines many different kinds of actors with a variety of motivations, and everyone involved gets

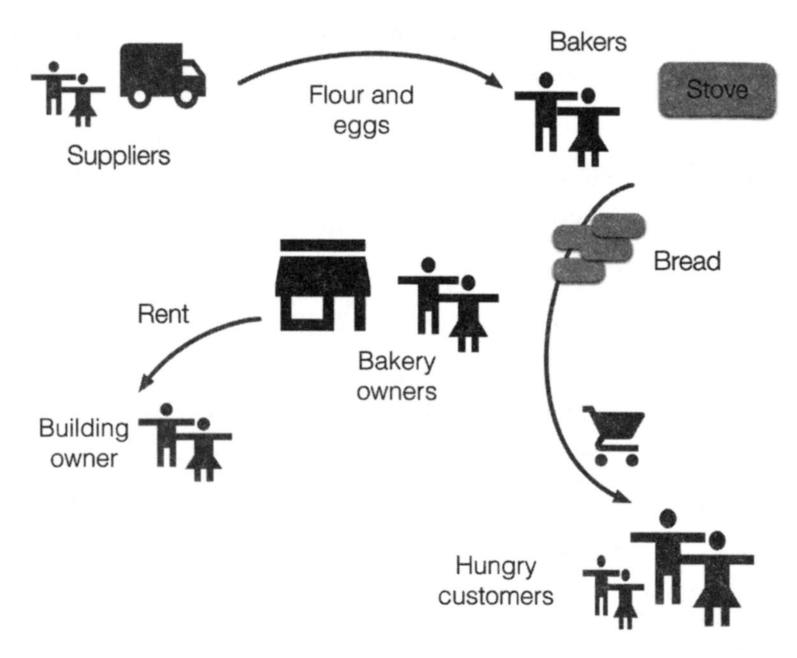

Figure 2.1. The diverse parts of a bakery's ecosystem

rewarded in some way. The bakers get to hone and practice their craft and be paid a salary. The suppliers make a profit on the goods they sell to the bakery. The business owner makes a profit on the bread and other products the bakery sells. The building owner finds a use for their property while gaining a steady rental income from it. And the hungry customers get fresh, tasty bread to eat and serve to friends and family. And it's the bakery ecosystem that connects all these different actors together, creating value for all of them.

ASSEMBLING LEGOS TO MAKE BETTER ECOSYSTEMS

> Simply defined, a system is a complex whole, the functioning of which depends on its parts and the interactions between parts.
>
> **—Michael C. Jackson[2]**

Because of its power to get big things done, it should be no surprise that ecosystem innovation is being increasingly embraced around the world. Used by individual innovators or large companies, startups, and nonprofits, it is a practical method to deliver innovations with impact—whether you're working on a messy challenge or a big opportunity.

If any of these scenarios resonate with you, then ecosystem innovation could be a game changer:

- You're taking on an issue that is particularly challenging—something that's both complex and too important to leave be.
- You're working in an organization that is reinventing itself, creating new products, and moving into new markets. Or you might be watching your organization decline year after year and you know you need to make some big changes to get back on top.

- Or it could be that you're an innovator with a great idea or a great invention that has the potential to create tremendous value when it's released into the world.

Ecosystem innovation helps you move from working on one small part of a challenge to shifting the whole proverbial mountain by considering all the parts. Essentially, you are building an ecosystem that works in the real world. Best of all, it's not rocket science; nor is it abstract material for a PhD thesis. At its core, ecosystem innovation is simply about assembling Lego blocks drawn from the world around us.

Maybe you enjoyed building things with Legos when you were a kid—houses, robots, spaceships—or perhaps your kids enjoy them today. Ecosystem innovation is kind of like building with those blocks, except the Legos you use are real-life people, organizations, or pieces of technology.

Our bakery's Legos included people such as bakers and customers, businesses such as the bakery itself and its suppliers, and even some government agencies. If we want to create a new bakery ecosystem, we could combine those living Lego blocks with technology and resources, such as ovens and flour. If we do a good job, the ecosystem we've designed will produce wonderful baked goods for families in the community, profits for the bakery owner, and rewarding jobs for the employees.

In the bakery, there may be rules that guide how everyone works together, but there are also choices being made within the ecosystem all the time. While the bakery owner might be able to tell the bakers what to do on a particular day—make more scones and fewer cupcakes—that owner isn't the boss of the customers, the building owner, the suppliers, or the local utility. They each make choices based on their own goals, priorities, and circumstances.

These characteristics inherent to ecosystem innovation create a natural flexibility to adapt and change that many traditional innovators envy. For example, what if our bakery owner noticed there was a late-night boutique bakery trend gaining popularity in all the big cities? While the bakery wasn't located in a big city, it *was* in a college town with thousands of ravenous students who were active at night—looking for something tasty and affordable to eat. For this reason and more, the owner believed the idea might create a good return on the time and money she would put into it.

The good news was that making this late-night boutique bakery idea would not require starting from scratch, because there would be no need to throw out the bakery's existing Legos—the bakers, ovens, physical storefront, and so forth. The bakery owner could simply add new pieces to the bakery's ecosystem, including such things as new lighting, seating for customers, night managers, an enticing selection of different late-night menu items, a home delivery service, and whatever else might be required. And so the innovative new late-night business wouldn't be just a single change—for example, keeping the bakery open late at night—but would combine all these different pieces to create a new ecosystem that could succeed in a new environment.

So you may be wondering *what* exactly you can do with ecosystem innovation and how it can help you and your organization overcome difficult challenges and turn opportunities into successes. In the following sections, we explore three uses that make it such a powerful approach:

1. You can tackle big problems.
2. You can reimagine organizations in a changing world.
3. You can make innovations work in the real world.

You Can Tackle Big Problems

> We have the perilous fortune to have been born into a historic moment—a decisive moment—when events and choices in our own lifetime will dictate the circumstances of many many lifetimes to come.
>
> **—Ian Goldin and Chris Kutarna[3]**

There are hard problems in the world that need solutions. Some of these, such as climate change, are global challenges that will literally determine the fate of future generations. But there are also hard problems that can be found everywhere around us—in our schools, our communities, our political institutions, businesses, and in the world at large.

Hard problems aren't hard simply because they are big. Problems are hard because they have many parts that are tangled up with one another. They are tied up in an ecosystem where lots of people are involved and participating, each bringing their own motivations and needs.

These kinds of hard problems can't be easily solved. This is because there isn't one simple fix that will make a difference for everyone who is a part of the ecosystem. A simple answer often only addresses one person's concerns or provides a solution for just one corner of the challenge. A lasting fix for these ecosystem problems requires all the different parts to come together in new ways. Even if a simple fix works for one or two groups, all the rest of the participants may still simply refuse to go along with the idea.

This is what Aravind successfully overcame when they created an ecosystem that could treat blindness across one of the world's most populous countries. They made lots of pieces fit together, from training nurses to manufacturing lenses. The whole ecosystem fit together and each of the participants benefited from being part of it. Later in this book, we'll take a deep dive into a wide range of hard problems that ecosystem innovators are particularly well suited to take on, including undertaking the monumental challenge of eradicating diseases; fundamentally changing the kind of cars we drive; and making education accessible, even to those displaced by wars.

If you choose to take on a hard, important problem like one of these, it's absolutely critical that you learn how to apply the power of ecosystem innovation. Good intentions are of little value if you can't deliver solutions that are big enough to matter out in the world we live in today.

WHEN TO TACKLE MESSY PROBLEMS WITH ECOSYSTEM INNOVATION

While there are many different situations where you might want to apply the principles of ecosystem innovation to take on a messy problem, in our experience, the following elements are particularly strong signs that you will need ecosystem innovation to be successful:

- *Others have made little progress.* Many well-recognized challenges (think climate change, ecological safeguarding) have seen frustratingly little progress. Despair isn't helpful. Instead, apply a more powerful set of creative tools, using ecosystem innovation to approach the challenge differently—and more effectively.
- *People are involved.* Ecosystem innovators recognize the key role people and organizations play in making things work in the real world. They happily use technology in exciting and creative ways, but they know that tech alone can't solve most hard problems—it takes *people.* Ecosystem innovation can get people into the heart of the solution.
- *There are a lot of gray areas and changes.* The real world doesn't explain itself or sit around waiting for people to design and implement ideas according to a project plan. A lot of great innovations fail because they are stuck waiting for clearer information, or the situation changes before the proverbial ink is dry. Ecosystem innovators expect and embrace uncertainty and change as part of the job.

You Can Reimagine Organizations in a Changing World

> [The Fourth Industrial Revolution] is disrupting almost every industry in every country. And the breadth and depth of these changes herald the transformation of entire systems of production, management, and governance.
>
> **—Klaus Schwab**[4]

A clever baker who sees their bakery as an ecosystem always has the opportunity to reimagine themselves. They can do more than survive in a changing world, they can thrive by doing something bold, new, and different. This is what the founder of Dollar Shave Club did, and it's the second powerful use of ecosystem innovation.

Today, if a leader doesn't want to see their business made obsolete, they're going to have to do more than simply improve and grow their operating performance. In the past, it was: "Can I get my numbers high enough for Wall Street this year?" "Can I continue to maintain my profit margin?" Now, the stakes are much higher. Every day, in almost every industry, you're looking at organizations being wiped off the face of the earth or commoditized to the point where they can't survive.

There are big global trends driving this rise of disruption and creative change across industries. To start, the world's box of Legos is getting bigger and more powerful every day. Of course, everyone knows that technologies are always getting faster and cheaper—it's been more than fifty years since Intel's Gordon Moore predicted that computing power would continue to exponentially grow while decreasing in relative cost.[5] But it's not just computer processors that are cheaper by the day. All sorts of technologies have similar growth curves. Since 2003, sequencing the human genome has gone from a one-off, multibillion-dollar project to a couple hundred dollars, with prices continuing to fall.[6]

Today's technological advances are about more than just increased power and reduction in cost. One of the things that's exciting about this moment in history is that we're throwing so many kinds of exceptionally powerful tools—more Legos—into our creative toolbox. The host of new, interconnected technologies includes things as diverse as genomic-driven medical breakthroughs, internet of things (IoT), digital sensing, widespread application of artificial intelligence (AI), new energy tech, autonomous vehicles, new power sources, 3D printing of everything, and much more. All these new Lego blocks enable—in fact, *demand*—organizations to be constantly reimagined.

In a world of supercharged creativity, it is important for successful organizations to remember another of Gordon Moore's observations, "Whatever has been done can be outdone."[7] Organizations that want to thrive in this world of change need to learn to move quickly and boldly, and in many cases, this requires that they reinvent themselves in some very fundamental ways.

Reimagining an organization isn't just something that commercial businesses need to do. In a changing world ecosystem innovation is a powerful tool for leaders in any type of organization. We've seen leaders reimagine big and small businesses, nonprofits, government agencies, and even community organizations. The basic principles are the same in every case, and the positive outcomes are long lasting.

WHEN TO REINVENT YOURSELF USING ECOSYSTEM INNOVATION

There are times when reinventing your organization faces challenges where you need the scale and power of change that ecosystem innovation makes possible:

- *You want to disrupt an industry or claim new game-changing opportunities.* This isn't just about being first; it's about being

continued

fundamentally different than everyone else (like Uber, Airbnb, Dollar Shave Club).

- *You are facing disruption and need to change.* The bus is about to run over your organization, and if you don't change it, you'll become irrelevant or profitless. This is about letting go of the status quo and doing something that changes how you work in the world (think traditional newspapers, universities, and the many small businesses being swept up in changes resulting from the way people shop, where they live, and how they work).
- *You want to continue to lead.* Even if you don't think about your goals as disrupting an industry, you will still want to move boldly and quickly to capture new opportunities and grow. This is about creating success for an organization when others are struggling, or creating the future before those around you do (like our little bakery toying with the idea of selling late-night buns).

You Can Make Innovations Work in the Real World

> The misconception that great ideas inevitably lead to success has prevailed for too long.
>
> **—Scott Belsky**[8]

The final powerful use of ecosystem innovation is focused on innovators and the challenge of bringing great ideas from concept into the world at large. Every day, pilot programs and prototypes are developed that generate exciting buzz, making both the innovator and their investors and other stakeholders feel that success is just around the corner. And then, far too often, the initiative stalls out or hits a wall.

This is often because innovative pilots and inventions are just one part of a complete solution that needs to be put into place. Solar Sister realized this. The organization's founders weren't satisfied with distributing useful pieces of solar technology to those who needed them. They went further by combining the physical parts of their solution with transportation, training, community meetings, financial support, and more. They realized that to make a successful and sustainable solution that would actually work for women living in a remote village, they would need to build an ecosystem.

This is a really hard lesson for innovators who have been raised on stories of people like Palmer Luckey. In case you don't know who Palmer Luckey is, he's the guy who—when he was just sixteen years old—started building remarkably innovative virtual reality (VR) headsets in the garage of his parents' home. A few years later, he founded Oculus VR, a business to produce his Oculus Rift headsets. He famously became a multimillionaire at age twenty-one when he sold the company to Facebook for $2 billion in cash and stock.[9] Inventors and pilot projects around the world are fueled by this kind of fairytale Silicon Valley storyline.

Too much importance is given to the singular brilliance of a creative hero, or the power of silver bullet technology—when far more often the actual story behind big successes involves more real-world messiness. How many brilliant inventors have you heard of diligently working away on something for years, but never finding success because they can't connect the dots?

And of course, even Palmer Luckey's story isn't so simple. Facebook became Meta and repositioned itself around the strategy of building a virtual reality ecosystem—a *metaverse*. The innovation that will change the world will be made from Meta's (or someone else's) VR ecosystem, one with a huge number of interconnected parts. The VR goggles were just one piece and can't make significant change on their own.

You might say that no invention is an island. To succeed, individual inventions must be part of an ecosystem of people, organizations, and technology. The third major use of ecosystem innovation is creating that supporting ecosystem for individual innovations. So often people see a piece of cutting-edge commercial technology like a new AI application, or a humanitarian invention like a new high-performance water filter, changing the world. It's easy to imagine that once a great idea is shown to work, the final step of widespread adoption can almost be taken for granted—a happy ending to the story.

This is, of course, rarely the case, and ironically, innovators and innovation labs haven't easily learned this lesson. They dump huge amounts of time, money, and hope into exciting ideas that don't have a path to impact and success. Executives in many organizations have become jaded and frustrated with innovation programs that never actually deliver ideas into practice, which is a tragedy since almost every organization needs more, not less support for innovation efforts. But it doesn't have to be that way. Ecosystem innovators can guide these promising but incomplete innovations to become fully realized solutions.

WHEN INNOVATIONS AND PILOTS NEED ECOSYSTEM INNOVATION

Simple innovations and pilots often fail to reach the stage where they can do big things in a sustainable, long-lasting way. Here are some times when you should consider leveraging ecosystem innovation to realize the full potential of your innovations and pilots:

- *You have a promising pilot or prototype.* You have an idea that has delivered promising results. Now you're at the wall. What's next? Ecosystem innovation can help you complete the whole working solution.
- *You have an incubator struggling to take ideas from pilot to adoption.* It's frustrating when committed investments in innovators and their ideas don't deliver real results in the end. Adding ecosystem

innovation to an incubator's approach can help break the cycle of failed pilots.

- *You are taking over an innovation and you want it to perform and grow.* If you take on the job of managing a new innovation in practice, you'll be constantly pushing uphill if it's missing key parts of its ecosystem. Putting all the needed pieces in place makes practical operations work.

THE INNOVATION IS THE ECOSYSTEM

So what ties all these challenges together? The big shift in thinking is to see that in every case the innovation *is* the ecosystem. Think about our bakery. We saw how the bakery ecosystem consisted of bread, bakers, flour producers, customers, and local health authorities. Taking on the challenge of selling late-night pastries is not a bun invention or some other individual change. Their innovation was a whole ecosystem. To put hot rolls in people's hands at midnight, everyone had to make changes and work together in new ways.

As an ecosystem innovator, your job is to create innovative ecosystems that work out in the real world. How you bring different parts together determines if you succeed or fail. This gives you the power to claim a big space to work if you want, building innovations—or ecosystems—from both the parts you control and the ones you don't. What you won't be doing is pursuing individual ideas or changes that stand alone.

We talk about this a lot more over the rest of the book, but as you read, it might be worth reminding yourself at different points that your innovation is an ecosystem—a whole ecosystem. In this chapter, we lay out the (hopefully persuasive) case that by embracing ecosystem innovation, you can do some remarkably powerful things wherever you are, with whatever resources are available to you. Ecosystem innovators have the ability to create new markets, reshape businesses, solve difficult challenges, and much more. They make inventions and people's good ideas work in the real world. And they can be at the forefront of dealing with hard problems—and leveraging big opportunities—both globally and very close to home.

So how can you deliver this kind of power? That's exactly what we explore in the next chapter.

THE FIVE SOURCES OF POWER

Airbnb now has more listings worldwide than
the top five hotel brands combined.

—Avery Hartmans[1]

You must have noticed by now that we are pretty excited about innovating with ecosystems, and it's because we have seen the significant value it creates for innovators and organizations around the world. So what is it about ecosystems that should get you excited? It's because ecosystems are an incredibly *powerful* way to create and shape the world around us. In our work, we have found that this immense capacity to solve challenges or leverage opportunities comes from five sources of power (see Figure 3.1):

Figure 3.1. Five sources of power in ecosystem innovation

1. *Lots of building blocks.* The huge selection of Legos we have at our disposal to create a new powerful ecosystem.
2. *Built-in motivations.* Diverse, sustainable rewards that get and keep people involved in your change.
3. *Rule-breaking.* Breaking rules and dodging barriers to challenges, rather than getting stuck and failing.
4. *Magical synergies.* The ability to create synergies among participants and amplify their combined impact.
5. *Adaptive flexibility.* Being able to vary, adapt, and stretch innovations in a fast-changing world for greater value and success.

As we do a deeper dive into these five elements, we weave in the example of Airbnb, which leveraged each of them to become bigger than the top five hotel brands in the world combined.

THE FIRST SOURCE OF POWER: LOTS OF LEGOS

> When a new building block is discovered, the result is usually a range of innovations.
>
> **—John Henry Holland[2]**

We've said that ecosystems are like building with Legos. If you take a moment or two to think about that, you'll realize that means we really have the entire world at our disposal. We can draw from whatever Legos we want (people, technology, resources) to build our ecosystems, allowing us to bring all sorts of things together. And there are new Legos being created all the time, even as others fade from relevance.

Unfortunately, many conventional innovators limit themselves to a narrowly defined set of possibilities for their ideas. Technologists, for example, might just look at a single piece of technology—say, a new mobile device or an AI program. Process designers, on the other hand, might focus on fine-tuning the people or processes within an organization. And executives might only look at their business's existing products and service offerings when expanding markets.

This limited point of view allows them to think about only what's related to the Legos they've already got, making their ability to create new value quite small. If you break out of this narrow focus, you can build, change, and innovate by connecting different people, organizations, technologies, and resources from anywhere around you as you build entire new ecosystems. And because many of these Legos are already working out in the world, you can create powerful solutions without having to build each piece yourself.

When you draw on this wide diversity of pieces, you can bring them together in new ways. This is how Aravind Eye Care System, Dollar Shave Club, Harry's, and Solar Sister found tremendous success. It's also at the heart of Airbnb's winning idea.

In 2007, Brian Chesky and Joe Gebbia decided to make a few bucks by renting out three air mattresses on the floor of their San Francisco loft during a design conference.[3] The success of this small venture led them to found Airbnb (originally, Airbed & Breakfast), which at the time of this writing has six million active listings worldwide[4] and is worth $68.2 billion.[5] Airbnb succeeded because the founders built an impactful, real-world ecosystem by connecting people, places, and technology in an original way.

They looked out in the world and saw many different Lego blocks available for them to pull together. Airbnb's founders saw a person who had a vacant, spare bedroom—or an empty apartment or house (a *frozen asset*)—that created no ongoing value. They also saw a person who wanted to travel to an area where the hotels were all booked up and there were no other options for lodging. The founders realized they had these initial Lego blocks—people with an empty room, apartment, or house, and people looking for a place to stay—and they could connect them together.

But to build an ecosystem that would create large-scale value, they knew they had to add more pieces, including a platform to connect the blocks, a sense of safety for the traveler and the owner with a rating system that fostered trust, and so on.

Some would say the innovation that made Airbnb succeed was the technology platform. While their technology was a key part of what made Airbnb work, it would be a mistake to see software as the sole reason for Airbnb's success. Stepping back, we can see that they are just like the bakery—everything works because it includes a variety of people, businesses, and resources all working together. Travelers, the destination homes, their homeowners, and local businesses—such as restaurants and taxicabs—are all essential parts of the ecosystem.

The Lego blocks they drew on were always available. But in creating Airbnb, Chesky and Gebbia (and a third cofounder, former roommate Nathan Blecharczyk) took these blocks and connected them together in a new way. The result was an ecosystem that created benefits for all the people who participated. It's not like the value was sitting there already—it emerged from putting the different parts in a new configuration, thereby creating new sources of value for everyone.

This is one of the things that's truly amazing about ecosystems. When you start bringing the pieces together, new sources of value emerge just by combining them together in new ways. In essence, Airbnb found a way to unfreeze a huge pool of assets—unoccupied and underutilized real estate—with a new ecosystem, just as Uber and Lyft unfroze a different pool of assets—people's cars—with their own ecosystems, unleashing tremendous value in the process.

Every day in every industry, new Legos are becoming available. It's not just underutilized assets that can be used to assemble an ecosystem.

People are learning new skills, and revolutionary technologies are regularly bursting onto the scene. New businesses are being set up in countries across the globe that can become potential partners, and increasingly the lines that used to separate government, commercial, and nonprofit organizations are being blurred or erased so they can share their capabilities when tackling challenges.

The Legos available to you are more varied and more powerful than at any time in history.

TECHNOLOGY MAKES POWERFUL LEGO BLOCKS

It's easy to see technology as the center of innovation. Most people would probably say that the revolutionary part of Uber's disruptive entry in the taxi business was their mobile ride reservation app. But that would miss all the other parts of their rideshare ecosystem, the shifts they made to individual car ownership, the new ways of doing pricing, and more.

Ecosystem Innovators know that technology is just one part of what makes new ecosystems work. That doesn't mean you shouldn't be fired up about all the new inventions emerging every day. After all, each new technology offers another Lego block that you can put together to create powerful ecosystems. What's particularly exciting about today's technologies is that these blocks can be connected in ways that amplify their combined impact.

For example, what if you wanted to know if someone was experiencing a medical emergency on a crowded street and then quickly do something about it? As you can see in Figure 3.2, a collection of rapidly developing technologies could become Legos connected in an ecosystem to do just this. Sensors embedded in IoT devices could allow you to have an awareness of the shifting crowds of people on a

continued

street. And all that awareness could be connected through the cloud, bringing it together in one place as big data collection. And then that data could feed an AI system which identifies someone in distress and make an informed choice about what to do. Then the AI could take action, perhaps sending an emergency autonomous vehicle to help.

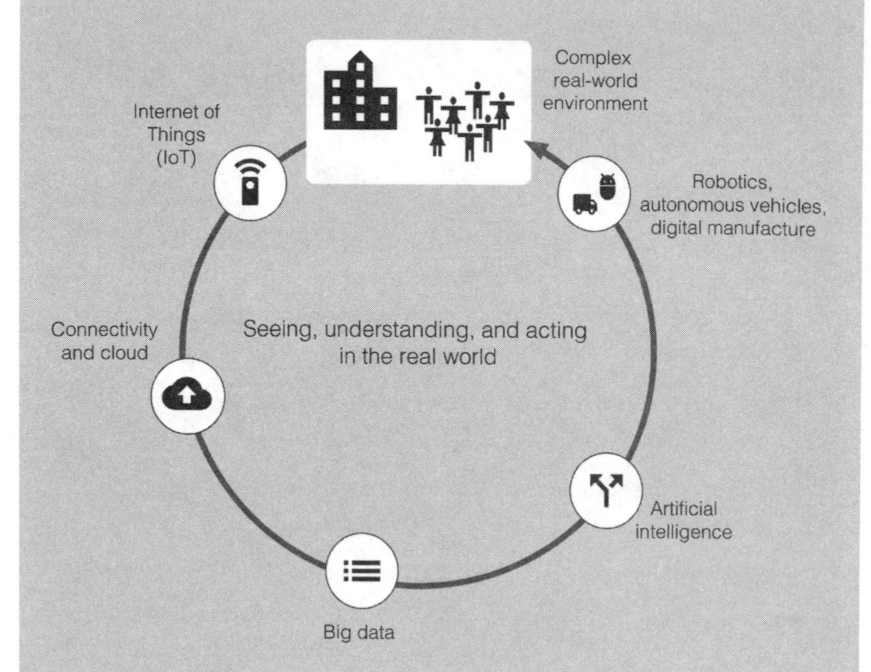

Figure 3.2. Connecting technology like Legos in an ecosystem

Any one of these technologies is useful, but it's when they plug together that you really see their impact. Of course, once you start plugging together new technologies, you'll often encounter new challenges. For example, because this ecosystem involves people out on public streets, you'll also have to think about how to manage privacy and any misuse of information. Because innovations so often push into new areas, there will often be ethical questions that should be asked. The good news is that you are in a good position to step back and see these issues, and then do something meaningful to address them.

THE SECOND SOURCE OF POWER: BUILT-IN MOTIVATION

> Truly successful collaborations have an inherent quid pro quo—that is, the collaborators all know that their individual contributions are meaningful, essential, and acknowledgeable.
>
> **—Michael Schrage[6]**

One of the things that really sets ecosystems apart is that participants can be motivated to act and make their own choices. While on the surface this might seem like an invitation to chaos—or at least the beginnings of a painful migraine—it's actually incredibly powerful.

The reality is when you bring people, organizations, and communities together, they aren't like a clock that mindlessly runs in the exact way you want or expect once you wind it up. Instead, ecosystems allow you to bring together very different kinds of people and organizations—each of whom often have very different motivations.

They can (and often do) demand a reason to be involved in your innovation. Everyone needs an incentive to participate. Some might say this is a burden for an innovator, but it is actually a powerful advantage for you. In simple, machine-like systems, you must continually put resources in to make things work. The competition for the same limited resources can be quite fierce. A business, for example, has only so much budget to go around, so one person's benefit comes out of someone else's reward. It's a win-lose, zero-sum game where one person gets the money and the other person doesn't.

Ecosystems, on the other hand, offer more options. The different people supporting your ecosystem can (and likely will) have different priorities. They can also have different capabilities to build what you need. Some people may be motivated by profit, for example, while others may not care about profit but instead want to change their part of the world for the better. One person might be a marketing maven, while another loves working with numbers or has a strong mechanical aptitude. An ecosystem can bring together people and organizations so they're doing things that matter to them, combining and leveraging their different capabilities in a unique way where everyone benefits.

When you've got people who have different motivations and who want different rewards, then you can say Person A gets this, Organization B gets that, and Government C gets this other thing. Because there are many different potential rewards in an ecosystem, it's possible to find win-win solutions where one thing is traded for another. Make no mistake: there are still trade-offs. But when you've got lots of actors with lots of different motivations, they don't all have to fight over the same slice of cake. Instead of having one whole carrot cake, you can share slices of several different desserts together like ice cream cake, cheesecake, and chocolate mousse. More cakes + more diversity = more and bigger wins.

Providing diverse, meaningful rewards makes it possible to create naturally growing ecosystems—everyone in them is incentivized to energetically participate. It's like ecosystems come with their own kind of renewable fuel. You can see how this is clearly the case with the various actors in the Airbnb ecosystem. Not everyone has the same motivation. Travelers want a safe place to stay at a reasonable price, homeowners or renters have a place they want to rent out for extra income, cleaning businesses want to make a profit while providing steady work to employees, Airbnb insurance providers want to support people to feel safe in renting out their houses, and so on. These are all very different actors, but they all benefit in their own way by participating in this ecosystem.

In fact, increasing the diversity and variation among participants can make ecosystems even more powerful. If you take a closer look at each of the different kinds of actors in Airbnb's ecosystem, you'll find that even similar actors are different from one another. This would be a problem for

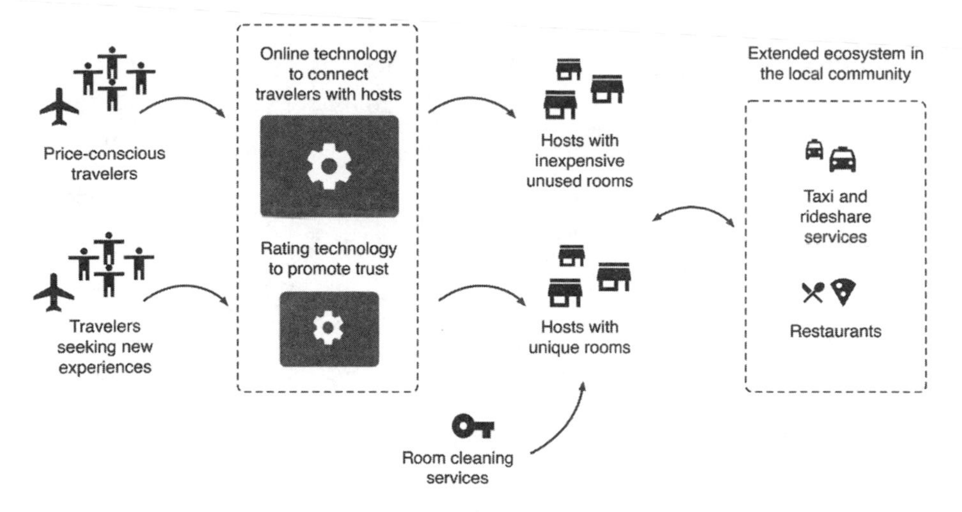

Figure 3.3. Airbnb's ecosystem, built from diverse blocks

machine-like operations where everything is supposed to be done according to a fixed set of rules. But ecosystems revel in variation. For example, one traveler might want an inexpensive place to stay, while another one might want luxury digs. One traveler might want to rent a place close to the airport, while another wants to be on the beach. And so you have many different types of people who can be accommodated within a single, flexible ecosystem, as shown in Figure 3.3.

Meaningful rewards for actors become fuel for an ecosystem's engine of operation and growth. This has made it possible for Airbnb to build on a global community of people who love the idea of opening their homes and sharing them with the world, and travelers who want to experience the places they visit. Of course, a complex new ecosystem like this comes with challenges too—issues that need to be addressed alongside the benefits. There will be neighbors whose day-to-day lives are disrupted by a steady flow of short-term renters (and sometimes, late-night parties) and families who see housing prices skyrocket in their neighborhoods and cities because of short-term rental investment strategies. While Airbnb continues to grow because of the passionate members of its ecosystem, it also continues to face challenges from other participants—groups as diverse as mothers' networks, local governments, climate organizations, and homelessness alliances. Thinking about how to manage and appropriately share both benefits and costs across the whole ecosystem is part of what's needed to make a new ecosystem thrive and grow over time.

THE THIRD SOURCE OF POWER: RULE-BREAKING

> New techniques, new approaches, new technologies can upset the old order, mandate a new set of rules, and create an entirely new climate in which to do business.
>
> **—Andrew Grove**[7]

Perhaps it's no big surprise, but conventional innovators are often closely bound to the status quo. They take the status quo as a given and work around the edges—adding something new to one part of the ecosystem, making an adjustment to another part of the ecosystem, and maybe taking away a bit here or there. But for the most part, they leave in place much of the ecosystem that exists today.

In this way, they're always limited by an existing web of interconnected constraints, so you often hear innovators say, "There's a limit to what we can do, because there are rules that we can't change." Or, they'll explain, "We'll never be able to get past this barrier." And that's true. When they work within the status quo, they must live by the rules that govern how things work now.

But what if you could throw out all those old rules that constrain your decisions and how things work, and play an entirely new game? When you reimagine an ecosystem, you can do exactly that. You can move the parts, rewire the connections, and change the rules. The new ecosystem doesn't have to work the same way the old system did.

If you're a tall, skinny guy, you might not be a particularly good rugby player, given that sport's demand for bulky mass. But you could imagine a different game, mounting baskets on top of ten-foot poles, which would turn out to be a much better sport for someone with your physique. And ta-dah! Suddenly instead of being a mediocre rugby player, you're a global basketball superstar.

It's the same kind of idea with ecosystems. You can change the rules to fit your capabilities and break the dependencies and the barriers that constrain you today. When Airbnb's founders created their own travel ecosystem, they changed the rules that had long constrained the hotel industry. First, they didn't have to invest time and money building their own hotel or motel rooms, because they had a nearly endless supply of accommodations provided by homeowners and renters. This change of rules flowed through to the company's economic models—Airbnb doesn't have to pay for unoccupied rooms or keep mostly empty buildings staffed during tourist low seasons. In fact, Airbnb does everything—managing its six million listings, in more than 220 countries and regions worldwide—with a little more than six thousand employees.[8]

Airbnb also used their ecosystem innovation to dodge around barriers that held others back. For example, today's travelers look for variety in lodging. Traditional chains like Marriott, Hilton, Wyndham, Accor, and InterContinental have been forced to spend huge sums of money to add new brands and update their hotels, which has been an uphill struggle because their ecosystem is set up to profit from standardization.

Airbnb doesn't face this barrier at all. Instead of being limited to half a dozen types of lodging experiences—a studio with two queen beds or a junior suite with a desk—they can offer as many different housing choices as there are people who have homes.

There's another advantage when you change the rules: entrenched incumbents who continue to play by the old rules won't be able to catch up with you. Not simply because you had the opportunity to leap out in front of them but because their old rules and constraints don't apply to your new system. This allows you to grow with exceptional speed. By creating a new ecosystem with different rules and constraints, Airbnb was able to move quickly to compete with—and overtake—previously invulnerable hotel industry juggernauts.

Of course, rule-breaking doesn't mean breaking laws or being unethical. You can (and should) set a really high bar for your ethics, so even though you break with the way things work today, you don't do things that make the world worse. Ecosystem innovators, even more than most other innovators in the world, must realize their creative freedom is not the freedom to do anything they want, regardless of the consequences to others.

THE FOURTH SOURCE OF POWER: MAGICAL SYNERGIES

> Synergy is the highest activity in all life. . . . It catalyzes, unifies, and unleashes the greatest powers within people.
>
> **—Stephen Covey**[9]

Most innovations, and most businesses, are designed to do one task well. A newly designed pair of sunglasses aspires to keep the sun out of your eyes in a fashionable way, but that's about it. This desire to narrow attention should be no big surprise since businesses—and the people who run them—have for years been told by management consultants that they should focus on one thing at a time. They don't encourage you to create something really different like Dollar Shave Club. Instead, they want you to just focus on slightly improving the razor bit by bit.

Many companies have come to believe that changing many different parts of a system at once, like Dollar Shave Club did, is a recipe for confusion. As a result, they intentionally narrow their focus so that each change they make serves just one need, one user/person, or one solution. This focus misses a powerful opportunity, a chance to create magic through new synergies. What is this magic? It is a superpower of ecosystems, where the whole ecosystem can be greater than the sum of its parts.

For example, imagine you have four individual singers. Each one of them could be an excellent performer. However, when you bring them together, new possibilities emerge. They can sing harmonies and play different rhythms against each other. Their choir is not simply the sum of four vocalists; it's something more that would be impossible to achieve as soloists.

Synergies emerge from systems to increase their impact and growth. Often no other investment is needed to get this added value; the magic happens simply by bringing everyone together. Ecosystem innovators can tap this source of free value.

Have you ever noticed the growth of restaurants in areas where Airbnbs became popular? Restaurants and Airbnb rooms work fine on their own, but when they come together in the same ecosystem, they create synergies that benefit each other.

When Airbnb travelers eat at local restaurants, the restaurants do better, which encourages the creation of more restaurants. These new restaurants attract even more visitors, which prompts more people to put their places up for rent on Airbnb. This becomes a positive feedback loop of growth (as shown in Figure 3.4)—a virtuous circle that costs neither the restaurant owner nor the Airbnb owners anything.

One of the other great things about ecosystems is that they're kind of loose around the edges, so you can continue to amplify and extend them in almost any direction, anytime. Because they don't have rigid boundaries, you can expand the value of an ecosystem simply by including more

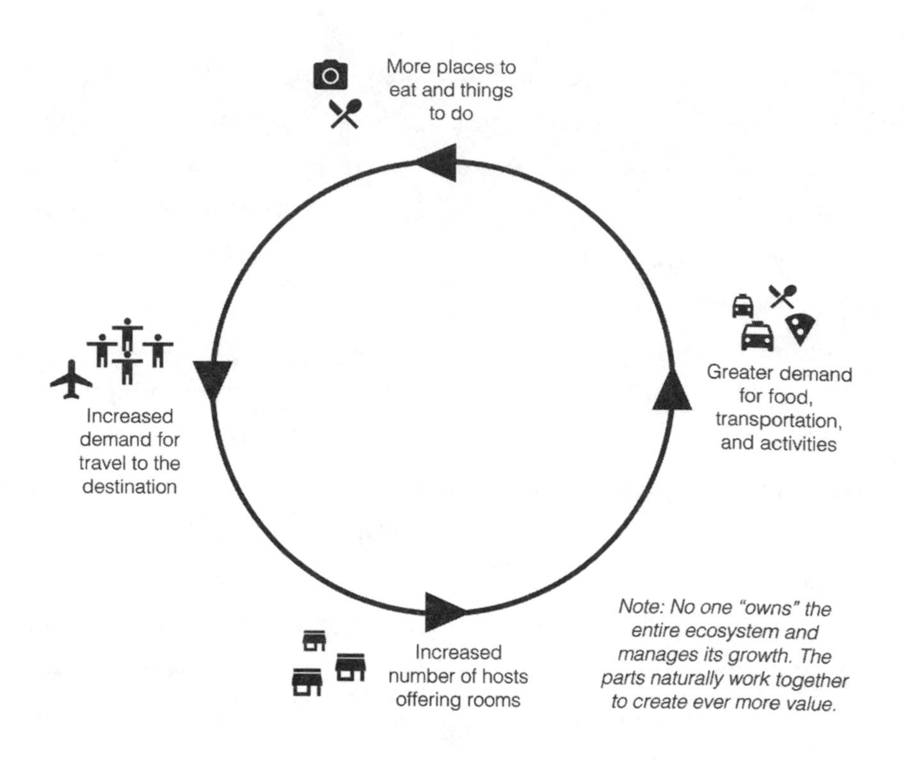

Figure 3.4. Positive feedback loops naturally drive growth in the Airbnb travel ecosystem.

participants or adding new connections. For example, both travelers and hosts benefit when the Airbnb ecosystem includes cleaning businesses that service the accommodation, or insurance mechanisms that keep them both safe.

And it's not necessary for someone to own the entire ecosystem to get these shared benefits. For example, Airbnb and its hosts may have nothing to do with creating added experiences for travelers when they arrive at their destination. But the whole travel ecosystem becomes more valuable when others offer experiences from kayaking with whales, to cuddling goats on a local farm, to participating in a downtown ghost tour. These unique experiences now appear on Airbnb for those using the platform, and so the ecosystem grows, while those new participants in it thrive.

THE FIFTH SOURCE OF POWER: ADAPTIVE FLEXIBILITY

> Problems and solutions are in constant flux; hence problems do not stay solved.
>
> **—Russell Lincoln Ackoff[10]**

For the better part of the twentieth century, the conventional approach to building a business was to make it as rigid and robust as possible. Why? So that it would be able to grow predictably and withstand big (and small) changes in the business environment. It was sort of like building an oceanside home, made from reinforced concrete and steel instead of wood and drywall—strong enough to survive the hurricanes or typhoons that might sweep the area.

The thinking was that by making your company rigid and robust, when change came, you would be able to weather the new competitive challenges; and that stability would allow executives to optimize how they made their existing products. The idea was that if you could resist change, perhaps even control change, you could give all your attention to becoming very good at whatever it was you were doing.

That is, of course, unrealistic in today's world. You cannot assume you can either resist or control change in the organizations, communities, or the broader world in which you live. In every industry there are drivers of deep change pushing organizations into new spaces. As we explained earlier, these big changes are coming faster than ever before, and no one has the luxury of simply ignoring them or taking years to adapt and respond.

Fortunately, ecosystem innovation has the ability to quickly adapt and respond. Ecosystems aren't rigid machines operating by fixed rules, and the parts can shift in response to new conditions or challenges. New Legos and connections can be added as necessary, resulting in an ecosystem that can bend and adapt like the proverbial green reed bending in the wind, rather than breaking, when facing a challenge.

For example, as Airbnb developed it found ways to provide flexibility and options for those in the ecosystem. It can support someone who occasionally rents out a spare bedroom, or a property investor who owns hundreds of apartments or properties they need to keep constantly rented. The ecosystem is remarkably flexible and can serve the needs of both kinds of people, and many more.

Airbnb is adaptable to different conditions too. With operations in more than 100,000 cities and towns, in over 220 countries and regions around the world,[11] the company must routinely adapt to different regulations, cultures, and contexts—often in real time.

The flexibility of ecosystem innovation is also a powerful tool for responding to new challenges. Consider the example of Airbnb.org, which can take Airbnb's ecosystem of hosts and homes and repurpose it to provide housing during a crisis response. Since 2012, more than two hundred thousand people—including refugees, relief workers, and those displaced by natural disasters—have found a comfortable, safe, and free place to stay through the work of Airbnb's nonprofit arm. In 2022 alone, the organization helped one hundred thousand people fleeing warfare in Ukraine find temporary housing.[12]

Few business owners would think, "I've got this company, and I can use it next week to respond to a hurricane." Yet that's what the flexibility of Airbnb's ecosystem allows the company to do.

TAKING ADVANTAGE OF THE FIVE SOURCES OF POWER

Airbnb drew from all five of these sources of power to create a remarkable ecosystem that reimagined the hotel industry. They unlocked a tremendous pool of previously underutilized assets while creating value for all the different participants in the system. Airbnb isn't just a one-shot invention, like a new heated razor (yes, Gillette sells such a product, which retails for a mere $200). Instead, it's an entire ecosystem brought together in a way that is sustainable and can respond to changes in the environment as they occur.

This is powerfully creative stuff, and it's not only available to entrepreneurs who are featured on the front page of the *Wall Street Journal*. You can build new ecosystems to shift the way your business competes in your industry. This could be done on a global scale of Airbnb, or a much smaller scale of a family business that wants to reimagine itself in a changing marketplace.

These five elements allow you to rise to any of the three big uses (or challenges) that are laid out in Chapter 2. In fact, it's hard to find people taking on important challenges who couldn't take advantage of the power of ecosystems. Yet, perhaps not surprisingly, most organizations today turn to innovation practices that seem easier and less risky, even though they actually deliver less real impact on the possibilities that matter most. In the next chapter, we dig into this well-intentioned, but limiting pursuit of simplicity that so many innovators and changemakers do every day—often leading to failed or disappointing efforts.

THE INNOVATION PRACTICE SPACE

No tool is omnicompetent. There is no such thing as a master-key that will unlock *all* doors.

—Arnold Toynbee[1]

So by now, you might be asking yourself, "If this approach to innovation is so great, why isn't *everybody* doing it?" The problem is that, over the years, most people have learned and adopted other ways of doing innovation that were designed to tackle simpler challenges. When we talk with people about ecosystem innovation, they'll often tell us, "Well, we already know how to do innovation." But what they often mean is "We know how to do a particular form of innovation, and we assume it will apply to all the challenges we face."

The danger of automatically relying on a familiar innovation practice was on display when Dan was invited to Whitehall in London for a meeting of UK government and international aid sector innovators. The setting was a fitting place for bold thinking—the room was where, two hundred years earlier, Admiral Horatio Nelson's body had been brought after he was fatally wounded at the Battle of Trafalgar. Nelson, outnumbered with his twenty-seven ships to a formidable thirty-three opposing ships, chose an innovative battle strategy and decimated the opposition. The greater force just wasn't prepared to counter his daring new maneuver.

The challenge confronted at the meeting was that far too many of the aid sector's promising pilot innovations were failing to be adopted and scaled. This mattered because humanitarian aid brings together many of the world's most difficult challenges—from the provision of clean water to dealing with gender-based violence—with all the work done in volatile, fast-moving contexts. The number of people affected is staggering. If you could bring together all the people around the globe who are facing a humanitarian crisis at any given time, it would represent the eleventh most populous country in the world.

The leading agencies and funders of international aid who attended the meeting had developed major innovation programs building on the latest high-profile innovation practices of the time. These were based on the fast-moving pilots championed by Silicon Valley technology startups.

They set up far-reaching programs and incubators focusing on social and humanitarian innovation. Many were being launched, including two hundred innovation programs in Jordan alone. Innovation pilots were like breeding baby bunnies—but while many were being born, very few were growing up.

This wasn't because they were doing a bad job with their innovation programs. These aid organizations followed the Silicon Valley technologists' playbook to a T—they were doing all the right things, including failing fast and learning quickly. But they were still struggling to scale any of the innovations to create real impact.

Instead, the problem the group faced was deeply rooted in the nature of fast-moving pilots. They were using a targeted approach to innovation on problems that weren't simple or small but had lots of complexity and real-world messiness.

Stepping back, the group could see the disconnect. Providing clean water to a community in crisis was not just about prototyping yet another brilliant water filter, and rates of gender-based violence for displaced people wouldn't be changed solely by the introduction of a new mobile app for reporting the crimes. These problems were too big and too messy for such specific solutions. And yet the intentionally simplified innovation approach they had adopted—where agile pilots limited the scope of the innovation and avoided doing the hard stuff that would slow them down during their pilot—was repeatedly taking them away from the kind of solutions they needed to create.

This is just one example of the challenges you can face when the type of innovation you use doesn't match your challenge. It's important to pick the right innovation practice for what you are doing, and for that you'll need to understand the strengths and limitations of today's four major innovation practices. This will also explain why, for so many of the important challenges and high-value solutions you face, relying on familiar practices can so often lead to failure. Let's start by looking more closely at why those baby-bunny pilots failed to deliver value in the real world.

AGILE PRODUCT INNOVATORS: LEARNING QUICKLY AND CLAIMING UNEXPLORED TERRITORY

> The fundamental activity of a startup is to turn ideas into products, measure how customers respond, and then learn whether to pivot or persevere.
>
> **—Eric Ries[2]**

In the early 2000s, the emergence of online commerce and mobile phones created environments where quickly trying out new ideas and really pushing the envelope was required to succeed. These markets were still mostly unexplored—no one really knew the full potential of the internet, or how it would one day extend its tentacles into almost every aspect of our organizations and lives. And few people imagined how mobile phones would one day become *smart*phones—handheld, web-enabled microcomputers—transforming the world in the process. It was all new; a blank map of possibilities with no boundaries drawn in.

So if you wanted to make a creative leap and enter these new unexplored markets, how exactly did you do that? There were fortunes to be made by those who were the first to discover and claim opportunities in these greenfield spaces—spaces that weren't previously developed.

With no track record of what works to rely on, these technology innovators needed a method for doing innovation that was suited to the fast-moving job of exploring untested opportunities. Their real need was to quickly pilot ideas, answer key questions about whether an opportunity existed, and if it did, rapidly develop the best solution for capitalizing on it—all without putting too much money into possibilities that would ultimately go nowhere.

This approach to innovation was popularized by Eric Ries in his widely read book, *The Lean Startup*. The book was based on several key principles for creating pilots to explore new and untested opportunities:

- Generate many ideas.
- Make the first trial of an idea as small as possible and test it as quickly as possible—creating a minimum viable product (MVP) to see if an idea works.
- Fail fast—quickly abandon failed ideas.
- But also learn from failures and pivot as necessary.
- Then double down and focus on winning ideas.

The idea of rapid exploration only works by keeping things small. If you were talking about something that involved a $100 million investment and ten years' worth of work before you even knew if it would work, you would never be able to take advantage of the opportunity before your competition. Figure 4.1 illustrates how this approach to innovation works.

One example of great success with this method is the Finnish company Rovio Entertainment. We'll bet you've heard of (and maybe even played) its most famous product: *Angry Birds*. Rovio was founded in 2003 in Finland by three university students and focused on creating games for mobile phones. By 2009, the company had developed fifty-one games—and was close to going bankrupt. Says cofounder Niklas Hed, "We knew we were able to make the best games in the world, but the problem was that you had to do loads of versions to support all the different handsets. So our development time and overheads were getting worse and worse."[3] They weren't moving quickly enough. Most of the company's staff had been let go, and only twelve employees remained.

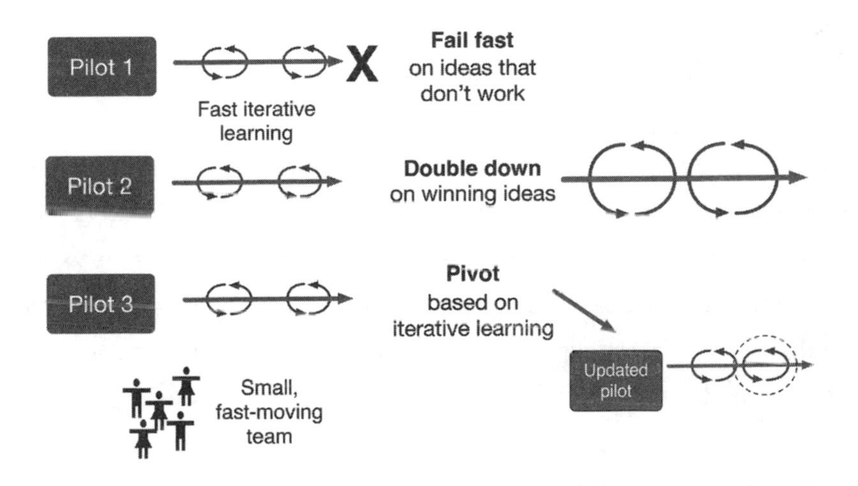

Figure 4.1. Agile pilots and products—quickly exploring new spaces

Rovio's leadership team made the decision to build one more game, but this time to focus on just one mobile platform: the Apple iPhone, which had been introduced in 2007, simplifying the pilot. Rovio's developers proposed many ideas for this game, but in testing they were shot down for being too simple, too complicated, or simply too boring. That is, until developer Jaakko Iisalo sketched the foundation of a new game: a flock of fat, wingless birds with big, yellow beaks and no feet, large eyebrows, and angry expressions.

About eight months later, the new game—*Angry Birds*—was introduced to the world on the Apple App Store. It soon became the iPhone's most popular app, with billions of downloads to date for the original and more than twenty versions of the games in the series.

The founders and developers at Rovio learned that they had to move fast. They were in an unexplored space, and saw their greatest success when they came up with something fairly simple and small—an addictive gaming app. They came up with lots of ideas, experimented, discarded ones that didn't work, learned lessons along the way, and tried again. And after fifty-one attempts, they eventually came up with *Angry Birds*. Since each game was its own thing, they could throw different ones against that wall to see what would stick without negatively affecting other games in the company's pipeline.

Tech startups naturally flocked to this innovation approach because it was fast, cheap, and promoted as *easy*. The mobile applications and websites that worked well with this method focused on specific people's unmet needs, building on the practice of user-centered design that asked straightforward questions to the innovation's users: Is there someone who has this need/problem? Do they really care about it? Can we delight them with our solution?

Perhaps surprisingly, large, well-established enterprises adopted it as well—finding that small, fast-moving, independent pilots gave them an opportunity to do creative innovation without disrupting much of their core business. Corporate innovation labs sprang up—special areas where teams could do all the pilot innovation stuff neatly sequestered away from the rest of the organization.

This agile pilot methodology works well for simple challenges or innovation by limiting the size of what you are able to do, so you can move fast, learn with simple metrics, and move on. This is an innovation model that can be done on a small enough scale that you can hide it in a closet. The problem with pilots is they deliberately avoid complexity or big challenges by intentionally simplifying the problem and the solution.

The method works when you can focus on one or two user needs or simplify a problem into one or two basic elements. But when your problem or innovation is so small, there's only so much you can do to work on harder or messier challenges. For any innovations, changes, or challenges that aren't simple, you need to work with multiple parts together, rather than working on one narrow challenge at a time.

This innovation approach says, if you want to build a car, you start with a skateboard, then you build a motorcycle, and then you get a car. Make it simple and then add more parts. But in the real world, if you want to build a car, you can't start with a skateboard. A skateboard is a simplification of something on wheels that is cheap, easy, and fast. You can do easy tests, fail fast, and learn basic lessons with a skateboard, but you will never build a car. If you start with a skateboard, you have already lost sight of what you actually need to do: work out how to build a complete working car.

The first Tesla was a two-seat roadster with an electric powertrain and lithium-ion batteries jammed into a modified version of the sophisticated Lotus chassis that went from zero to sixty miles per hour in under four seconds,[4] and there was nary a skateboard in sight. These interconnected complexities are the kinds of inconvenient things that pilots conveniently ignore, often simplifying so much that when real-life complexity is finally required, they fail to get implemented or the project ends. This creates a wall that stops pilot innovators in their tracks. It's what made so many of the humanitarian pilot innovations fail. If you avoid doing hard stuff by starting in the simplest way, it's often the most important stuff that gets left out, such as integrating with other systems, building support and getting approvals for change, negotiating hard trade-offs, or building a revenue model that works.

Agile pilots succeed when nimbly exploring untested possibilities for small or simple innovations. But they stumble when trying to put bigger, more complicated solutions in place. Does that mean innovators have always just ignored larger challenges? Of course not. In fact, the oldest, most well-established form of innovation was specifically designed to take on big projects that are far from small or simple.

ENGINEERING/REDUCTIONIST INNOVATORS: BREAKING UP COMPLICATED PROJECTS

> In the Machine Age messy problematic situations were approached analytically. They were broken down into simpler discrete problems that were often believed to be capable of being solved independently of one another. We are learning that such a procedure not only usually fails to solve the individual problems that are involved, but often intensifies the mess.
>
> **—Russell Lincoln Ackoff**[5]

At 2,717 feet tall, the Burj Khalifa skyscraper in Dubai was built as the tallest building in the world when it was finished. Building a structure like this, more than half a mile in height, is a remarkably complicated problem to be solved, and an engineering tour de force—one part meticulous planning and execution, one part applying existing technologies in new ways, and one part appealing to national pride. Referring to Sheikh Mohammed bin Rashid Al Maktoum, ruler of Dubai, a Dubai-based property developer said, "He wanted to put Dubai on the map with something really sensational."[6] And with the Burj Khalifa, which opened to the public in 2010, that goal was accomplished—and more.

Of course, the tallest building in the world doesn't get built in one day. Developers faced a building site where temperatures often surpassed 50 degrees Celsius, desert conditions that, next to the sea, produced violent sandstorms. The underlying rock was very weak, so given the extreme weight of the building, fifty-meter-deep pilings were needed.[7] Special concrete mixes had to be developed and poured at night to avoid high daytime temperatures, which could cause the concrete to cure too quickly and possibly crack.[8]

Incredible engineering innovations need precise planning. So, before anyone ever approved buying a bag of cement for the project, there was an extremely thorough analysis. A nearly endless list of things had to be considered, but for the most part, they were technical challenges that could be well understood based on experience and sophisticated engineering knowledge. The primary contractor for the project—Samsung C&T—played a role in the construction of the Taipei 101 skyscraper, which at 1,667 feet, was the world's tallest until Burj Khalifa was completed in 2010.[9] And, of course, people have been successfully building skyscrapers for more than a hundred years.

What needed to be used here is the reductionist approach to innovation. It's what engineers and detailed project management teams use to build large, complicated things—from spacecraft to nuclear power plants and much more. For this method to work, it must be possible to:

- Break the innovation into parts with clear boundaries between the pieces.

- Analyze each part in detail.
- Create a detailed plan that can be executed without significant deviations.
- Bring all the parts together in the end.

As you can see in Figure 4.2, this approach to innovation is well suited to doing really big projects that can be thoroughly understood up front and won't change significantly by the end of the project. Because all the parts are being designed to a fixed specification, it is really important for the design to be locked down and correct early on. Changes made later, say when half the tower is built, can undermine all the rest of the work.

As a result, reductionist innovators tightly control work with fixed *stage gates* to lock down choices and plans at each phase of work. Ideally, once you pass a stage gate there's no turning back. It's like you fall over the edge of a series of waterfalls, which is why this is sometimes called a waterfall approach when applied to software development.

Early automakers were champions of applying reductionist principles to all parts of their business. Henry Ford created and perfected mass-production automobile assembly lines, which broke down the assembly

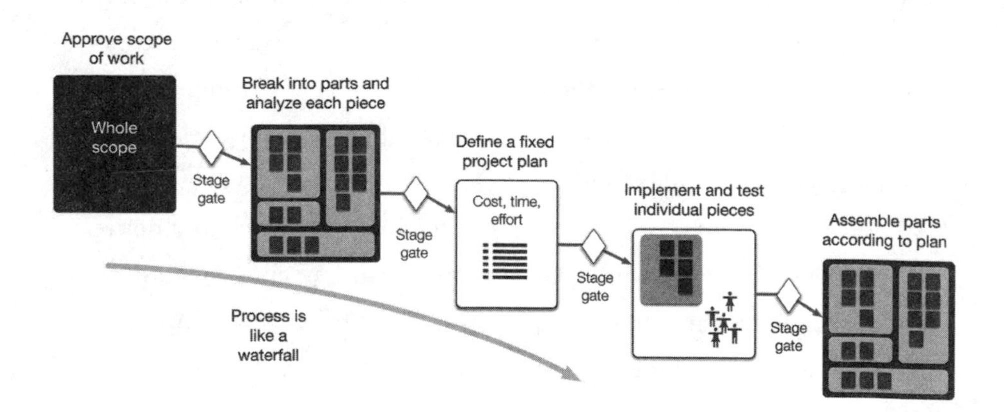

Figure 4.2. Reductionist innovation—tightly planned waterfall project delivery

of cars into a series of discrete steps. Assembly of a Model T, for example, took eighty-four steps, and specific workers were trained to complete each one of these steps.[10] Henry Ford hired the famed industrial engineer Frederick Winslow Taylor to observe workers and suggest ways to design a production line with peak efficiency and productivity.

The kind of innovation that Taylor advocated was based on the belief that efficiency could be increased through detailed analysis of activities that eliminated wasteful time and motion. People were given specialized jobs on the production line—say, bolting wheels onto a car's axle. As Taylor said, "All we want of them is to obey the orders we give them, do what we say, and do it quick."[11] When production lines were treated like machines, this really worked, even if it didn't make for rewarding jobs. The amount of time it took to assemble a Ford automobile plunged from more than twelve hours to just one hour and thirty-three minutes.[12]

It wasn't just the factory production line that could be broken down into discrete pieces. At General Motors in the 1920s, then–company president Alfred Sloan pioneered top-down management control and business silos. He divided his increasingly complicated business into distinct parts that could be designed around specific functions and operated for peak performance. His approach set the standard for business management that dominated the rest of the twentieth century.

This thinking enabled manufacturing to grow explosively for decades. Throughout the twentieth century, the requirements for reductionist design—the ability to tackle stable, well-understood problems that could be analyzed in detail—were built into the fabric of many of the world's largest organizations.

But the approach stumbled badly when the world began to change more rapidly. By the turn of the twenty-first century, the industrial leaders who relied on this rigorous approach were in trouble. At this time, Dan was working with a range of global automobile manufacturers, and he saw how this fixation on detailed analysis and control drove policies that were counterproductive in a more dynamic world. Even when American automakers faced increased global competition and waves of new technologies that left them floundering in the late 2000s—with General Motors and Chrysler both filing for Chapter 11 bankruptcy in 2009 and Ford taking a $6 billion Department of Energy loan—they held on to their tightly controlled engineering model for dear life.

They limited the scope of projects to one business silo rather than cutting across the company. They intentionally left messy users out of program design because their varied voices would make it hard to settle on specific requirements. One project specifically designed to support dealerships chose not to engage thousands of dealerships in the program design. One company even went as far as to remove the spot for forecasting new revenue on project approval forms because projections of future growth were too hard to document. As a result, even as the automotive industry was being reinvented around them, rigorously studied cost reductions became the preferred justification for new projects.

This is the Achilles' heel of reductionist innovation and those who love detailed project management. The approach can't cope with a messy, changing world, where complex problems can't be completely analyzed and planned out in advance. Those fixed plans and waterfall approvals make it impossible to respond to unexpected problems or take advantage of unanticipated opportunities. Ironically, big reductionist projects often fail because of their dedication to rigorous design and planning.

OPTIMIZATION INNOVATORS

> No more than 10 percent of innovation investments at global companies are currently focused on developing new business models.
>
> **—Mark Johnson[13]**

It would be wrong to assume that automotive companies were not innovative. Even as many managers were insisting on well-planned reductionist projects, there was someone working on how to make automakers more innovative in a different way. W. Edwards Deming made Toyota a great global competitor by democratizing innovation—developing a third form of innovation where everyday workers on the ground became a valued source of good ideas. This was an innovation approach for businesses that were intent on incrementally improving their production processes.

This practice emerged in the years following World War II, when manufacturing firms were using reductionist practices to design and build more and more factories. During the 1950s and 1960s, the big US automakers—General Motors (GM), Ford, Chrysler, and American Motors—came to dominate the global industry. In their arrogance, they decided that to build even more factories, they had to find a way to sell even more cars. To achieve this they developed the strategy of *planned obsolescence*, which meant that quality and durability weren't at the top of their list of priorities. Instead, the idea was to make the car you just bought undesirable and unfashionable within a few years, so the company could introduce flashy new models with dazzling bells and whistles—prompting you to trade in your frumpy old car for a shiny new one.

As Harley Earl, GM's head of design, said in 1955, "Our big job is to hasten obsolescence. In 1934 the average car ownership span was 5 years: now it is 2 years. When it is 1 year, we will have a perfect score."[14] If Earl got his wish, they could build more factories, to make more cars, which they would sell to their ever-growing market.

In the wake of World War II, Japanese automakers, which lagged behind US and European firms, realized they needed to compete on something different, and the something different they decided to compete on was improving cost and quality. They would make a better car that cost less. Instead of building more and more new factories they would make each factory work better and better every day.

Deming led this revolution, and his philosophy was quite different from the one promoted by Taylor. Deming didn't think any process was ever perfect. Instead, he saw people as active contributors to ongoing efforts to improve both quality and cost. Toyota's Total Quality Management (TQM) program was about people continually working to optimize and improve the performance of the current process.

Essentially, instead of having specialized experts design every process and lock it down, ideas for incremental improvement were solicited across the organization, encouraging widespread creativity and getting suggestions and ideas from people who were closest to the problem. They didn't make big changes, like rebuilding a production line from scratch, but this democratization of innovation could provide a stream of new ideas that improved quality and optimized efficiency one step at a time.

The methodology works like this: First, you measure the baseline of how a status quo operation or product works. Then you make an incremental change and measure again to see whether there was enough of an improvement to justify a permanent change. If not, you discard the idea. But if it works, you implement it, as illustrated in Figure 4.3.

This formal, repeatable model works well, because the way things work *right now* can be thoroughly understood and measured. This provides a baseline that can be used to test improvements, while checking for impact from each new idea. Once the testing is complete, the best ideas can be implemented. This provides a great example of Pareto's 80-20 rule, where 80 percent of value is said to come from 20 percent of actions. A Total Quality Management team's job then is to generate lots of ideas and use rigorous measurement to pick the ones that deliver the most value.

At its essence, this approach to innovation is a simple, predictable methodology for making small improvements to the status quo. Its true

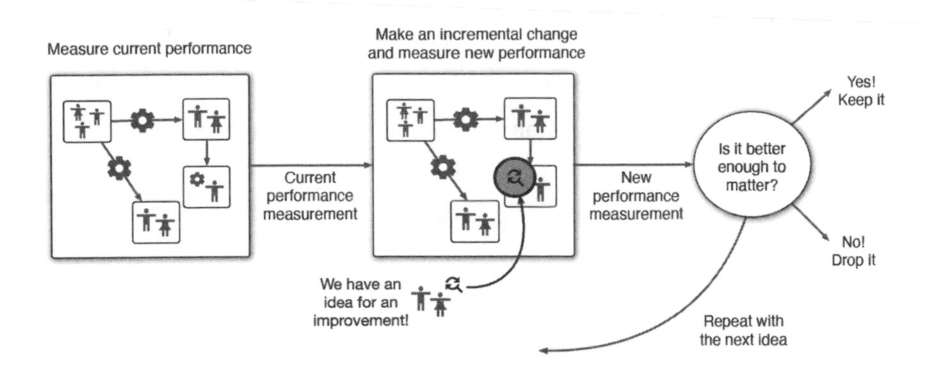

Figure 4.3. Incremental optimization—measure and test new ideas

power comes from the ability to make these improvements continuously, so things can always be getting a bit better. And it works. Optimization makes operations and products better, which is incredibly important for businesses working in industries where the standard of performance is consistently and incrementally being raised. This incremental innovation practice has become a big part of innovation culture, with examples of Deming's approach to incremental improvement found across different organizations that have standardized operations.

There are TQM shop floor programs that engage workers in the mission to improve operational performance. There are also customer engagement programs where organizations ask customers for ideas and suggestions on how products can be improved. In recent years organizations have begun hosting exciting innovation events—hackathons and innovation fairs designed to tap creative energy and solicit ideas for improvements that come from across the entire organization.

That said, there are clearly limits to incremental improvement, especially when it comes to organizations that want to take bigger leaps forward, are under threat from disruptive competitors, or face major changes in their sector.

Incremental improvement makes the basic assumption that it's good enough to make the status quo a little bit better, one small step at a time. But as we've said, in every industry today, emerging competitors are making current providers obsolete. Ultimately, it doesn't matter how much you've optimized performance if no one wants what you're offering. If you are about to be hit by that bus, crawling slowly off the road is not going to save you.

THE INNOVATION PRACTICE SPACE

> Seek simplicity and distrust it.
>
> —**Alfred North Whitehead**[15]

Each of the innovation methodologies we explore here—agile pilots, reductionist engineering, incremental improvement—works in specific circumstances. For example, agile pilots are excellent for quickly exploring and testing ideas in a new area where there is little understanding, with relatively small products. Reductionist engineering is effective for large, complicated projects in areas of limited change, which can be analyzed in detail up front. And incremental innovation is useful when there is a working status quo that can be improved bit by bit.

You can see in Figure 4.4 how each of these approaches sits in the innovation practice space. They all lean on simplicity of some sort—rather than dealing with messy, changing issues.

There is a seduction to this simplicity; it's comforting to think you can deal with something simple rather than face something messy. But the reality is, when you use tools that make something look simple when it is not, you will likely fail. The same is true if you pretend that everything can be understood up front and won't change, or that everything can be a simple test when it isn't. This is a problem, because today's messy, big opportunities, complex challenges, and high-impact

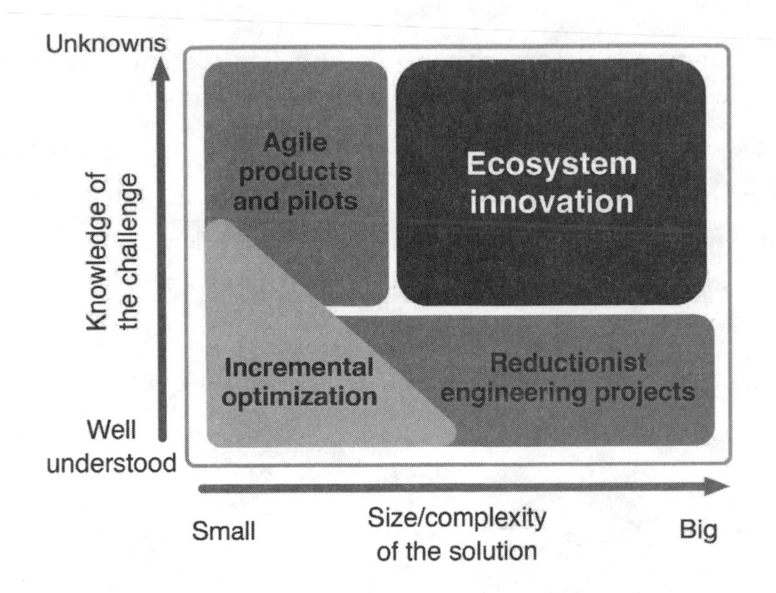

Figure 4.4. A variety of approaches to innovation—different tools for different jobs

innovations sit in the upper right of the practice space, the area where ecosystem innovation lives.

Even well-trained innovators are often unaware of the limitations of their approach. You will often find experts in these practices still telling you that you should follow their methods as it will reduce your risk of failure with your work, no matter what you are working on. But as we've seen, each of these innovation approaches stumbles in areas where they don't fit. Unfortunately, the combination of experts and the familiarity of these practices creates a false sense of certainty and control. This comfort quickly disappears when your work hits the gray areas that are not well understood.

We're not saying you don't need these other innovation methods—they are very useful where they apply. They just aren't the tools suited for today's most important innovative work. If you're going to do bigger things, you need to work with the reality of what you have, and you need the power to work in today's messy spaces. This is where the big opportunities are, the ones that matter the most across any industry. And this is what ecosystem innovation does well.

Now that you know there is a method for pursuing big ideas and dealing with more challenging problems, you are probably wondering what comes next. Part II is about how you rise to the challenge.

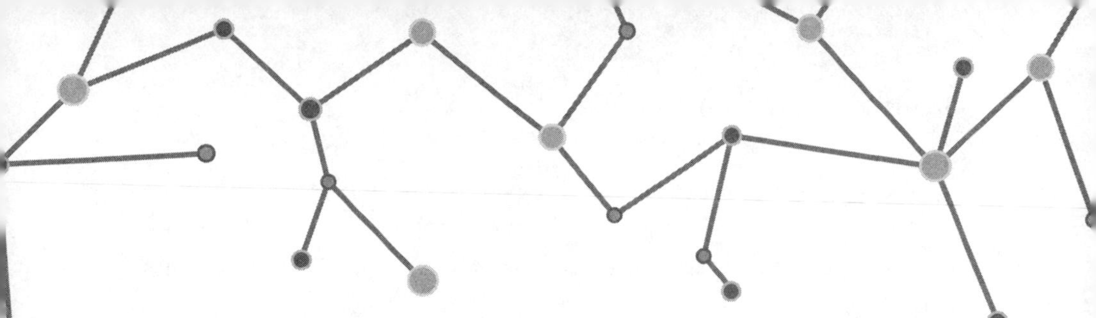

PART II

THE PEOPLE

Innovation distinguishes between a leader and a follower.

—Steve Jobs[1]

So what does it take to successfully use ecosystem innovation on the important challenges and exciting opportunities around you? Innovation can't be a mysterious thing that only a handful of special people in exceptional circumstances can do. You need to be able to step up to a problem worthy of your effort and deliver results with lasting impact. You need to have a practical approach that you can confidently use whenever the occasion demands it.

Fortunately, as you may have guessed, ecosystem innovation isn't magic. There are people all over the world using the resources and skills they have at hand with ecosystem innovation, and succeeding. Once you understand what must be done, you can choose to claim this work.

In this part of the book, we dive into what it takes for you to be successful as we explore the emerging role of an innovation choreographer. Choreographers help shape a future vision for the ecosystem and are powerful storytellers—going from place to place, describing their innovation, and making the case for its success. They lead everyone involved on a creative journey that makes the world work differently. We can tell you from personal experience that it is an amazing job to have—a fantastic role to play.

You might well be one of these choreographers, or you might be a leader who needs choreographers on their team to succeed. Either way, you'll want to understand the big-picture thinking, connection building, and rule-breaking that are needed to tackle important challenges, reimagine businesses, and make innovations work in the real world.

THE CHOREOGRAPHERS

As soon as I knew it was a profession, I knew it was mine.

—Jessica Chastain[1]

If you look at a satellite photo of the twin cities of Laredo and Nuevo Laredo, they appear to be one big city, a singular metropolitan area. However, look closer, and you'll see that Laredo is in the United States and Nuevo Laredo is in Mexico, and the two cities are divided by a wide moat filled with slow-moving, chocolate-brown water—the Rio Grande.

Despite this physical and international separation—rigorously enforced by the US Border Patrol—in many ways these cities function as one, with approximately ten thousand people crossing the border each day to work, shop, go to school, get medical care, visit family, and more. Says Dr. Victor Treviño, who led the Laredo Health Authority during the COVID-19 crisis, "Laredo has always had a rich history as a border city that has always been intertwined in culture, commerce, and family with its sister city of Nuevo Laredo."[2]

During the pandemic, as vaccines were rolled out around the globe, the availability varied widely based on where you lived. In Laredo, on the US side of the river, vaccines became widely available and most anyone who wanted to be vaccinated could—while vaccines were in short supply in Nuevo Laredo. By mid-2021, approximately 7 percent of Nuevo Laredo residents were vaccinated, compared to roughly 70 percent in Laredo.[3]

As it turned out, there was an ample supply of surplus vaccine doses in Texas that were not being used. Given their limited shelf life, these unused vaccines would normally be destroyed—representing many thousands of missed opportunities to save lives and reduce human suffering. What if these surplus vaccines could be repurposed, provided for free to the people in Nuevo Laredo who so desperately wanted them? A good idea, but since the vaccines couldn't be transported from the United States to Mexico—political realities wouldn't allow that—what if someone created an ecosystem to bring those people who needed them most to the vaccines?

Dr. Treviño worked with the Mexican consulate general, Laredo fire chief, and Laredo health director to create an ecosystem designed to distribute the surplus vaccines. Buses were arranged to pick people up in Nuevo Laredo and drive them to the center of the bridge between the two countries. Then teams of medical professionals would move quickly through the bus, providing injections.

This is a classic case where existing Lego blocks were used in creative ways to solve a big problem. The vaccines existed—in fact, these surplus doses would have been thrown away if not used before their expiration dates. The buses that transported people to the vaccination site were readily available, and a bus full of fifty to sixty people could be vaccinated in just seven and a half minutes using shallow plastic tubs suspended from the neck that are commonly used by children to sell gum, candy, and other snacks to people in their cars in Mexico.[4] Then the buses would quickly return and pick up another group. By March 2022, about two hundred thousand doses had been administered to residents of Nuevo Laredo, and the overall vaccination rate for the city jumped to 50 percent.[5]

Dig down behind the most inspiring ecosystem innovation stories, and you'll find there is a person, someone who sees the big picture, builds bridges, and solves messy problems. They are regular people who have claimed a new but real job at the center of ecosystem innovation. The role is called an innovation choreographer, and it's one that you can pursue as a career. In the pages ahead we help you find out if you are a choreographer or what you need to do to hire one.

Whether they knew it or not, Dr. Treviño and his son, Victor Treviño Jr., who led the mass vaccination program, were acting as choreographers. They imagined an innovative ecosystem and then pulled together all the different parts—the vaccines, the politicians and government authorities whose approval they needed, the medical workers and volunteers who administered the vaccines, and those who received the vaccine. They cut across traditional boundaries—physical, political, and bureaucratic—and created a working ecosystem with real-world impact.

Choreographers are making the world work in new ways, often without traditional levers of power or deep pockets, as the story of Dr. Victor Treviño illustrates. The Treviños didn't have a huge budget; they didn't have federal or even Texas state government approval; and they didn't have a model to follow. But they had the vision to see the big picture, the ability to get others on board through powerful storytelling, and the drive to create an innovative ecosystem that worked with what they had at hand.

The great news is, if you are energized by messy challenges and passionate about ambitious ideas, then this is a job you can claim. You can be a choreographer of innovation—a master of messy, creative action—doing big things out in the real world. It's also good news if you're an executive or leader charged with making big things happen, because you know who you need to put on your team to succeed.

THE IMPACT OF A CHOREOGRAPHER

> We're going to create a new class of artisans . . . inventing new jobs that hadn't been imagined a year before.
>
> **—Cory Doctorow**[6]

In the arts, a choreographer is someone who arranges the performance of a group of dancers to achieve a creative vision. You might think of this as a niche profession, but step back and you'll see that bringing together the talents of many people to deliver on a big vision isn't limited to the dance studio. For example, you could be the choreographer of a global initiative to eradicate malaria or the choreographer leading a new business innovation that creatively connects people, organizations, and technology.

Leaders know that having the right people in key roles is the secret sauce for success. This is certainly true with messy work. A choreographer at the heart of your journey makes it possible to do any of the following:

- *Pursue bigger dreams.* They're going to make it possible to drive bigger ideas, go after more important problems, and discover more ambitious solutions.
- *Have a more successful journey.* In the wandering path toward a successful innovation, the choreographer helps navigate a journey of learning and adaptation. They also will get you closer to success faster.
- *Circumvent barriers/change.* Choreographers can use a big-picture view to circumvent barriers and deal with change in a complex world, increasing your chances of success.

To fill this exciting position, it won't do to utilize a professional who is specifically trained to avoid risks with a work plan spelled out in painful detail—like a traditional project manager. This is because all their years of training and natural intuition will consistently lead them in the wrong direction. To be successful, you need a big-picture thinker, a boundary crosser, who can build toward a bold vision.

CONTINUING A HISTORY OF NEW INNOVATION ROLES

The history of innovation practices shows that as a new way of innovating takes hold, each methodology creates a demand for people with specific skills to make the practice work. While at first, the emerging roles seem strange and unconventional, they eventually become an established part of college curriculums and organizations' hiring practices, as illustrated in Figure 5.1.

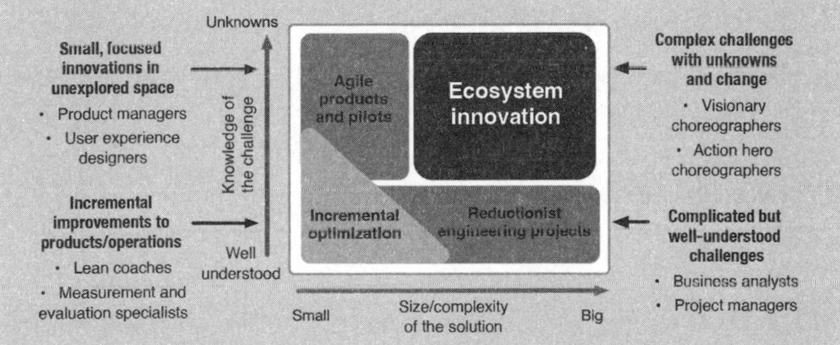

Figure 5.1. Creative roles emerge with each new innovation practice.

For example, looking to the twentieth century, the increased reliance on engineering/reductionist innovation (the lower-right corner of our innovation map) created a need for an innovation leader who could track and manage the details of big, complicated projects such as building bridges and developing business software. The professional project manager emerged as a key role, becoming a widely recognized profession in the 1990s.

When innovators began to focus on optimization—where the goal is to make things incrementally better, or cheaper, or with more consistent quality (the lower-left corner of the innovation map)—a different

continued

kind of specialist was needed to coach teams so they could identify and test improvement ideas. Because data on performance is key to this practice, lean coaches were supported by specialists in measurement and evaluation.

Exploratory product innovation meant the agile pilots (upper-left corner of our innovation map) needed nimble designers who could target new user needs and then progressively design products and services to meet them. The demands of this work led to the creation of a pair of new roles: user experience designer and product manager. This latest generation of positions, which emerged after the turn of the twenty-first century, became the darlings of both technology and business organizations as they rushed to create technology products in response to waves of opportunities in the digital economy.

In this history of new creative roles, choreographers have been the latest to emerge. This means you may find there isn't the same level of recognition as these other positions, but that's okay. It takes time for roles to emerge after each new kind of innovation becomes established. For example, for several years after the initial revolution of online business opportunities, and even after the explosion of digital products in 2007 with the iPhone release, there often weren't recognized roles for the UX (user experience) designer or product manager. However, that has changed—big time. By 2020, there were nearly seven hundred thousand product managers on LinkedIn[7] and over two hundred thousand UX designers in the United States.[8]

RECOGNIZE A CHOREOGRAPHER'S UNIQUE TALENTS

> How do you innovate? First try to get in trouble. I mean serious, but not terminal, trouble.
>
> **—Nassim Nicholas Taleb[9]**

So are you a choreographer? Let's dig a bit deeper to find out. A choreographer's job is not simply a matter of rebranding an existing role. We have learned, for example, that a good project manager who is organized and methodical can make a bad agile product manager, because they need to be fast-moving and adaptive. Likewise, we're going to find that choreographers need five distinct talents and skills:

1. *Big-picture thinking.* When you master this, you will see across an entire challenge and be able to step back to imagine new possibilities for an innovative ecosystem.
2. *Crosscutting bridge-building.* When you realize you don't live inside the box, you can cut across boundaries to weave things together in new ways.
3. *Strategic rule-breaking.* Mastery of this skill gives you the courage to act on your inner rebel, breaking with the status quo when it's necessary to imagine something new.
4. *Adaptive problem-solving.* This skill helps you take action even with unknowns and uncertainty as you use your problem-solving skills to keep moving forward.
5. *Powerful storytelling.* Once you have this down, you can paint a picture of a better future, bringing others along on a creative journey.

To support this kind of work, choreographers need to be generalists, not specialists. Specialists know a lot about the way things work now—their expertise is based on proven practices and what they already know. Because they value deep, detailed knowledge, they generally view knowledge outside their field as a distraction.

In contrast, generalists leverage a broad, mixed set of knowledge. They leverage a portfolio of ideas where the parts may often be unrelated. And as a result, choreographers will naturally accumulate a background that's full of lots of different things. One of the best choreographers Dan ever worked with had his undergraduate degree in classical Greek languages, which is not a credential many organizations are recruiting for. He wasn't alone. Fruit salad resumes are common among choreographers, where degrees in seemingly unrelated fields are mixed in with jobs that hop, skip, and jump across different industries.

What many organizations fail to realize is this diverse knowledge is an extremely powerful tool. The more different things you know, the more Lego blocks you've got to work with. The phrase "jack of all trades but master of none" misses the point. A generalist choreographer has the tools to be a creative expert in the big picture—and so, because of that, you can be extremely skilled at combining knowledge in new and creative ways.

A choreographer naturally spends a lot of time on this big-picture view. Instead of approaching a challenge from the bottom up, getting every detail in place, they tend to start with a broad view of relationships, trends, and actors. However, they aren't just about the top-down view; they can access details when they need to. They can nimbly move from the balcony to the dance floor—they ground their thinking by looking out at the big picture, get down into the details, and then jump back up to the big picture. Because they have the big picture to hold onto, they can be comfortable making this shift back and forth, from broad view to detailed view, over and over again.

VISIONARIES AND ACTION HEROES

You'll find that it's good to have other choreographers working side by side with you. This offers the benefit of giving you a chance to spread the work around, and there will be plenty of work if you have a big, ambitious idea to pursue. But having creative partners can also help you focus your own attention where you work best. The five major choreographer skills can be daunting, and while you may be able to rise to each challenge if pressed, most people excel in some skills more than others. As a result, in practice we've found that there are two distinct types of choreographer.

Back in 2002, when Dan was working with Dawn Kurc—another scrappy choreographer—they came up with names for these two breeds of choreographer: visionaries and action heroes. The first role, the visionary choreographer, is most comfortable with big-picture thinking about challenges and creating the vision for the innovative ecosystem. They want to design and architect the future but have less interest in the often messy journey to implement the vision. These big-picture thinkers really enjoy setting big goals, understanding complex challenges, and creating a future vision.

The second breed of choreographer, the action hero, is often a bit impatient with the strategizing bits of the process, and more naturally sets their priorities on driving forward to action. They're energized by putting ideas into practice, planning the journey, and then taking action to use the innovation in the real world. Negotiating trade-offs, removing barriers, and solving problems in real time are all things that get them up in the morning with a fire in their bellies.

Both kinds of choreographers are generalists and dedicated ecosystem innovators. They each see the big picture and break rules. But there is a difference in practice. Visionary choreographers get their best energy from doing big-picture imagination, while the action hero is revved up by taking action. You can see how these could make a powerful pair, so it's no surprise that we often see visionary and action hero choreographers teaming up. In fact, on our own team, Dan is very much a natural visionary, while Jenny leans powerfully into the action hero role.

GIVE THE PROFESSION A NAME

While other innovation roles exist across many organizations, there are still comparatively few clearly defined roles for choreographers. While we find natural choreographers across the businesses we work with, these people have often improvised their own personal approach to the work. They frequently wrestle with two issues:

1. Inventing an approach to what they do (ecosystem innovation)
2. The job they perform (choreographer) hasn't always had a name that everyone knows and uses.

That's a problem, because if you don't have a name for what you do, no one can create the right position to hire you, and you can't find other people like you for learning and support. It's also a problem for the leaders of organizations who desperately need to hire someone to do bigger things inside their organizations.

It's interesting that while there are many well-recognized roles like a choreographer in the arts, similar positions in the world of business are uncommon. Business roles tend to support the idea of breaking the work into pieces and performing specific responsibilities—often within strictly defined organizational silos. In the arts, however, there are many roles where people need to have ownership of a collaborative effort, pulling together a lot of different parts into a complete vision. Film directors, TV showrunners, music orchestrators, and of course dance choreographers are all responsible for taking multiple parts, pulling them together, and creating a high-value whole.

So after years of working to shape and define this role in ecosystem innovation, we landed on the name *choreographer*. Early on, when we mentioned it to people, it resonated with them—it clicked. For most people, it seems the name intuitively reflects the creative job of coordinating different participants, parts, and actions within a broader vision.

A name is a starting place for creating a role, but it's hardly the only hurdle. Organizations need to embrace the skills and talents that make choreographers successful. For years, traditional organizations have valued attention to detail and the ability to organize work within a set structure, which means they are biased toward specialists and top-down managers. Even as the world changes, they have tended to hire employees based on a twentieth-century factory model that puts a high value on people who are good at delivering work according to an unchanging plan. And throughout the nineteenth and twentieth centuries, most public schools were set up to hone, measure, and deliver workers with just these kinds of skills. And that's a problem—but fortunately one we can solve.

EMBRACE THE ROLE OF CREATIVE REBEL

> Truth tellers are genuinely passionate about solving big problems. . . . They are not model employees—their true loyalty is to the future.
>
> **—Larry Downes and Paul Nunes[10]**

People in traditional organizations are expected to stay in their lane, and many "high-performing" organizations have intentionally defined silos and roles designed to consistently deliver what the status quo does well. To be successful as a choreographer, you need to envision yourself as a well-intentioned shaker-upper. This isn't simply a personality trait; crossing boundaries and challenging the way things are done is at the heart of your job.

Ironically, many people have been taught that skills like this, which are most important for their success, are faults they need to fix or hide away. Don't listen to the people who only want you to fit in their box. You'll be a lot more successful if you don't yield to their pressure and instead lean into the talents of a creative rebel. This kind of independence isn't about tearing things down; it's about doing what's needed to build something new.

Let's explore three ways these choreographers get big things done. Creative rebels must:

1. Work across boundaries
2. Be courageous and independent
3. Bring people along

Work across boundaries. Choreographers have the exciting job of assembling the Lego blocks of the world in new ways. You routinely reshape the status quo, intentionally working across silos and breaking with existing roles and practices. Think of fundamentally acting *horizontally*, across organizations. Most business organizations are set up to operate vertically—decisions and information flow from the top of the organization down, and then back up to the top, often in rigid silos that are hard to break down. Choreographers, on the other hand, are oriented to work across an organization and even across multiple organizations and groups.

Ironically, because this crosscutting work can be seen as disruptive, in many organizations the innovation team charged with doing game-changing innovation is often tucked away in a corner. Even though the team is asked to create something groundbreaking, no one actually spends much time working with the people outside their small team. Many of us know this is a recipe for failure, because when a big idea finally emerges, the rest of the organization won't be ready to join in and things rapidly grind to a halt.

Be courageous and independent. If you're pursuing meaningful innovation, you'll probably find there isn't a natural boss to oversee such far-flung work. This means you'll need the confidence and maturity to do challenging work without the common structure or formal direction that exists in most organizations today. This isn't always an easy thing to do.

Ambiguity and change will shift and redefine what your job is from week to week. Every day, you're going to have to figure out what you need to do to make your innovation work, and then have the determination and independence to push it forward.

It takes courage to act without the comfort of formal permission from those in charge. While some people may complain, "My boss won't let me do this," or "My boss won't let me do that," the truth is, they find it reassuring to be in a position where their boss takes responsibility for giving permission and making them feel safe.

To be successful you will have to have both the courage and the mature independence to keep pushing forward in a messy, fast-changing environment. Jenny has a friend who worked with the National Health Service in the UK doing an incredible piece of research. At some point during the project, three National Health Service group leaders told her, "You can't do this. You need to speak to us first." Faced with pushback from multiple nationwide agencies, other people might have put on the brakes. Instead, the friend took a choreographer's persistent approach. She didn't stop her work. She kept pushing ahead, pulling the different people and pieces together toward the long-term vision. Along the way she reached out to the group leaders, finding a way to add them as new collaborators. Her opposition stopped being barriers, and instead became part of a growing solution.

Bring people along. Ecosystems are built around diverse people and organizations working together. Because you see the big picture, you are in a unique position to inspire everyone to continue to move forward (as Jenny's friend did), even if things look bleak, which of course, they sometimes will.

Choreographers act as stewards of a future hope, and it will often be up to you to continue to push forward when others are churning in uncertainty. Because you may not have the same formal authority that people in the organization's hierarchy do, you must use your skills, personality, insights, and ability to sell possibilities and solve problems to get things done.

You help others get around barriers and fears by making a compelling case to step into the future, often without hard evidence or proof, and no guarantee that everything is going to go well. This isn't the kind of pitch you can make with a stack of spreadsheets.

Instead, it requires you to develop the skills of a persuasive storyteller, distilling and telling a story for change in powerful ways that people understand. In short, you must pull a clear melody out of the messy noise of change. You won't do this just once. The experts in this work often have empathy for the challenges each listener faces, adapting the story to focus on each person's unique concerns and opportunities.

FIND THE RIGHT KIND OF BOSS

> What set Silicon Valley apart was not just Stanford University or the warm climate. It was that the place was open to and supportive of the creative, the different, and the downright weird.
>
> **—Richard Florida**[11]

For all the challenges routinely faced, it's enormously helpful to have good bosses—sponsoring leaders who aren't going to demand top-down control. The best bosses guide and protect choreographers in their organization without preventing them from doing what they need to do. They use their political and positional power to create a dome of safety over the work, within which the choreographer can move.

This doesn't mean that you can do anything you want. The boss who creates this dome of safety also has the responsibility to let us know where the boundaries are—the limits to the amount of disruption the organization can tolerate, or the sacred cows that can't be attacked. With this knowledge in hand, you know when and where to stop pushing so you don't inadvertently step over the line and begin to take on too much personal and professional risk.

INTENTIONALLY HIRE CHOREOGRAPHERS

> I am convinced of one thing—that in the future, talent, more than capital, will represent the critical factor of production.
>
> **—Klaus Schwab**[12]

For years people have been doing this kind of work almost as insurgents. They were putting together different parts into a broader vision, crossing boundaries, building incredible things—but without a formal name for it, or formal recognition for what they were doing. Organizations had few choreographer-type roles and often didn't even know who the people with choreographer skills were inside their own walls. Now, as the need for more sophisticated innovations grows, organizations face an urgent need to intentionally create a space for choreographers and to hire them to fill these crucial roles.

So if you are an organizational leader, how do you find a choreographer? In our experience, the characteristic most frequently mentioned when seeking out innovators is being "creative," closely followed by "problem-solver." These are important, and so you may assume that everybody who's in innovation is a creative problem-solver. The thing is, there are problems, and there are *problems*. We have already discussed how other forms of innovation have problems that are tidier and neater than the ones you are likely encountering if you are reading this book. You need to find someone who can rise to these challenges.

The good news is, there are lots of things an organization can do to hire and retain the kind of skilled professional who will be a good choreographer. Here's our top-five list:

1. *Promote the real job.* Confidently describe the real role of a choreographer and design the criteria for hiring to get the right talent in the door. People really want this work if you spell it out. We worked with a client to hire a very senior role in this position. And one of the things they heard from people applying for the job was "Finally! This is the work I actually do, written down on a piece of paper." So choreographers are going to be excited about the opportunity if you clearly describe the position.

2. *Don't mislabel the work.* Don't compromise by using a more familiar job title that is wrong—or just sort of right. Many organizations already have choreographers, but they're often hidden under different job titles. They're given names like lean innovation coach, product manager, or business strategist—all of which may have other meanings unrelated to the actual responsibilities of a choreographer. They sort of fit, but not really. Recognize that just because it might be easier to call someone a product manager, those names imply other skill sets and demands, making it more difficult to find and inspire the person you actually need.

3. *Apply the right criteria.* Traditional firms will often end up failing to consider skilled choreographers because they are looking for the wrong thing. A traditional hiring manager might prioritize expertise in a technical field like insurance underwriting, when what is most important is experience with big-picture thinking. Sadly, bad priorities are often baked into many organizations' formal evaluation criteria.

4. *Look for hidden talent.* Many organizations already have choreographers, but they're often not formally recognized. Sometimes you'll find choreographers in completely inappropriate roles—such as audit—that have little to do with their real skills. Ironically, great choreographers can underperform in more detail-focused roles, since they bristle at having to live their lives in structured detail. And so some of the best choreographer candidates may not look like stars in their current positions.

5. *Provide the right work.* Once your new choreographer gets in the door, you need to give them the right kind of work and support them while they're doing it. Hiring someone as a choreographer and then asking them to be a detail-focused project manager is almost guaranteed to lose them—both mentally and, eventually, physically. Don't assume that just because they're doing some kind of innovation, it will work. Just like other roles, choreographers need a space that's designed for them to succeed.

LEARN TO SELL YOUR TRUE GIFTS

> Tell a story that is worth sharing. Tell a story that's unforgettable. And tell a story that makes things better.
>
> **—Seth Godin**[13]

When we talk with people in group settings about this idea of choreographers, they often run up to us, excited because what they've been doing for years has finally been given a name. They have hope and feel they can stop hiding in job roles that don't recognize their talent. Now, finally, they can claim a role that empowers them to make their unique mark in the world.

To help find those roles, you also need to do your part. This begins by helping educate hiring organizations and leaders. To sell your gifts, you need to be able to:

- *Target a worthy challenge.* Explore the kinds of important but challenging problems the employer needs to address. (Hint: Look for messy, high-value opportunities that require bold thinking and an ability to break from the status quo.)
- *Show what's needed.* Explain what you do and why it's needed for success in their bold challenge. (Hint: Talk about addressing messy problems together, shaping practical solutions across boundaries, and the stories of creative success that makes it possible.)

- *Explain why you.* Show why this type of innovation needs somebody like you in the role. (Hint: Tell your story as a history of tackling complex challenges and big opportunities.)

Choreographer careers seldom follow a conventional, stable job progression—they tend to jump around, moving from challenge to challenge. So you should talk about the types of skills and the big themes that run through your experience. Instead of focusing on specific subject matter expertise, try framing your mix of experiences as a continuing journey of big-picture thinking, crosscutting complex problem-solving, and the ability to inspire and lead change.

DO WORK WORTHY OF YOUR TALENT

> The best way to change a life of frustration into a life of mastery is by developing talents and strengths, not just shoring up weakness.
>
> **—Edward Hallowell**[14]

One of the most empowering events in Dan's career came to him by way of a coworker who was an action hero choreographer. It had been a really bad day on their ecosystem innovation project—an audacious attempt to rewire one of the largest businesses in the world—but with each meeting it seemed like the ambitions just kept getting smaller and smaller. It felt like everyone was questioning why the vision had to be so big, or why familiar processes couldn't be more closely followed. Dan and Julie were dispirited, close to feeling like they should apologize for offering their time and best talents on a multimillion-dollar challenge for a company that was in crisis and on the verge of bankruptcy.

Julie turned to him and said, "We deserve work worthy of our talent." And she was right. The unique, if unconventional, talents you have are legitimate, honest gifts that make essential contributions to important work. You shouldn't twist your career and life into knots, sacrificing your talents on smaller conservative assignments, even when the headwinds—schools, friends, employers—may push you toward a more traditional job.

This work is too important to ignore. It would be a tremendous waste to keep people who have these exceptional gifts from using them or force them to accept positions that don't include their skills in the job description. We face a unique moment in history when our creative potential is unprecedented, as we face bigger, more difficult challenges than ever before.

CREATING A CHOREOGRAPHER PROFESSION

- Recognize the choreographer's unique talents.
- Give the profession a name.
- Embrace the role of creative rebel.
- Find the right kind of boss.
- Intentionally hire choreographers.
- Learn to sell your true gifts.
- Do work worthy of your talent.

YOUR NEXT STEP

In the depths of frustration, Dan found truth in the words "We deserve work worthy of our talent." His colleague was right: we must not settle for less. As you begin the next chapter, imagine the dream that fuels your ambition—the problem you want to solve, the business you want to reimagine, the innovation you want to thrive. To succeed with this vision, you have three crucial jobs you'll need to perform. You must create a complete solution, inspire others to join your cause, and navigate uncertainty through action.

WHAT IT TAKES TO BE SUCCESSFUL

> Today, functional problems are becoming less simple all the time. But designers rarely confess their inability to solve them.
>
> **—Christopher Alexander**[1]

When you choose to step into the messiness of real-world challenges, taking on an ecosystem innovation, what do you need to do to be successful? When you boil things down, there are really just three main jobs. You need to be able to:

1. *Create a complete solution.* Select the right parts or Legos and arrange them in innovative ways that work in practice.
2. *Make sure everyone gets a pony.* Motivate people and organizations to embrace your innovation to make it work.
3. *Take action and adapt.* Work with the unavoidable uncertainty and unknowns of the real world and take creative action.

We walk through each of these three jobs using the example of education. Years ago, Jenny worked to set up a network of global humanitarian innovation labs to tackle challenges people face in crisis. During one of her trips to Iraq, she was in a refugee camp in the desert trying to understand the challenges and opportunities that mattered to people. The refugee camp was made up of row after row of emergency shelters as far as you could see. Those who lived there had crossed the border from Syria seeking safety from the war. They came with very little, and received food, water, clothing, and incidental items to meet basic needs.

As Jenny walked through the camp, a woman in her late fifties invited her into her shelter. The woman had been a French teacher in Syria, her husband a tailor, and her two daughters had almost finished high school. In Syria, they had a nice house in a nice town, and they enjoyed a stable, middle-class life. She had planned for her daughters to go to college. That is, until war came and the conflict found its way to their front door. They didn't want to leave. They had built their lives there. But they "had to let that life go."

Now, sitting in a shelter that was just over twenty square meters, she heard that the average time someone was in a refugee camp was seventeen years. Looking at her situation and age, she told Jenny, "Forget about us. Forget about me. Forget about my husband. Our time is done."

She paused for a moment and then continued. "I need to change the future of my daughters. They need to get out of this camp. They are smart and can have a good life if they get a university education, but they can't do that here. They can't even take university entrance tests."

All she could dream of was her daughters getting out of the camp. She knew if they had the opportunity to get a university education, they could build another life. They were smart, they could do amazing things in the world, but they needed the opportunity, the access. That was a future she could hold onto.

This is the kind of big important problem where ecosystem innovation can make a difference. How do we provide an education that prepares someone for a real role in today's global work, but from a place where there's a strain to meet many of the basic needs of day-to-day life? Let's explore the jobs to do to create a successful ecosystem for these girls and others around the world.

JOB 1: CREATE A COMPLETE SOLUTION

> A city sidewalk by itself is nothing. It is an abstraction. It means something only in conjunction with the buildings and other uses that border it, or border other sidewalks very near it. The same might be said of streets.
>
> **—Jane Jacobs**[2]

Seeing a complete, big-picture view of your innovation is your first job. You need to grasp all the parts and how they connect in the ecosystem you are working on. To do this, step back from thinking about just a small fix or change and look at the whole thing. We talked earlier about avoiding simplicity and living in the reality of the messy world. Well, here is the key: Don't get tripped up on small inventions or individual actions. Instead, zoom out and imagine a whole picture of what you are working on with all its connected Legos.

For example, it wouldn't be unreasonable to think that technology might offer a silver-bullet solution to the girls' education problem. For decades now, a growing online learning revolution has been sweeping the world, and there are many real successes. A fifteen-year-old Mongolian boy, Battushig Myanganbayar, was recognized in the *New York Times* when he used online courses to study remotely from his home in central Asia, achieving a perfect score in a difficult Massachusetts Institute of Technology (MIT) course in circuits and electronics. He later built on this success to apply to MIT and be accepted.[3]

Stories like this are exciting, but the unused educational technology littering the backs of classrooms highlights that making education work in real life requires far more than a magical bit of technology. So let's take a closer look behind the scenes at Battushig's inspiring story, examining the ecosystem that made it possible to turn his hard work into academic success.

You will find there was a whole web of Lego pieces that were connected that supported Battushig's success. First, Mongolia devoted a lot of time and money in building a modern information technology infrastructure, including a 3G mobile phone network. Mobile phones are ubiquitous throughout the country, and most homes are connected to the internet, so that "even on the steppe, with only sheep in sight, you can get a signal."[4]

Second, as Justin Reich, director of the Teaching Systems Lab at MIT, points out in an article, there was "a community of people working together to raise the quality of education in Mongolia."[5] This community of people included the school's principal—Enkhmunkh Zurgaanjin, the first Mongolian graduate of MIT—who offered the class that Battushig took. It also included Tony Kim, a Stanford electrical engineering student working on his PhD, who for ten weeks assisted in the running of educational classes in Mongolia. And it built on learning experiences from a network of formal and informal satellite classes that use curriculums based on free online edX courses to target a "small, defined, often face-to-face cohort of students."[6]

This really highlights how building and connecting all the different parts of an ecosystem enables you to do incredible things. In this instance, the remote learning technology was important, but it wasn't enough by itself. The complete ecosystem also included a Mongolian school principal, a graduate student from Stanford, and a broadly available internet infrastructure, empowering Battushig to work from a high school in Mongolia and to succeed in prestigious and difficult courses at MIT.

You Can't Leave Pieces Out

You need to be able to see the big picture and you need to make sure that all the parts are in place for the ecosystem innovation to work. Even one missing part can be a showstopper. Take the young women in Iraq looking to get a college education in their refugee camp. Before they can participate in any classes, they'll need access to technology (computers or phones), electricity to power the technology, and internet connectivity just to sign in. If even one piece is missing, it all fails, as shown in Figure 6.1.

You don't have to go to a refugee camp, however, to see this kind of challenge. A technology-driven educational divide exists in all sorts of communities. A UNICEF study found that worldwide nearly two-thirds of school-aged children were disconnected from education at home, with poor and rural communities being particularly left out of the digital education ecosystem.[7]

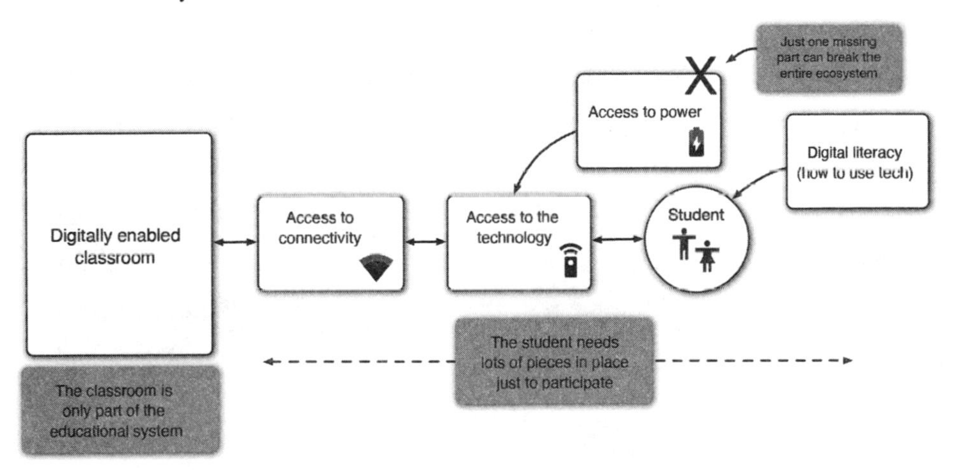

Figure 6.1. Having most of an ecosystem isn't enough—you can't leave pieces out.

Lessons from Job 1: Create a Complete Solution

- *See the big picture.* Ecosystems are built from many different parts. To get greater value and impact, you need to move beyond simple incremental solutions and bring together multiple pieces.
- *The connections matter.* It's not just about the parts. It's how the parts are connected to each other that creates value. You gain immense power by seeing and shaping those connections.
- *Don't leave pieces out.* You can't leave out parts and expect the innovation to work. Often an ecosystem won't work if a key piece is missing.

JOB 2: MAKE SURE EVERYONE GETS A PONY

> If we don't understand the forces of resistance, we end up placing the blame on the people and institutions that reject our ideas and not the dark forces that undermine them.
>
> **—Loran Nordgren and David Schonthal**[8]

We like to say, "Everyone gets a pony." This concept is at the heart of your second job. When you create an ecosystem innovation, you also need to make sure the different goals, motivations, and capabilities of the people who are part of your innovation are recognized and addressed. If you don't, they won't participate in making it a success.

This is one of the things that sets ecosystem innovation apart from technical engineering. If you are building a machine—a clock, for example—you might argue that the machine you're building meets all the prime conditions of an ecosystem. A clock has lots of parts and all those parts connect to do a job—tell time. What makes an ecosystem different is that the pieces in it aren't just gears or cogs or springs. The most important contributors are people and organizations with their own reasons for taking action and expectations of their unique benefits and costs.

Dan was working with the UN and their innovation programs on the main challenges innovators faced in global disasters. At a workshop in Geneva that brought together experts from all around the world, Dan asked, "What's the biggest barrier you face?" His assumption was that the most common answers were going to be lack of funding or the difficulty of setting things up in conflict areas, which are hard and complex things for everyone. To Dan's surprise, almost everyone's answer was something along the lines of: "Someone's going to tell me no. It might be someone in my organization, or a donor, or someone else."

He was truly stunned, because these were not lightweight innovators. They were all heavy hitters with access to international partners and skilled teams. But their biggest barrier was that someone was going to tell them, "No, you can't do that." Even if the innovation worked, there was the issue of funding and capability, and even if it was clearly a good idea, people still needed to be persuaded to participate. This scenario plays out in organizations and businesses all around the world, all the time. It can make it seem that there's always someone there waiting to stand in your way.

After working so hard on an innovation, it is easy to blame the people who refuse to change, seeing them as backward-thinking sticks-in-the-mud. They are the problem and not the innovation, right? But that is seldom the whole story. More often this failure occurs because someone has failed to give that person a pony.

Everyone Needs a Reward That Matters

It's important for you to constantly remember that every person or organization in your ecosystem has a choice, a vote on whether they will work with your innovation or not. You can't assume that people or organizations will be dutiful gears in the machine and agree with everything you want to put in place. You should expect that they will each require a reward for their particular contribution of time, money, attention, or participation. And those who aren't given a reason to participate may well become your opposition.

Unfortunately, innovators often focus on giving rewards to the people they care about and neglect thinking about and providing rewards to the people they don't like or don't think should matter. And then they're surprised when their initiatives fail. And yet the reason their solutions don't get adopted is simple: they gave a reason to participate to just half of the people that mattered.

Getting this right sounds hard, so it can be tempting to simplify the job by relying on one person in power to steer the ship and make the choice for everyone. Unfortunately, even if it seems they have the authority to enforce choices or actions, this seldom leads to success. A heavy hand might work for a short while, but eventually people will do what they want and may even abandon your ship if they feel ignored.

But here's the great part: Ecosystems are often able to generate a whole range of benefits for different participants. For example, teachers deserve fair pay for their work, but this isn't their only reward. Teachers also get satisfaction from seeing students learn and grow. So if better pay isn't an option at that point, perhaps finding ways to deliver better student participation and success is.

Often you don't need to be responsible for creating these incentives, someone else participating in the ecosystem can. This means you don't need to end up in battles for how to divide up limited resources—you can use your creativity to find ways to generate and share motivations and incentives among the different participants in your ecosystem.

UNLEARNING NARROW DESIGN FOCUS

For years, business innovators were accused of working in ivory towers. They were seen as remote experts who sat in R&D labs or corporate strategists in board rooms—people with no real contact with those the organization ultimately served. There was more than a little truth to this accusation. In fact, according to research conducted by HubSpot, 42 percent of companies do not survey their customers or collect feedback.[9]

So it's clearly been a step forward over the last twenty years when innovators have come to see the importance of actively involving the users of an innovation in its design. It makes no sense to create solutions without talking to the people who are actually living with the challenge. The company IDEO has been well recognized for its efforts to promote the concept of *design thinking*, which they define as "a human-centered approach to innovation—anchored in understanding customer's needs, rapid prototyping, and generating creative ideas."[10]

Considering user needs when doing an innovation is obviously a good idea, but in practice it can be done in a way that leads to problems with hard or messy challenges. In the past, innovators using design thinking have often been instructed to focus on solving a particular issue for a designated user. While you are listening to someone's real needs, you are giving all your attention to one primary person.

Zooming in on a problem like this provides the innovator with clarity and focus, which is really useful if you are going to design something like a piece of new technology. You have one user voice to listen to. So if you wanted to design a piece of educational technology you might focus your attention on talking with students, the users who need to get an education.

However, when working with messy problems that have multiple types of people involved, such as a teacher, a student, a mother, and an educational content creator, you need to engage different people across an entire ecosystem. For most messy or complex challenges

continued

there is no one user or one need that can be the focus of attention. An ecosystem innovator can't narrow their focus, even if this is a best practice for other innovation practitioners. You obviously must care about the needs and desires of people and organizations. They are what make up your ecosystem, but you can't focus on just one person or one concern. Everyone matters.

Lessons from Job 2: Make Sure Everyone Gets a Pony

- *Provide rewards to everyone.* People and organizations need a reason to work in your ecosystem. You can't treat people like parts of a machine.
- *Recognize different motivations.* Not everyone is the same. Rewards need to match the motivations of each participant.
- *Anyone can create rewards.* Don't just fight over fixed resources. Create and use diverse incentives from participants across the ecosystem to generate rewards and build win-win situations.

JOB 3: TAKE ACTION AND ADAPT

> A plan that is too specific will soon lie in tatters. Daily plans are tidy, but life is messy.
>
> **—Tim Harford**[11]

If you are working on a challenge like delivering education in a refugee camp, you can't know everything up front. There is no way you can look inside someone's mind, or into the workings of an organization, and know exactly how they will respond to something new. This reality drives your third job—the need to take action even when you are wrestling with a challenge that has unknowns and uncertainty. Imagine if every morning you opened the front door, but there was a heavy fog outside. You could wait until everything was clear, but then there is a good chance you would *never* begin.

To be successful you must be comfortable with taking steps forward, even when there's a fog of unknowns. Let's imagine how you could see if a new educational innovation was going to be embraced by students, teachers, and parents. There are a lot of uncertainties and unknowns, so instead of trying to analyze each piece, you could set up a small version of the classroom and the families of the students, give them an early version of your innovation, and see what happens. When you start doing the learning in real life, things might go very differently from how you expect. That's okay: as the students, teachers, and parents interact, you'll discover both problems *and* opportunities.

The secret here is you don't have to give up if things don't go according to plan. You can adapt as you go, navigating through your innovation's unknowns. Because you have the courage to step into the fog and begin, your innovation can evolve through a continuous cycle of learning and adapting. With each new version of your ecosystem (*your innovation*), you might add new Lego blocks as you go or change the way participants work with each other. Or you could shift people's rewards. You become a master at adapting as you go, rather than depending on rigorous planning and analysis before the initiative starts.

Learning in a Changing World

There is something you need to be careful of in this process. Taking action to learn is a powerful tool for dealing with unknowns, but change comes with a cost. You can't simply go out and change the way the world works over and over again, expecting it to be the same every time. With each experiment you run, there will be repercussions that shift the options you'll have in the future.

This isn't true for other innovators working with simpler innovations. For example, web developers can run thousands or even millions of tests to see which website design or ad campaign works best with their users. If they want to know whether an ad should feature a dog instead of a cat, they can easily test the question. For example, repeated online testing was able to show that dogs are better for selling cars and cats are more persuasive for mutual fund investors.[12] During this testing, there is very little cost to either the product innovator or the reader of the ad. If one ad doesn't work, they try another, over and over. The price they pay for learning is exceptionally low.

In ecosystem innovation you can't simply repeat tests, because each test potentially changes the world around you. Imagine you're trying to make a choice between College Degree 1 and College Degree 2. You are basically picking between two future ecosystems for your life. Like the web designer, it'd be nice to simply make the decision over and over again and see which choice produced the best results. But because you are making changes in the real world, picking one college degree means you will pay a real price to change your choice and move to the other degree.

This is called *path dependence*, and it creates a cost for learning when working with bigger problems in the real world. You can and should plan to explore unknowns by testing how your innovation works. But know that each experiment has the potential to change the future options you have as an innovator. So you also must get good at adapting your innovation, *the ecosystem*, even as the world changes your future options.

Lessons from Job 3: Embrace Unknowns, Uncertainty, and Change

- *Take action in uncertainty.* Ecosystems will always have unknowns and change. You can't wait to know everything before taking action.

- *Manage risk by adapting.* The way to manage the risk of unknowns and uncertainty is to continuously learn how your innovation works and adapt with each new insight.
- *Recognize the cost of learning.* Be aware of path dependence when taking actions. Each change that produces learning also changes your future options.

THE STEP-BY-STEP PRACTICE THAT DRIVES SUCCESS

When you can master these three key jobs, then doing really big things doesn't require some kind of magic. In Part III, it's time to show you how to get those jobs done, by focusing on the all-important question of how.

In Part III, we no longer discuss concepts, because it's time to dive into the realm of action and execution. This is the part of the book where innovators like yourself turn dreams into reality. In the pages ahead, we give you a practical step-by-step process to implement ecosystem innovation successfully. We guide you through the five major tasks that are crucial to delivering an impactful ecosystem innovation. And by the time you finish this book, these tasks will provide you with the framework you need to tackle the biggest and most fascinating challenges and opportunities in our world.

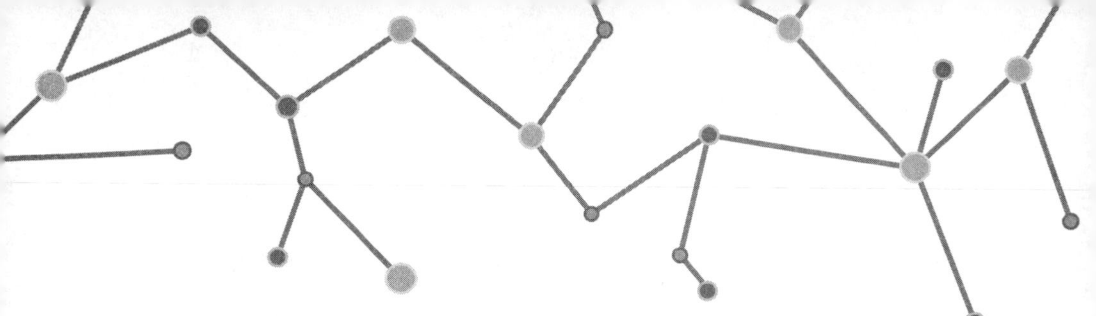

PART III

THE PRACTICE

> It turns out that "having the idea" is just a small part of the process, perhaps only 1 percent of the journey.
>
> —**Scott Belsky**[1]

Now that you know all about the *what*, *why*, and *who* of ecosystem innovation, it's time for the *how*. In Parts I and II, we took a deep dive into new opportunities for ambitious innovators, introducing you to examples of people successfully using ecosystem innovation to do big things and have a tremendous impact on the world around them. We defined ecosystem innovation, dug into the roots of its remarkable power, explored what you need to do to be an ecosystem innovator, and considered how it differs from the most common approaches to doing innovation today.

Now, if you're ready to innovate with ecosystems, it's time to take the next big step, putting concepts into practice. And that's what Part III is all about. This part lays out a clear and practical approach to take on big and interesting opportunities in your world. It's not magic. A lot of the concepts and techniques that we describe draw on familiar innovation practices, but there are also fundamental differences that make doing ecosystem innovation exciting work.

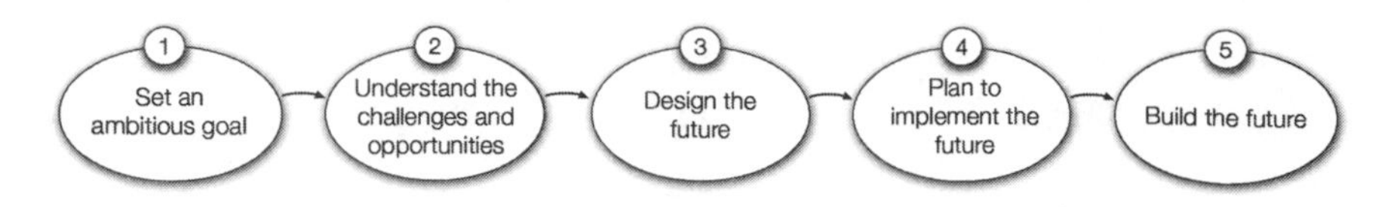

Figure III.1. The ecosystem innovation journey

To deliver an impactful innovation, you'll need to work through five major tasks (see Figure III.1), which we describe in each of the chapters in Part III:

1. Set an ambitious goal.
2. Understand the challenges and opportunities.
3. Design the future.
4. Plan to implement the future.
5. Build the future.

To help you work through these tasks, each chapter walks you through a challenge that must be addressed and the steps you need to take to tackle it. In each chapter, we provide you with:

- *The job to be done.* This is the core thing you need to do in the task.
- *The steps to follow.* A practical set of things you can do to successfully complete each step.
- *A checklist.* If you find yourself wondering what you should do in practice, this quick checklist will get you on the right track.

The five tasks that we explore in Part III will take you on a journey that begins by creating a powerful goal, then shapes a vision for your ecosystem innovation, and finally takes action to make that ecosystem real. Each task builds on the ones before it, so the work you do at the beginning lays important groundwork for the later tasks. That said, ecosystem innovation is not a waterfall process where once you complete a task the results are set in stone. Over time you will likely need to go back and forth across the different tasks, making changes to what you've already done based on new things that you learn and discover. It isn't a failure. It's a key opportunity to learn and adapt, so that you can dodge barriers and move more quickly and strategically toward an ambitious goal.

Let's begin the journey with the foundational task, setting a shared ambitious goal.

7

SET AN AMBITIOUS GOAL

Houston, Tranquility Base here. The Eagle has landed.

—Neil Armstrong[1]

Bold goals drive the creation of powerful ecosystem innovations. They provide the fuel and direction for people to work together to achieve great ambitions. And this is what we will be covering when we go over the first task: set an ambitious goal that aligns actions. This is what US President John F. Kennedy did in the 1960s, using a pair of famous speeches to call for a great collective effort to land humans on the surface of the moon and safely bring them back home to earth by the end of the decade.

On May 25, 1961—the date Kennedy first publicly set this goal in an address to a joint session of Congress—the United States was losing its space race with the Soviet Union. On October 4, 1957, the Soviet Union had launched the first human-made object to orbit the earth—Sputnik 1—and a month later, they launched the first living creature into space, a dog named Laika. By 1959, the Soviet Luna 2 probe became the first human-built object to land on the moon, and on April 12, 1961, Soviet cosmonaut Yuri Gagarin became the first man in space—making a single orbit around the earth.[2]

The Soviet Union had a huge lead when it came to all things space, and everyone knew it. From this lagging position, it would take a bold goal to inspire the American people and align them in action, so that the country could really compete in the space race. It was against this background that President Kennedy made his address to Congress in May 1961. In part this was a request for funding, but he took the opportunity to call for a much greater commitment than simply a budget line item. His goal was to spark the bold, aligned action of an entire nation.

> I believe that this nation should commit itself to achieving the goal, before this decade is out, of landing a man on the moon and returning him safely to the earth. No single space project in this period will be more impressive to mankind, or more important for the long-range exploration of space; and none will be so difficult or expensive to accomplish. . . . In a very real sense, it will not be one man going to the moon—if we make this judgment affirmatively, it will be an entire nation. For all of us must work to put him there.[3]

One of the powers of an inspiring goal is that it can be built on and retold, rekindling excitement. So it wasn't a surprise that a little over a year later—on September 12, 1962—President Kennedy doubled down on his call for aligned action in a speech at Rice University in Houston, Texas.

> We choose to go to the moon in this decade and do the other things, not because they are easy, but because they are hard, because that goal will serve to organize and measure the best of our energies and skills, because that challenge is one that we are willing to accept, one we are unwilling to postpone, and one which we intend to win, and the others, too.[4]

In a fairy tale, this kind of powerful speech would be told and then the heroine would go straight on to triumph—confidently sailing the stormy ocean and rescuing the prince. But in real life, there are many ups and downs on the quest to pursue such a big idea. The international competition to push boundaries in space was intense. Less than a year after Kennedy's Rice University speech, on June 16, 1963, Soviet cosmonaut Valentina Tereshkova became the first woman in space. Her mission lasted a total of three days, during which time she orbited our planet forty-eight times.[5]

Yet hard challenges don't have to be the end of the story. Kennedy's speeches stand as supreme examples of storytelling that aligns action around a big goal. He was able to tell an inspirational story about his goal that could spur a nation to action. It was more than a simple "We're going to the moon in ten years." He doesn't make the journey ahead sound easy. Instead, he lays out how it would feel to have a country work together toward high ambitions and act with urgency.

It is remembered today because it's such a compelling story for taking action. And because it worked. On July 20, 1969, Neil Armstrong climbed down the ladder of the Apollo 11 lunar module—located at Tranquility Base—and became the first human to set foot on the surface of the moon.

SETTING BIG GOALS

Kennedy did two important things with his speeches: He focused a diverse group of people and organizations on a goal, and he inspired them to take action. This is one of the key jobs of a leader who wants to take advantage of ecosystem innovation, and it lays the foundation for the work that follows.

In this chapter, you will learn how to define a playing field that aligns collaborative action by setting ambitious goals and clear guardrails. This is how you move mountains, enlisting many different actors and resources outside your direct control.

Why Is This Important?

- *It inspires bold action.* An ambitious goal inspires people and organizations to pursue and prioritize actions that make bigger things happen.
- *It draws in diverse participants.* A compelling goal helps you engage more talent, drawing in diverse people and organizations so you have more capabilities to draw on to create more powerful solutions.
- *It aligns collaborators.* Shared goals help participants drive in the same direction toward the result you want, so you can use the full power of your enterprise and its collaborators.
- *It empowers autonomy.* Knowing the goal makes it possible for people to independently make informed choices and use their knowledge, so you can move faster and more effectively toward your goal.
- *It guides good choices.* Shared guardrails reduce the risk of rogue behaviors and ensure your values and principles are not lost in the creative process.

THE CHALLENGE: ALIGNING ACTION ACROSS THE INNOVATION

> When people know the desired destination, they're free to improvise as needed in arriving there.
>
> **—Chip and Dan Heath**[6]

Think for a moment about just how difficult it was to get a man on the moon—238,855 miles away, give or take—and then bring him back home safe and sound.[7] The effort had to bring together the most brilliant people across the United States (and around the world) and support collaboration across hundreds of different organizations. The challenge required an ecosystem of widely different participants—each with their own priorities and challenges—to work toward an ambitious goal that required all their interconnected efforts.

Now, you might not be trying to put a person on the moon, but *your* ecosystem innovation will also have many different participants. What you're creating is an interconnected web of pieces, where everyone must ultimately be part of a shared idea—a shared future. You're not going to make that kind of ambitious change alone, so your big job with this first task is to get other people aligned around the effort.

What's the best way to do this? You might trust everyone to just go out and take action on some important piece of work without setting a goal to point toward. That could seem quite empowering, the kind of thing an enlightened leader would do. But when dealing with a big challenge, so much freedom without direction is likely to produce disappointing results. While everyone may do something important, all that furious action will point in different directions. As shown in Figure 7.1, there may be lots of change from how things work today, but it doesn't easily come together to lead to a new and better solution.

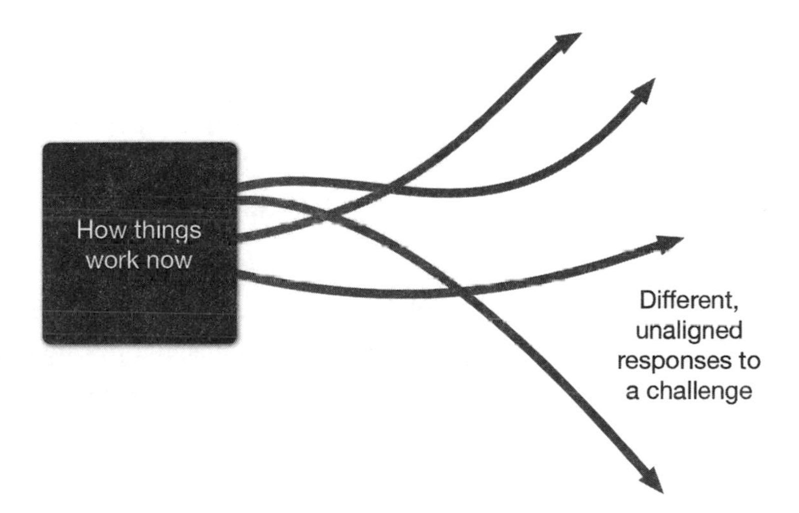

Figure 7.1. Freedom without direction leads to energetic but unaligned action.

As an alternative, you could choose to go in the other direction, appointing yourself the boss of everyone, but you know how that works. Think back to the last time someone just assumed top-down control of a messy challenge, handing out assignments and directing the work of everyone in the room. Rebellion or desertion likely followed close behind. Even in business environments, where top-down control is the norm for many everyday operations, it's hard to make top-down control work when building something big and messy. A boss sending instructions from above will be too slow and too ill-informed, and the talented people receiving those directives will resent the fact that they have little to no say in the matter.

When control is centralized, there's little expectation of individual initiative on the part of those people who are farther down in the organization. You lose the opportunity to tap their insights and creative solutions, but this is exactly the kind of support you'll need as you work to shape and build your innovation.

Step 1: Create an Inspiring Big Goal

> All companies have goals. But there is a difference between merely having a goal and becoming committed to a huge, daunting challenge—like a big mountain to climb.
>
> **—Jim Collins and Jerry Porras**[8]

Instead of setting everyone free to do whatever they want, or being a top-down autocrat dictating specific instructions, imagine you are putting a sports team onto a playing field. You want everyone to bring their best talent to a shared effort at winning the game. As a leader, your first job is telling them which game they're playing and where the bounds of play are.

This is how Kennedy aligned action within NASA, a sprawling government agency with hundreds of thousands of agency and contractor employees working on a variety of different projects.[9] He set an inspiring big goal, so that while NASA was hard at work getting a man to the moon, everyone within the agency was aligned on that mission—from the very top of the organization to the very bottom. Mark Zuckerberg tells this apocryphal story from the early days of the moon mission: "One of my favorite stories is when John F. Kennedy visited the NASA space center, he saw a janitor carrying a broom and walked over and asked what he was doing. The janitor responded: 'Mr. President, I'm helping put a man on the moon.'"[10]

President Kennedy didn't lay out one particular solution that would become a straitjacket for future imagination and exploration. Nor did he slip into language like "You've got to pick the one, most important problem," or "You have to focus on this particular solution." That is the way many traditional innovators talk when they are targeting simpler problems.

Instead, he provided a big vision—the goal of putting a man on the moon, a destination that guided and motivated the work of everyone involved. NASA, like many other government agencies, could have focused on a list of concrete actions they wanted to perform, such as securing funds, ordering rocket parts, and designing futuristic-looking space suits, but that would have neither inspired dedicated action nor kept everyone in hundreds of different work lines moving toward the same shared goal.

Big goals lay the foundation for your innovation. The best goals not only define the innovator's playing field; they also serve as a call to action to do things that really matter. They are inspiring and have the power to pull people forcefully into the future, embracing changes that break with the status quo. These big goals also boldly announce where everyone is going and fire up the courage required to take the journey.

Jim Collins coined the term Big Hairy Audacious Goal (BHAG) to describe this kind of challenging and bold vision. Collins explains, "The best BHAGs require both building for the long term AND exuding a relentless sense of urgency: What do we need to do today, with monomaniacal focus, and tomorrow, and the next day, to defy the probabilities and ultimately achieve our BHAG?"[11]

While Collins originally applied this term to commercial businesses, it can be the start of *any* ambitious innovation. You need a big goal whether the innovation is being shaped by a business, an innovation team, or a community creating social change. Not coincidentally, this is the same idea behind today's approaches to progressive leadership—moving from command-and-control management to providing employees with opportunities to create autonomy and alignment. This isn't freedom without direction. Instead, in fast-moving, complex markets, organizations hire smart people, give them a compelling goal, inform them of the guardrails, and let them loose on an important challenge, supporting their efforts along the way.

Conventional innovators spend a lot of time worrying about goals being *too* big, which is ironic. We often need to be visionary game changers, but it's not uncommon to find innovators spending a lot of time worrying that their goal will cost too much, or they won't get the right approvals. We worry about disrupting the status quo or taking on too much risk. As a result, we can come up with ideas that aren't as big as they could and should be.

Instead, we should look at big, important challenges and see that being timid has its own risks. If the goals aren't big enough, the problems the organization faces may never be solved, and new opportunities might never be pursued. You can help others come along with you by asking, "What's the danger of not making enough change? What's the danger of being too timid?"

AN AUDACIOUS BAKERY'S BIG GOAL

Our bakery owner from Chapter 2 isn't trying to put someone in space, at least not that we're aware of, but they should have a bold goal to align efforts toward a new ecosystem. Let's see how their big goal might evolve as they think through it.

- *Begin with a simple goal.* Their goal to "make a profitable bakery that delivers healthy food to the community" is not particularly inspiring. That's because it doesn't really point to the future. It's more like a performance target for the manager.
- *Try again.* Make the goal bolder and future focused. If you stretch the vision and say something like "Transform our conventional bakery into a nighttime bakery that serves students from the university," you're getting closer. But it's still pretty specific. This phrasing points to the future—but a narrowly defined one. As time goes on, it won't invite in different ideas or guide what happens after the night bakery is open.
- *Consider an inspiring goal with the flexibility to grow over time.* A more flexible goal could be "We believe great baked goods bring happiness whenever you have them, so we want to be pioneers of providing this joy in more parts of people's lives." This goal certainly includes the possibility of becoming a nocturnal bakery, but it also allows people to think more broadly. It doesn't box you in to a specific project. Even after the nighttime bakery is a success, it creates space for future possibilities (perhaps fresh-baked croissants delivered by drone?).
- *Test whether the goal is exciting to others.* Could you, for example, use it to sell someone on taking a job to be part of the adventure?

Note that while it is thrilling to imagine a big goal that's powerfully inspiring, you also need to actually make your vision work. So while you want to take on challenges that are big enough to matter, you don't want to claim ideas that are too big to get your arms around and succeed. For example, Kennedy didn't propose to start the space program by going to Mars. Instead, he set a goal that was both ambitious and potentially within reach.

Ironically, a more focused goal can often turn out to be far more powerful than a goal that is drawn too broadly. Consider, for example, the community activist group called Elevated Chicago that Dan had a chance to collaborate with.[12] Their goal was to help neighborhoods that have been bypassed by the prosperity that other parts of their city enjoy. It's a worthy goal in the third largest US city, but also one that is incredibly broad. In this instance, so many different things could be done to help achieve this goal that it would be difficult for local groups and organizations to come together on a specific set of paths for action.

Instead of embracing an all-encompassing view of the problem, Elevated Chicago focused on opportunities to shift transportation policies and investments in support of these communities. A more tightly bounded playing field provided focus for everyone working on the challenge. Their underlying motivation was the same—to help communities left behind in urban growth—but now they could target their partnerships and action around innovations to the transportation ecosystem. This positioned them to be much more effective and successful innovators.

Step 2: Define Guardrails on Must Do's and Must Not Do's

> Our history is based on extending the brand to categories within the guardrails of Starbucks.
>
> **—Howard Schultz**[13]

Being able to shape the future also makes us responsible for the future we create. One of the great powers of ecosystem innovation is its ability to break rules and reinvent the way things work. Of course, there are real-world implications to your work. You're changing rules and making choices about things in people's lives. The act of doing this kind of work can engage people in deeply intimate ways that affect their lives into the future, and that's a big responsibility.

You need to set guardrails on the type of innovation you create. Consider, for example, the ethical challenges Uber and other rideshare companies faced as they pioneered a different kind of urban transportation ecosystem. For sure, they created an extremely financially successful innovation, but they also had to wrestle with questions about how they would address costs for its willing and unwilling participants. Observers were concerned that much of their success was made possible by exploitive labor practices, such as treating drivers as independent contractors instead of employees, paying them less than minimum wage, and leaving people out of the new transport ecosystem by not having options for disabled people or those with children. Thinking about how you view these big issues up front helps make sure the innovation you create also aligns with your principles and values.

When so much is possible, guardrails help ensure there is shared agreement on where everyone will and won't go as the innovation evolves. The default assumption for collaborators is that everyone should have a lot of freedom to do what they think is best to make the innovation successful. But there need to be certain things that, no matter what, will or won't be done. These are the guardrails on your actions. For example, a "won't do" might be something like the innovation won't violate community standards or break laws. And a "will do" could specify that your innovation will respect data privacy.

Guardrails can help make sure you don't violate ethics, beliefs, or policies. Once you've set your goals and guardrails, you empower other people to work with greater autonomy and alignment toward realizing the innovation. When combined with strong goals, the guardrails fully define the

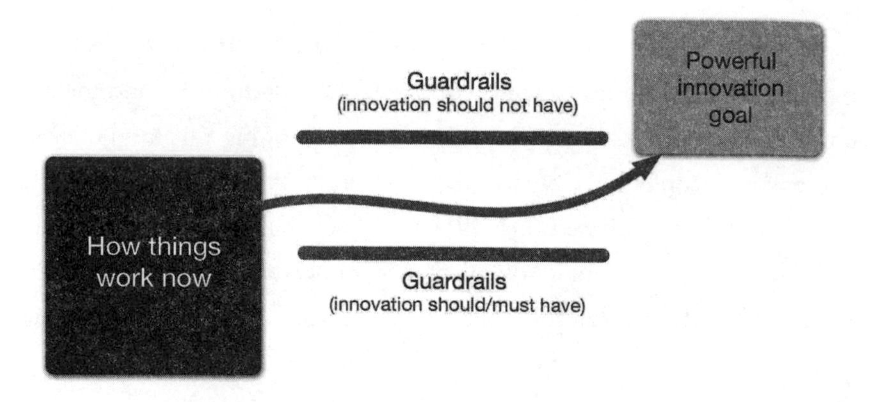

Figure 7.2. Goals and guardrails work together to define the playing field for the innovation.

playing field for the innovation, as shown in Figure 7.2. Everyone can be aligned and moving in the same direction, while also keeping people from making unacceptable choices and doing things they shouldn't be doing.

For your guardrails to be most effective, distill and focus them, and make them as practical as possible. In our experience, people either neglect to create guardrails, or they overdevelop them. Overdeveloped guardrails have lists of dozens of items (sometimes more!) that all need to be considered. That said, it's extremely difficult to rein in the urge to overdo guardrails. The thing is, everyone has something they think is really important to add. And it probably is. But, if you don't distill and focus your guardrails, they lose their impact.

In just one example, the International Committee of the Red Cross published a three-hundred-page *Handbook on Data Protection in Humanitarian Action*, containing all the things you should do and not do when it comes to the safe use of data.[14] Obviously, that kind of detail would be very useful when someone does a detailed assessment of an innovation. However, when aligning the work of many participants across a new ecosystem, a few well-framed guardrails will be far more effective than three hundred pages of detailed points that are likely to be overlooked by most people.

A BAKERY'S GUARDRAILS

Putting guardrails in place allows you to set the rules that those involved must respect. For our bakery owners, they could set things like:

- Must do: Always provide employees with a good living.
- Must do: Always use quality ingredients.
- Must not do: Violate rules or regulations.
- Must not do: Things that undermine our good reputation.

Any new bakery ecosystem would then be checked against these guardrails. For example, a proposed new line of discount muffins made with low-quality, cheap ingredients would be rejected, even if projections show it could be very successful. However, a new line of premium muffins using the very best ingredients would be considered.

Being able to set guardrails is a special benefit for ecosystem innovators. Other innovators often don't get to be intentional about these choices. Someone inventing a new piece of technology can't say how it will or won't be used. Ecosystem innovators, however, have the opportunity to build these choices into their innovation from the outset.

Step 3: Support a Big Goal with a Powerful Story

> No leader needs to be able to deliver a great speech, but every leader has to have a great speech to deliver.
>
> **—Watts Wacker and Jim Taylor**[15]

Costco CEO Craig Jelinek clearly stated the company's pressing strategic challenge at the 2016 shareholder meeting: "We cannot get enough organics to stay in business day in and day out."[16] While you might not think of Costco as a bastion of organic food, in 2015, the company became

America's number one retailer in this product category. That was the year that it registered more than $4 billion in sales of organic food—passing up Whole Foods, the previous number one retailer.

But being the number one retailer of organic food puts you in a precarious position. It wasn't enough for Costco to make their supply chain operate more efficiently; there was simply not enough organic food to go around. So leaders told a story for change that would give permission for the organization to look for bolder, more original solutions to their supply problems.

Jeff Lyons, Costco's senior VP of fresh food, made it clear that they wanted people to ask big questions and to have the courage to think like ecosystem innovators. "What do we see down the road that could be a challenge in terms of supply? And what can we put in place today to grow that particular scarce resource?"[17]

They ended up pushing boundaries with new ecosystem innovations. With one program, Costco decided to get in the farming business. Not directly, but by helping farmers buy equipment and land to produce organic food. According to an article in the *Seattle Times*, Costco loaned money to San Diego–based farmers Andrew and Williamson Fresh Produce to help them buy equipment and 1,200 acres of land in Baja California.[18]

That's a bold move that under normal circumstances most supply chain managers would hesitate to make. However, Costco's senior leadership made it clear that they expected and would embrace bigger change. Lyons said, "By helping them with financing, we got access to and purchased about 145,000 cases of organic raspberries that we normally would not have access to because they normally would not have done the deal or could not have done it. Or, if they could have, we may not have gotten first dibs."[19] In the years since, Costco has greatly expanded this program—developing an ever-expanding ecosystem of new organic food sources.

Effective ecosystem innovators know it's not enough to make a poster with a big goal and put it on the wall. Words are cheap and people will be skeptical. Far too many leaders have a history of setting goals and plans and then failing to rise to the challenge, or even worse, betraying those who embraced big, difficult changes. The bolder the goal, the more likely it is to inspire, but also the more likely it is there will be doubters.

So when a message challenges the comfort, familiarity, and habits of the status quo, there must be a powerful story that explains why it is important to step up and take action. This is a story that makes it clear why the big goal matters and then gives people permission to take courageous action—or even better, that they have the duty to be part of creating a new future.

When writing your big goal and the story behind it, a good structure includes:

- *Why you must act.* What's happening in the world that drives the need for change?
- *What you must do.* What do you and others hope to achieve? What does your successful future look like?
- *Why you/why now?* This is the urgency that drives *you and others* to action, and the practical truth of why *you* specifically can succeed in this venture.

A good, powerful story can be told over and over again, by anyone and everyone, but it is particularly important that the story be heard loud and clear from leaders. In fact, this is one of the principal roles a leader has in ecosystem innovation. They aren't the boss who makes every key decision. Instead, it's their duty to stand on the mountaintop and call for change in a loud and clear voice, so that an entire ecosystem of people and organizations is inspired to take action together.

POWERFUL STORIES THAT AREN'T MUSHY

While we're on the topic of big goals, we feel the need to alert you to a common problem we've seen over and over in organizations of all kinds: mushy mission statements. They're far too passive, far too fuzzy, far too flat, and they describe who they are, not where they are going.

Organizations have long posted big goals or mission statements on their walls that neither inspire nor lead to an interesting future. When you take a closer look, they seem to be designed mainly to provide a clear definition of the management-approved current state, which is to be maintained, not disrupted. They set a standard for performance, not a reason or direction to succeed in the future or to create great change.

Here are some things to keep in mind for creating powerful stories that aren't mushy:

- *Good stories demand action.* A powerful story demands action that delivers results. "We need to do this, to get to that place, for this reason."
- *Good stories are aspirational.* They point to a future that is beyond the current state, a vision for a better future: "If we achieve this big goal, we'll prevent thousands of children from going to bed hungry every night."
- *Good stories draw people in.* One way to test the strength of your goal is to tack it onto the end of this phrase: "Come join us, because we are going to ___________" or "It will be an amazing journey because we will ___________." Is your story exciting and engaging enough to get people to jump on board with you? If not, try again.

If you take another look at the excerpts from President Kennedy's two speeches in the beginning of this chapter, you'll see that he did all these things. The big goal he set got the attention of the American public and legislators, it provided them with an inspiring vision of a future they wanted to be part of, and it sparked action.

TAKE ACTION ON THE BIG GOAL

A big goal enables you to align efforts to create an ecosystem innovation across a wide community of people. These bold ideas are captured in a story that promises opportunity and change, and they are told by respected senior leaders who proclaim them consistently and loudly.

Now it's time to drive those powerful inspiring goals into action, and that's what the next four chapters are about: how we take these bold, aspirational visions of the kind of world we want to create and then create an ecosystem that makes it happen.

CHECKLIST FOR TASK 1: SET AN AMBITIOUS GOAL THAT ALIGNS ACTION

- Step 1: Create an inspiring big goal.
- Step 2: Define guardrails on must do's and must not do's.
- Step 3: Support a big goal with a powerful story.

UNDERSTAND THE CHALLENGES AND OPPORTUNITIES

If you really want to change the world you have to understand it.

—Hans Rosling[1]

During the global COVID-19 pandemic, there was an urgent need to get people around the world vaccinated. In the rush to act, many obvious problems were identified and often given high-profile coverage by governments and the media. Over and over, the message was "If this could be done simply, then the problem would be solved." More vaccines, more doctors, faster supply chains, faster production of testing units. Each of these single problems—and many more—were called out as *the* key to solving the entire COVID-19 pandemic.

Of course, the problems weren't so easily put into neat little boxes. For example, vaccination was broadly seen as a strategic game changer in the fight against COVID-19. A successful vaccine can stop people from getting really sick and help keep the disease from spreading. But tapping the power of vaccines isn't just a matter of inventing an effective shot, as shown in Figure 8.1.

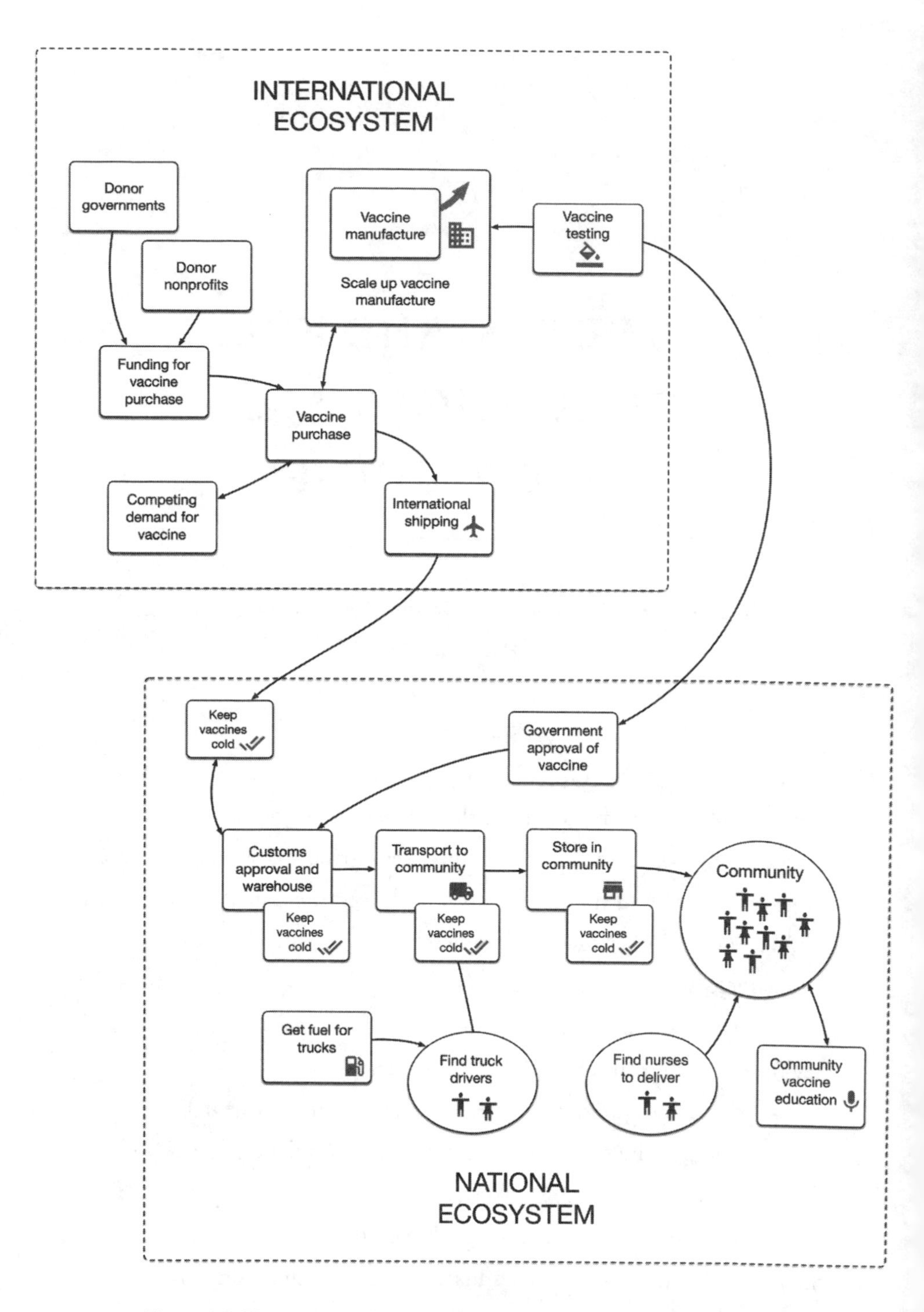

Figure 8.1. The ecosystem for international vaccine delivery has many parts.

Once a vaccine is developed (a truly impressive technical feat) it needs to be tested for effectiveness and safety, and the tests need to be verified, before being rushed into mass production. Distribution and delivery are equally challenging and deciding who will be responsible for paying for the vaccines opens even more questions. Do governments pay? Health insurance companies? Medical providers? Individuals? Then you need to get the vaccine into people's arms safely and effectively.

Consider the case of the African country Chad. In June 2021, one hundred thousand doses of the Pfizer COVID-19 vaccine were paid for and delivered to the country, which seemed to be a major challenge addressed. However, five weeks after the vaccines arrived in Chad, only six thousand doses had been administered and the remaining unused doses were at risk of spoiling. According to a *New York Times* article, "As it is, some countries, like Chad, cannot move Pfizer doses outside major cities."[2]

If you look at all the Legos that needed to be in place to get shots into the arms of the people of Chad, then this outcome is not surprising. An ecosystem of community educators, medical staff, government customs officials, truck drivers, trucks, gasoline supplies, and cold storage all need to perform time-sensitive work together during the middle of a pandemic.[3]

Effectively responding to this kind of complex crisis requires seeing how many interconnected parts of ecosystems work—or don't work—together.

SEEING THE BIG PICTURE

In this chapter you will learn how to claim an important problem by seeing the bigger picture. This matters because it allows you to see more of the real problem. When you step back, you can see what's really happening. Taking time to build a bigger view lets you better understand the messy reality that underlies most important challenges and then take advantage of that complexity.

Why Is This Important?

- *It focuses on important challenges.* This helps you find higher-value problems and avoid the danger of focusing on small or obvious challenges. You don't want to begin with a small problem, because everything that follows will be small too.
- *It takes advantage of the hard bits.* Everyone runs into difficult, gray, messy areas. Rather than trying to ignore these, or barrel straight through them, you get to capitalize on the power that comes from the complex parts of your work, to unlock bigger, more important innovations.
- *It synthesizes insights from everyone.* Instead of trying to understand the problem on your own, you can build a better understanding of what you are working on by harnessing diverse people's wisdom and knowledge, integrated into one brilliant picture.
- *It builds support for action.* A clear view of the challenge makes it possible to tell a compelling story and bring others along. Because you've thought deeply about a problem, you can more easily make the case for needing the innovation, find funding, and encourage action across many actors.

THE CHALLENGE: SEEING BEYOND OBVIOUS PROBLEMS

> It's easy to feel overwhelmed by the world's problems. It's harder to pinpoint the systems responsible for creating them.
>
> **—Apple+ promo for *The Problem with Jon Stewart*[4]**

In this chapter, you take on the second task in your journey: really understanding what's behind a challenge. This will require a fundamental departure from the way most innovators have been trained to target specific problems. Instead of trying to identify the one specific issue, you'll step back to see a big-picture view of the interconnected problems and opportunities you're dealing with.

You will actually draw a big-picture view of how the world works today, so you can think about why different problems exist and explore opportunities to make powerful changes. In the next chapter, you'll use this broad understanding to make sure you don't focus on just one specific problem or one fix. Instead, you will have the tools to design an innovation that addresses issues and possibilities together to create greater impact.

People are naturally drawn to clearly defined problems. And when we understand a problem, we often want to move from the problem to a solution as quickly as possible without giving it deep thought. For example, if you need more places to stay for travelers (problem), the quick solution is building more hotels. If you need to treat more patients with cataracts (problem), the obvious solution is finding more surgeons. Problem, solution; problem, solution; and so it continues.

But this focus on specific problems and quick solutions often means you miss the chance to make more significant and meaningful change. You will never create Airbnb, or Aravind Eye Care, or revolutionize your sector. And ironically you are much more likely to fail or be lost in the crowd because you are competing head on with everyone else's small and obvious solutions.

Consider this example from the book *Factfulness*. Many people would likely assume that to get better medical outcomes, you should focus on providing better technology or more advanced treatment. However, this is not the case when it comes to the problem of saving the lives of low-income mothers getting C-sections. In *Factfulness*, Dr. Hans Rosling says, "The most valuable intervention for saving the lives of the poorest mothers is not training more local nurses to perform C-sections, or better treatment of severe bleeding or infections, but the availability of transport to the local hospital."[5] All the trained and capable doctors and nurses, and all the beautiful, well-supplied hospitals in the world, are of no use if the women who need them most can't get to them. A bigger view—one where you can see all the different pieces needed for a mother's health—lets you see this.

There's a second big advantage to seeing a big-picture view of how the world works today. You can see lots of different problems and opportunities at the same time. You don't have to pick one problem, or one opportunity, to focus on. By seeing a collection of interconnected challenges, you lay the foundation for imagining a new ecosystem that deals with them together. And you will be able to think much more broadly about where impactful opportunities can be found to create something far more powerful and valuable.

Consider the example of Uber and the other rideshare companies. They exploded on the scene, outnumbering New York City cabs within just five years after beginning to offer rides in the Big Apple.[6] These companies were able to disrupt the deeply entrenched taxicab status quo because the new ecosystem they offered (their innovation) didn't solve just one problem, but was able to address a host of issues for many different people.

RIDESHARING DIDN'T SOLVE JUST ONE PROBLEM

Many people assume the mobile app that allows you to schedule a ride is the secret sauce behind the success of Uber. It is certainly more convenient, but why couldn't taxi companies do the same thing? In fact, many traditional taxis have introduced their own ride-hailing apps. If it was just about the one problem—hailing a cab—then the big, established taxi businesses should have easily beaten out the rideshare upstarts.

What's missing from this story is the host of other problems and opportunities that were addressed by the new rideshare ecosystem. Uber, Lyft, and the rest didn't solve just one problem. They created a new ecosystem that addressed lots of different people's needs. This wasn't something that taxi companies could easily replicate, and so the new rideshare ecosystem innovation thrived.

Look at all the different kinds of challenges they addressed:

- Predictable scheduling of rides (rider)
- Ability to stay inside out of the rain (or weather) while waiting for a car (rider)
- Flexibility to take driving shifts when they want them (drivers)
- Less time wasted cruising around looking for fares (drivers)
- Ability to put more cars on the roads at peak times (drivers and riders)
- No need to pay hundreds of thousands of dollars for taxi permits (the cost of a New York City taxi medallion, which is required to legally drive a taxi in the city, was at one time over $1 million)[7] (drivers, rideshare companies)
- No need to invest in a bunch of new taxis to scale up services in a city (rideshare companies)
- Providing more access to rides in neighborhoods outside the city center (riders, neighborhood residents)

The rideshare companies didn't see problems one at a time. Instead, they stepped back and saw a big-picture view of how the taxi ecosystem worked. There were lots of interconnected needs and opportunities. This broad understanding made it possible for them to imagine a new ecosystem with a new way of offering rides that created value for all sorts of people.

So what does it mean to see the big picture? Seeing the big picture means you step back and look at the area you are working on as a whole. It's a picture of what the real world looks like right now. You see all the parts connected in an ecosystem: the people, organizations, and resources that work together (or don't work together).

This might sound awfully ambitious, particularly if you've ever been part of some huge study that gets stuck in the weeds trying to dig up every single detail on a complex challenge. Fortunately, that's not what we need to do. You don't need to know everything about everything to get useful insights on challenges and opportunities that exist across an ecosystem.

Instead of trying to analyze everything in detail, you can say, "We're going to look at many things and understand how they are connected but explore each one in less depth." Your goal is to paint a broad picture of how the world works in your area of interest, without necessarily diving down into the details of every single piece and connection.

The metaphor we sometimes use is that you can hear the melody in a song without knowing every note in the arrangement. The same is true when looking at the way the world works around us. You can see the big themes in the way things work together, without understanding every detail.

Now let's look at how you create a big-picture view of your work today, which is directed by the big goal you created in the previous chapter. We're going to call this big picture the *current ecosystem*, and with it you will be able to think much more broadly about where the most impactful opportunities are.

Step 1: Intentionally Cast a Wide Net for Insights

> We have become not a melting pot but a beautiful mosaic. Different people, different beliefs, different yearnings, different hopes, different dreams.
>
> **—Jimmy Carter**[8]

To really see the big picture, you'll want to begin by casting a wide net for insights into how the world works related to your goal. Think like you're a hungry goat at dinnertime, consuming lots of different things. Your aim is to create a rich picture of how the world works, wandering widely through all sorts of sources of insight, without being too concerned up front about how they will all come together.

One of the best innovation practices to come out of the last twenty years has been the commitment to bring together varied voices, perspectives, and insights when developing innovations. This approach took over from the long-held idea that innovators are experts, best solving problems while sitting alone in an ivory tower.

Applying more people to a problem or opportunity naturally leads to more ideas when brainstorming. Having more people also helps make sure that no one is left out of the creative process. These are all good things, but for you the real benefit is that when you bring in lots of people who are part of the area you are working on, you have an opportunity to see a bigger and richer view of the world.

There are many ways to cast a wide net. When doing a workshop, invite people from different fields—not just the obvious choices or specialists. Think about who actually participates in your challenge today—your ecosystem of people and organizations—and invite that wide mix of people to join the exploration.

Every new voice—particularly someone who has often been excluded from the discussion—is a chance to see how the world works in a different way. You intentionally choose to utilize the extra messiness and complexity rather than ignore it. For example, your wide net could also include people at different levels of responsibility. A big boss and a person on the front lines of a problem each have their own insights into how things work in the real world.

But casting a wide net doesn't necessarily mean you have to get everyone in the same room at the same time. Group workshops can be a lot of fun. Who doesn't love putting Post-it notes up on the wall? But we've found that it's not necessary, or particularly useful, to rely only on meetings where everyone is participating at the same time. That kind of workshop has a huge cost in time and dollars and it often tries to rush insights and decisions that are best given more time.

Fortunately, when you're trying to build a big-picture view of how the world works, you can get a lot from side meetings and informal conversations that take place over a coffee or a video call on the other side of the world. Each new meeting adds to an increasingly rich view of what the world looks like today as you explore the mix of problems and opportunities in your area of interest. You can use the same wide net when trying to learn from materials like reports or articles. A solidly researched academic paper certainly has value, but remember the hungry goat and be sure to embrace other sources that reveal how the world works.

WICKED PROBLEMS: A BRIEF HISTORY

It can be interesting to look back and see how people have talked about complex, messy challenges in the past. Let's rewind to the mid-twentieth century. In the years following World War II, scientists and engineers had a lot of success using computers to solve complicated technical problems. As the power of computers continued to grow, people were thinking, "Wow, this is going to be so cool. We're gonna be able to take on all kinds of bigger and harder problems." And in many cases—for example, designing spacecraft that could make the journey to the moon and back—they were.

But then, beginning in the late 1960s, people with messier problems—urban planners, sociologists, and others—asked how they could use detailed computer analysis to solve their messy, difficult problems. They asked things like: How do you design a city? How do you create shared economic opportunity? What they found was the kinds of problems they were working with had attributes that made it impossible for them to create tidy mathematical models that you could put into a computer.

In a 1973 paper on urban planning, Horst Rittel and Melvin Webber used the term *wicked problems* to describe these messy challenges.[9] They said wicked problems weren't simply hard for computers to solve. Even with faster, more powerful processors, these problems were different in ways that would always make them impossible to solve with conventional technical analysis. They laid out ten reasons why working on these challenges wasn't suited to a rigorous analytical approach.

You must give them credit—"wicked problems" is a great name, and it's very memorable. But it might be just a bit too scary. The term tends to make people think they're looking at something that's incredibly hard, something no one could ever solve, something that's impossible.

Yet these are exactly the kinds of big problems you can take on with ecosystem innovation. All the examples of powerful ecosystem innovations we've discussed so far—from addressing blindness in India, to launching a new razor in a locked-down market, to bringing electricity to remote communities while growing entrepreneurship with women—might be labeled wicked problems. These innovators are proof, however, that even when you're faced with a wicked problem, it's possible to innovate with great success.

Step 2: Draw a Picture of How the World Works

> "Ah," remarked one of the guests when the topic arose. "You prefer not to see the gears of the clock, as to better tell the time."
>
> —**Erin Morgenstern**[10]

Now that you've talked to so many different people, how do you capture all those insights about how the world works? How do you see the bigger picture? How do all the different things you have heard and seen connect?

You don't want just a big pile of Post-it notes (which is what often comes out of innovation workshops). What you really need is a way to:

- Capture a lot of different pieces of information.
- Create your brilliant secret sauce knowledge by bringing the information and insights together.
- Share that knowledge with others.

The best way to do this is simply to draw a picture. There's a reason people say a picture is worth a thousand words. On a single page, it is possible to see many parts of a real-world ecosystem all connected (Figure 8.2). We call this a *current ecosystem map*. Rather than just writing ideas on individual Post-it notes with no connection to one another, you capture that knowledge by drawing a picture of how the world looks like right now for the area you are interested in. Instead of picking out a few individual ideas from the Post-it note pile, you take the time to synthesize all that knowledge in one place.

In a conventional innovation workshop, facing a wall of colored Post-it notes, you might ask, "Which Post-its are good and which are bad?" You then pick a few to examine further and throw out the rest. What a waste! If you want a big-picture view of how things work, it would be far better to ask, "How do we make sense of all these pieces of information at the same time?" You bring together all the insights in one place, keeping the varied knowledge in the room as opposed to throwing 95 percent of it into the trash.

To see how you would create a current ecosystem map in practice, let's look at a time when Jenny was working with a collection of organizations in South Sudan, a country about the size of France located in east-central Africa. The group was made up of a number of diverse participants—charity organizations, the UN, community organizations,

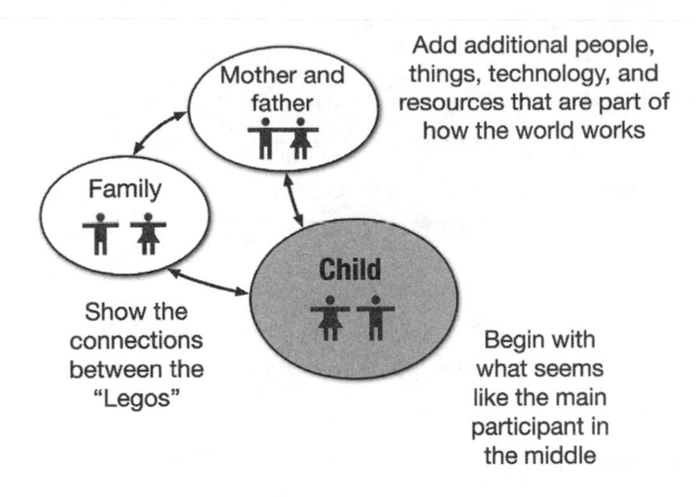

Figure 8.2. Starting an ecosystem map.

funding organizations, and others. This group was looking for ways to make an impact on child malnutrition, which was a tremendous challenge in South Sudan. After some discussion, a goal was set: create greater accuracy in monitoring children with malnutrition.

As Jenny asked what challenges came to mind for this goal, people moved quickly to very specific problems. One of the attendees jumped in: "We have volunteers who go from town to town, checking on children's malnutrition, one by one. But we don't have accurate data for the malnourished children. We need digital tablets for our volunteers to enter children's nutrition data. Then we can move resources where the kids need them." Many in the room agreed with the problem and the solution being proposed.

It would have been easy to go all-in on the tablet idea, create a project plan, and set out the next year of work. And that would have felt like a very successful workshop. But instead of rushing ahead, the group chose to step back and drew a picture of what the overall ecosystem looked like. They began by putting the child at risk in the middle of the picture and then mapped connections from there.

The first connection was to the caregiver (usually the mother in this case), then the immediate family, and then the community around them. They were then connected to community nutrition volunteers, who had an entire malnutrition screening process. They were also connected to a local health facility, which had a process for the treatment of malnutrition. And then lines were drawn to link up the health care system's efforts to identify and train nurses, nutritionists, and other health care workers, which were connected to the Ministry of Health, UN programs, local and global funders, and more. They quickly captured a working view of a sprawling, real-world ecosystem. This showed there were many parts that stretched far beyond the volunteers who would potentially carry around tablets to gather children's nutrition data, as shown in Figure 8.3.

In an ecosystem map, like the one in Figure 8.3, your Lego blocks are boxes. A box might show a person or an organization that is participating in the ecosystem. Boxes can also show where a piece of technology, product, or service plays a part. When different boxes work together, they are connected with a line or an arrow. You probably notice that we draw these kinds of ecosystem maps throughout this book.

One of the things that's particularly powerful about drawing an ecosystem map is that it's great for engaging people in thinking about messy problems. You might think that getting people into a room and allowing them to do free-form brainstorming would be the best way to get things going, but that's often not the case. Asking people to come up with original ideas out of thin air is a task that makes many people uncomfortable because there's nothing to provide grounding for their thinking.

On the other hand, asking people concrete questions about the things they know allows everyone to participate in a meaningful way. By asking, "How does the world work for *x* issue?" you empower people to draw on their real-world experience and knowledge to develop a picture of a complex and messy space.

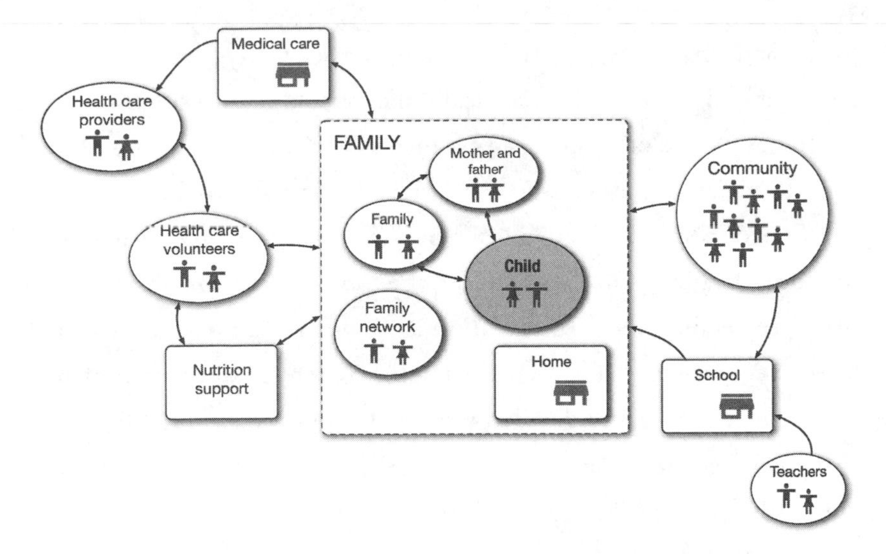

Figure 8.3. Expanding the ecosystem surrounding childhood nutrition.

This ecosystem map is like a blueprint showing the parts of the world around you. It provides a tangible foundation where diverse people can contribute their own thoughts and ideas, expanding everyone's understanding. Seeing everything brought together in one place helps people extend and adjust their view of how things are working today. You'll find people suddenly share aha moments about challenges that had previously seemed to be impossible to put their arms around.

Surprisingly, this process doesn't have to take a long time. We worked on ecosystem maps that had an initial draft within an hour. You don't need to be Picasso, and you don't need to get it perfectly right. As the saying goes, perfect is the enemy of done. What you're looking for here is a picture that captures lots of information about how the world works, with a kind of simple elegance.

In practice, too much detail can be harmful. It is certainly possible to keep adding details until the map is so thick with information that it's unusable. That dense mess might be technically correct but it won't be useful for diving into what actions you should take. Ecosystem maps should be simple and shareable. In fact, ideally, they should fit on a single page.

To get a sense of this, think of a map of the world. To be useful, you want to make sure every country is shown (big picture), but you don't really need to see every small town or back road. The same idea applies to your ecosystem map. You want it to be complete but you don't need to see every detail. If more information is needed for some particular part of your ecosystem you can create a second more detailed map of that specific area. This more detailed picture is like having a map for a city that you'll need to spend a lot of time driving around in. You can zoom out on the country map or zoom in on the city map depending on the level of detail you need.

DRAWING AN ECOSYSTEM MAP

So you want to draw your ecosystem? Here is a quick exercise to start. We recommend that you do the first draft of a map either by yourself or in a small group with one person drawing. We have drawn ecosystem maps in twenty minutes on the back of a napkin or done elaborate workshops lasting several days. Just remember every system map is a draft. The most important thing is to start, create something, and then grow it from there. Good enough at any point is right. You can start with as little as a pen and some paper or any kind of visual mapping software.

1. Start by writing a sentence that encapsulates the goal you are trying to achieve with the map. This provides you with a basic guideline for the scope of your map. It helps you think about what to include or not include as you begin.
2. Choose the main stakeholder you want to create value or impact for (e.g., the child at school, the injured worker, the adults looking for cheaper energy). Put them on the map as an icon with their stakeholder name above them. This does not need to be a hard

decision. It shouldn't take more than a couple minutes to decide. Just choose someone and get started.

3. Extend the map from the stakeholder you have drawn. Add what is around the stakeholder: actors, activities, resources. Use arrows, Post-it notes, and other icons to add and connect additional parts of the ecosystem. Focus on things that exist in the real world.
4. Keep adding actors, activities, resources, and connections. As the picture emerges, you can prompt additional insights by asking questions about a range of areas such as:
   - *Actors.* Who are the different actors in the ecosystem?
   - *Actions.* What are they doing and why are they doing it?
   - *Connections.* How do they interact with others and where are the connections?
   - *Gaps.* What pieces are missing from our picture?

Need help or inspiration? Have a look through the many ecosystem maps in this book.

Step 3: Understand Challenges and Opportunities

> Pull a thread here and you'll find it's attached to the rest of the world.
>
> **—Nadeem Aslam**[11]

You now have a high-level view of the challenge you are working on: today's ecosystem. This is a first iteration of seeing how the world works for the area you are hoping to transform. By creating this big-picture view of how the world works you've given yourself a broad foundation that can be used to see beyond the obvious challenges.

Now you can use this rich picture to explore the problems and opportunities in your ecosystem. Question the map you created and stretch your thinking to better understand why things work as they do. Find the opportunities that can make a real difference. Even if you think you have the challenge you will work on already chosen, it is important to step back and think more deeply about the problems and opportunities that are tangled up in your ecosystem.

This is what the team in South Sudan did when examining the challenge of childhood malnutrition. After creating a big picture of how the current ecosystem worked, it became increasingly clear to everyone that there were many other valuable opportunities, not at all tied to simply purchasing digital tablets to monitor children. These challenges were less obvious but could better play off the strengths of the individuals, communities, and organizations involved.

For example, after seeing the central role mothers and family played in the current ecosystem map, they thought about the problem in new ways. Instead of relying on an outside volunteer, who would only visit from time to time, the team considered if mothers might be in the best position to access additional food or nutrition support from health clinics. This perspective ultimately led them to propose cheap, easy-to-use tools that mothers could directly use to know when their child was malnourished.

By stepping back and seeing the big picture, the team challenged the underlying assumption that outsiders were needed to identify malnutrition. The ecosystem helped show where there might be different kinds of opportunities, such as putting more power in mothers' hands.

Just as the team used their map to explore other ways to address malnutrition, your current ecosystem map can become a tool for you to use when thinking about your complex challenge. For example, you may find that the map highlights pieces or connections that are missing. Or you may want to use your map to think about where it might be worth throwing out parts of the status quo and imagining a different ecosystem instead. Things that seem impossible based on your knowledge of the status quo today might later turn out to be within reach when you add more pieces, see beyond the obvious and familiar answers, or break some rules. Ecosystem innovators such as Uber and Dollar Shave Club didn't see an easy fix for their challenges. However, by creating ecosystems of their own they completely reinvented the creaky old systems for taxis and razors.

When you look at your current ecosystem map, you may be worried that it seems too complex. This is okay. Remember that you can use this complexity to develop powerful solutions and opportunities. So don't be afraid of seeing challenges for what they really are. Pretending that something is simple doesn't make the underlying complexity go away. The real world is filled with challenges and opportunities that are woven together. Seeing and understanding them gives you the knowledge you need to create significant successful innovations.

LOOKING DEEPER INTO CHALLENGES

A big view of the current ecosystem—the area you care about—allows you to better explore the real-world messiness that underlies challenges. Instead of trying to find the single issue that needs fixing, you can lean into exploring how problems exist in the real world. Use your current ecosystem map to dig deeper into challenges and opportunities. When using your map:

- *Follow the connections.* Ask yourself: What other parts of the ecosystem are driving your problem? If you have problems with product quality in a factory, could that be tied to issues with employee hiring and retention?
- *Uncover cascading effects.* Is there one part of the ecosystem that drives problems throughout the rest of the ecosystem? If you have problems with poverty, crime, and health in a community, could a lack of education be a problem that drives all the others?

continued

- *Listen for silent but important problems.* Are there problems that have a big impact on the overall ecosystem but haven't gotten visibility? Is an organization happy with its traditional operations because it is unaware of the broader industry movements where silent dangers exist from unrecognized competitors?
- *Recognize broad system failure.* Are there problems that spread across the entire ecosystem? These may be so fundamental to the way the ecosystem works that it's only by sweeping away the entire ecosystem that they can be addressed. Uber didn't simply improve the taxi service, it saw challenges across the entire ecosystem—from car ownership, to pricing, to ride hailing—so it created something completely different.
- *Look for missing ecosystems.* Are entire supporting ecosystems missing? Are things not working because there's nothing there to provide for a set of key needs? When Solar Sister wanted to empower women entrepreneurs to sell solar technology they had to address the problem that there simply wasn't an ecosystem in place to support much of the last mile of distribution, finance, and training.

Step 4: Evolve and Refine Your Big Picture

> A noble logical diagram once recorded will never die; long after we are gone it will be a living thing, asserting itself with ever-growing insistency.
>
> **—Daniel Burnham**[12]

Creating a current ecosystem map isn't something you do just to check the box in an innovation process. This picture of how the world works is a valuable tool that you'll continue to leverage as you imagine and develop your innovation. You are using it here to distill and structure information that comes from many different points of view. Later you'll use it to help guide the shaping and delivery of your innovation—*a new and better ecosystem.*

This current ecosystem is powerful because when you can clearly see how things fit together—complexity is no longer just a barrier in your way—it becomes a creative resource. Diverse people and organizations can work from a shared understanding. It's important to understand this is not something where you need to do everything in one workshop or one afternoon. Innovators have gotten into the bad habit of trying to do complex work all in a single afternoon with dozens of people in the room. That's a mistake (and often impossible). Thoughtful, significant work can seldom be done all at once with everyone sitting in a room getting progressively more tired.

So you should give it the time and space it deserves. Feel free to take time away from group sessions to synthesize materials and fine-tune your current ecosystem map. Your map may go through several iterations. Often, it's best to give one or two people (who are good at big-picture thinking) a chance to step back and think through the structure of the current ecosystem.

It's also important to believe that ecosystem maps are never really done. Views of ecosystems can be iteratively fine-tuned, so it's not necessary to get it perfect the first time. You can and should come back to add to the map and edit it. You'll probably find that a drawing is a great way to get additional input from others, since getting comments on a draft picture, which puts the world on one page, is far easier and more effective than asking someone to plod through piles of different facts and insights.

This practice of continual refinement takes a lot of pressure off your work. It gives you a chance to step back and think. It also allows you to get input later from people who weren't part of the ecosystem map's creation. Plus, as the world changes, the ecosystem map can continue to evolve to avoid becoming obsolete.

NEXT, IMAGINE A POWERFUL INNOVATION—YOUR FUTURE ECOSYSTEM

We end this chapter with a reminder that you can work at many different scales with this practice. While some ecosystem maps deal with big challenges such as global malnutrition, you can also focus on more limited challenges like exploring where there might be entrepreneurial opportunities for your family business.

Regardless of whether your current ecosystem is big or small, the concepts remain the same. Step back and see the big picture of how things work now in the real world. Then use that insight to think more broadly about what challenge or opportunity you can claim, one that will really matter.

Now that you understand the way things work today, it's time to think about designing the future. In the next chapter, we take a close look at how to create a new or improved ecosystem that has the power to transform the world—and those who live in it—for the better.

CHECKLIST FOR TASK 2: UNDERSTAND THE CHALLENGES AND OPPORTUNITIES

- Step 1: Intentionally cast a wide net for insights.
- Step 2: Draw a picture of how the world works.
- Step 3: Understand challenges and opportunities.
- Step 4: Evolve and refine your big picture.

DESIGN THE FUTURE

The future belongs to a very different kind of person with a very different kind of mind—creators and empathizers, pattern recognizers, and meaning makers.

—Daniel Pink[1]

In Chapter 8, we explore how to claim a worthy challenge by stepping back and looking at the big picture. Now it's time to explore the third task and design a solution that can change the game.

As you begin this work, you'll want to take an unexpected lesson from one of history's most prolific inventors, Thomas Edison. As you likely know, Edison did not invent the lightbulb. In fact, the electric arc lamp was invented in 1802 by inventor Sir Humphrey Davy, and many other inventors (some say more than twenty) created versions of the lightbulb before Edison created his own.[2]

However, Edison did do something important that the others didn't—he created an ecosystem around his invention. Knowing that his lightbulb was useless without electricity, Edison founded the Edison Illuminating Company of New York, which built the very first central electric power generation plant in the United States.

Edison's most impactful innovation was ultimately a real-world ecosystem. His power company didn't just end up providing electricity just to illuminate the lightbulbs he sold, but also powered a new generation of electric trains in New York and enabled a host of other innovations that forever transformed the world.

Thomas Edison's lightbulb took off where so many others failed because he realized that it wasn't just about the invention. It was also about building a complete ecosystem of power generation, transmission, and use with the lightbulb as one of many Lego blocks. This is what enabled his invention to scale and ultimately succeed. Of course, Edison didn't act alone to create this electrical network, but he did drive change with a clear, holistic vision. This vision allowed him and his team to develop parts and connect the pieces of his solution, ensuring that the whole lightbulb ecosystem was available to turn his lightbulbs on.

DESIGNING YOUR FUTURE ECOSYSTEM

In this chapter you will learn how to design a better future ecosystem that works in the real world. This is a hugely important task, which provides a foundation for your design trifecta—a future vision of how the world could work that is practical, ambitious, and creates significant value.

Why Is This Important?

- *It creates strategic impact.* You create more powerful solutions that do bigger things and create greater value.
- *There is less "feel good" wasted effort.* You avoid the feel-good temptation to pursue random, interesting, but disconnected work.
- *It offers whole solutions that work.* You design complete solutions that are able to succeed in a complex and changing world.
- *It offers improved adoption.* You avoid the heartbreak of people saying no, by spending time up front understanding what people need to be part of the future you imagine.

- *It dances around barriers.* Instead of running into walls where there is no path forward, you redefine the rules and constraints to circumvent barriers and change the game so that you are well positioned to win.
- *It creates more power.* By tapping the creative superpowers of ecosystems, features like synergies can amplify the impact and value of your innovation.

THE CHALLENGE: CREATING POWERFUL SOLUTIONS

> The "underlying problem" is difficult for people to address, either because it is obscure or costly to confront. So, people "shift the burden" of their problem to other solutions—well-intentioned, easy fixes.
>
> **—Peter Senge**[3]

Now is the time to create your powerful solution. You do bigger things by imagining your part of the world as an ecosystem where all the parts—organizations, technology, and people—work together in new and better ways. Just as Edison did with his lightbulb ecosystem.

For some innovators, particularly those who have been taught other, fast-moving innovation practices, it can feel natural to leap into action creating a hodgepodge of small, independent solutions that seem worthwhile and reasonable, one by one. The thinking goes, "I could fix this one little part, or I could make a bit of progress on this specific issue, or I could fix this thing over here right now, so why wait?" But these fragmented, individual innovations end up being poor tools for delivering impact or solving hard problems. This is because, as shown in Figure 9.1, you end up with a bunch of opportunistic actions. Fragmented innovations lack an end destination where they all come together for something bigger. It's a bit like the game Whac-A-Mole where you are

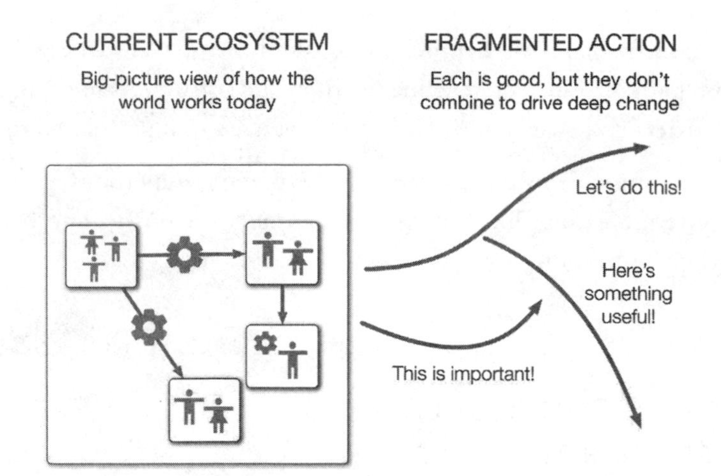

Figure 9.1. Fragmented innovations seldom lead to big solutions.

constantly hitting one thing after the other. You get a lot of small wins but seldom create something big enough to make a deeper change that could really matter.

In our work with social activists, we found that they often fall into this trap. Because they are passionate about dealing with urgent issues, they are driven to move quickly, identifying particular policies that must change right now or politicians who should be voted out of office without delay. They take on each pressing action and then look for the next urgent task. As each new problem pops up it's smacked down—only to be followed by yet another issue.

Of course, businesses and other organizations are drawn into this same rush to action. Yet in today's fast-changing world, everyone faces the same reality. When dealing with messy challenges or big opportunities, a basket full of small wins isn't enough. Whacking away at individual problems won't lead to the kind of impactful change that you need when looking to make bold changes. While each win feels good (we're getting stuff done!), they don't lead to a future where all the parts work together to make a meaningful difference.

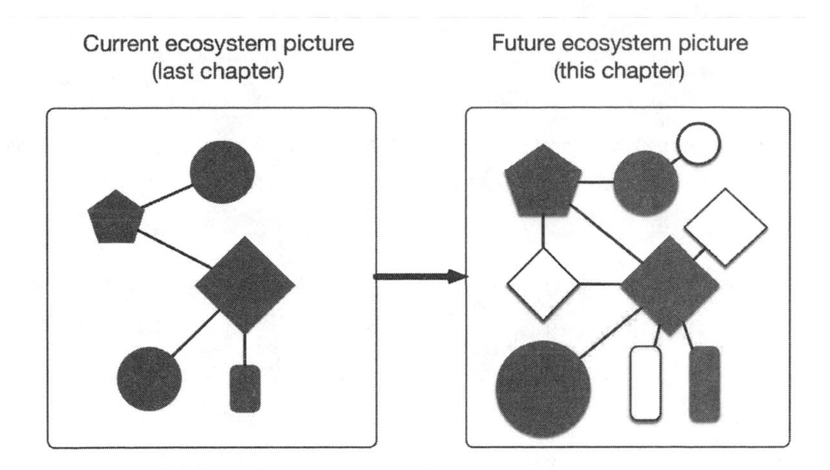

Figure 9.2. Current versus future ecosystem

You can escape this trap by taking a step back, this time seeing a big-picture view of the innovation you want to create. In the last chapter, you stepped back to understand the current ecosystem. In this chapter you'll imagine what a complete future ecosystem looks like (Figure 9.2). This future ecosystem provides you with a well-thought-out destination. Instead of fragmented actions it provides a complete picture that lets you make a jump forward into something significant and new, rather than just accumulating small incremental changes to the status quo. It's like a beacon sitting on a mountaintop that shows where you, and others who are part of the innovation, will aim your combined efforts.

Step 1: Create a Bold Future

> Seizing the white space requires new skills, new strengths, new ways to make money. It calls for the ability to innovate something more core than the core, for the ability to innovate the very theory of the business itself.
>
> —**Mark Johnson**[4]

Now is your chance to imagine an innovation that solves hard problems and takes advantage of exciting opportunities. Don't limit yourself to narrowing it down to five Post-it notes and then picking the best one to take action on. Your job is to imagine a future ecosystem—your innovation—which makes things work in new ways. You're not simply coming up with individual ideas, as often happens in many brainstorming sessions. Instead, you're moving things around, connecting them differently, adding new parts, and looking for ways to change the rules of the way the world works now.

This gives you enormous power, but don't mistake this for permission to be naively idealistic. You're not going to assume that people suddenly stop behaving like people, or that technology can do more than it can do. Remember the trifecta—aim for something that is practical, ambitious, and creates significant value.

This requires holistic, big-picture thinking. You'll want to draw inspiration for your future ecosystem design from a lot of places, so it's good to be a generalist who is always looking out across the world for ideas. Here are a few places you might look to drive your thinking:

- *Today's trends.* The world is changing in big ways all around you. Look for trends that create new needs or change what's possible. For example, one big trend is the growing ability to collaborate with people and organizations around the world. In his book *The Lexus and the Olive Tree*, Thomas Friedman points out that, more than any time in history, "individuals can increasingly act on the world stage directly."[5] How might current trends in the world open new possibilities for you?
- *New models.* A big-picture idea in one field can often be carried into an entirely different business or challenge. Both Uber and Airbnb draw on a new sharing economy ecosystem where individual frozen assets are brought to market—cars in one case and homes in the other. What new models or big ideas can you build on?

- *Untapped resources.* It's a sad fact that your current ecosystem may struggle to meet its goals while simultaneously leaving people, organizations, or resources on the sidelines. Look around and ask who could play a role in your future ecosystem but are woefully underutilized now. When Solar Sister looked for someone to sell solar technology, they didn't have to import business managers. Instead, they found and enlisted an energized community of women waiting for a chance to pursue new opportunities.
- *New technology.* Of course, new technology can often be part of innovations. Be careful to think big enough when you're considering new technology. Your job isn't just to imagine a way to apply the technology to improve existing operations (although technology is certainly good for this). Instead, you want to use technology to unlock bigger changes and opportunities. Look broadly—advances are exploding across a huge variety of fields, ranging from digital tools like artificial intelligence (AI) and biological advances in genomics, to on-the-ground infrastructure like clean energy tech.
- *Unmet needs.* People often ignore unmet needs and opportunities because they're simply too hard to deal with. If you're running a traditional cab company, for example, there's no easy way to let someone shelter inside a building while waiting for a cab. Riders must stand out in the rain to hail a car. Trying to serve an unmet need can push your future ecosystem into new areas, like making it possible to use an app to track when your car will arrive.

The most important thing about this creative process is that it is not done by Post-it note-voting, picking the best idea from the stack. Instead, it works best when you think about the whole challenge then look for ways to bring a range of ideas together into a future ecosystem that you could build in the real world. It's kind of like imagining a puzzle of ideas that you fit together to create something new and brilliant.

Step 2: Draw the Future Ecosystem

> A logical picture is easier to criticize than a vague picture since the assumptions it is based on are brought out into the open.
>
> **—Christopher Alexander**[6]

It should come as no surprise that we believe the best way to capture your future ecosystem is to draw it in the form of a picture. Just as the current ecosystem has a diagram that shows parts and relationships, your future ecosystem needs its own picture.

Doing this has all the same advantages we describe in Chapter 8. You can use it to capture many ideas on a simple and concise page. Then it can be laid side by side with the current ecosystem drawing to show how things would change and perhaps where they could stay the same. It also provides a powerful visual tool for examining your proposed future ecosystem, so that you find undetected gaps and untapped opportunities.

So what does a future ecosystem map look like? Figure 9.3 illustrates a simple example for a very complicated, important challenge: shifting from gasoline-powered vehicles to electric vehicles (EVs).

What are the pieces for a future ecosystem supporting electric vehicles? It may seem pretty obvious that we'll need someone to manufacture EVs—otherwise, there won't be any cars to buy and drive. We could start by drawing that factory.

Then we'll need people to buy those cars and put them into everyday use. That gets cars on the road but that won't be enough to make EV ownership practical. There must also be places to charge the electric vehicles—at home, at destinations (work, shopping, and so on), or along the road. Without chargers, EVs are useless. A quick sketch later and now we have the beginnings of a future ecosystem that lets people buy and drive EVs.

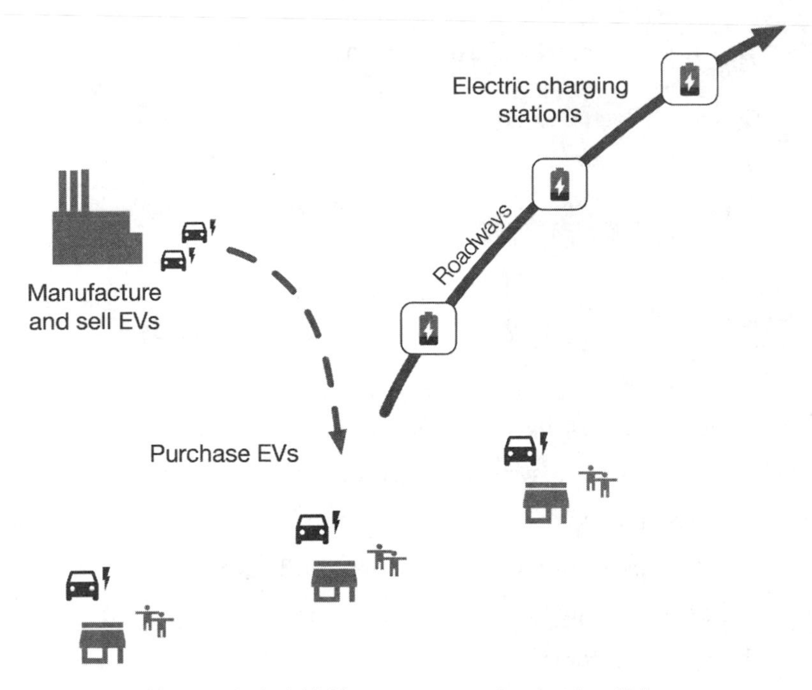

Figure 9.3. An initial future ecosystem for electric vehicles

After you have your initial sketch, don't stop there. Now it is time to imagine what an even better ecosystem would look like. Some things to consider: How will all the participants and parts work together? Where do technology and resources like funding or supply chains fit in? How is it all connected?

Putting together all the parts can seem daunting but it doesn't have to be done in one gigantic leap. Remember fundamentally you are building your vision from a world of Legos. Have fun with the process. Jenny's four-year-old daughter, for example, loves Legos and has one of those big boxes of assorted Lego blocks that she loves to build all kinds of different worlds with (dollhouse, zoo world, space adventures). Given some time to think and a willingness to try different combinations, you too can build big ideas from your own pile of Lego blocks.

Step 3: Make Sure the Future Ecosystem Works

> Copernicus complained . . . "it is as though an artist were to gather the hands, feet, head and other members for his images from diverse models, each part excellently drawn, but not related to a single body, and since they in no way match each other, the result would be monster rather than man."
>
> **—Thomas Kuhn**[7]

You can now start testing your innovation. While you don't need every detail of your future ecosystem figured out, it's important to make sure there are no major gaps or barriers to it working in practice. All the main parts of your ecosystem must be present for it to work in the real world. You need to ask, "Is my future ecosystem complete?"

To be complete, for example, our EV car would need to have charging capabilities everywhere, not just in dense, urban areas. It's not enough to say that you're going to have lots of charging stations—someone must build them, own them, and run them. That means the future ecosystem must imagine someone who would be willing to invest in installing these charging stations and then operating them over time so the ecosystem looks more complete, like Figure 9.4.

From time to time, you will want to step back and think about how the different parts of the future ecosystem will work together. For example, as the number of EVs increases, to maximize the climate benefits, you will want to power them with renewable energy generation such as solar and wind. That may require redesigning the electrical grid by placing new lines where they are needed and providing new capabilities to store electricity when it's generated in excess of immediate demand.

This completeness check is particularly important when working with innovations that have been developed in small, fast-moving pilot projects. Recall that the goal of a pilot is to validate key parts of an idea with

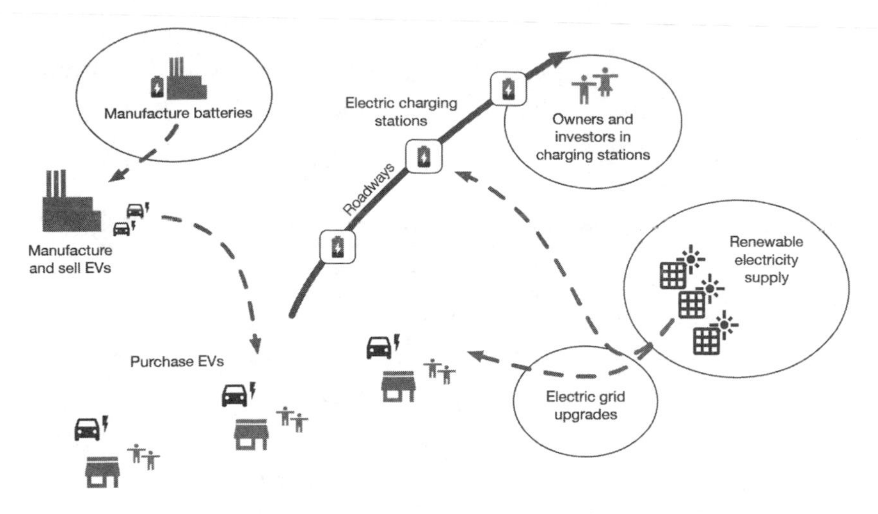

Figure 9.4. Making the future ecosystem of EVs more complete

minimum resources—learning quickly and failing fast. By design, they do not invest in developing a complete ecosystem design and so they may have a very incomplete view of the ecosystem to be built in the future.

Remember: You don't need to control all the parts in your future ecosystem and all the parts don't need to exist now. This is actually one of the powerful features of ecosystems. Other people can take on key roles in its creation and operation. For example, you don't need to be the company that manufactures EVs. But maybe your job is to create incredible viral marketing campaigns that entice people to buy them.

THE WEAK LINK: THE 1950S FAILURE OF 3D MOVIES

In the 1890s, film projectors were just a novelty but less than forty years later, movie innovators had developed a complete ecosystem of writers, actors, directors, film studies, movie houses, and celebrity magazines. During the Great Depression, 65 percent of Americans were going to the cinema to see movies every week on average.[8]

continued

However, by the 1950s, there was a shiny, new entertainment ecosystem in town—television—and it quickly became an existential threat to the film industry. Television viewers in the United States could choose from three different channels and watch them day or night in the comfort of their own home.

Because of this, the film industry decided it needed a big, bold invention to keep people firmly planted in their theater seats. That big, bold invention was 3D movies. 3D movies weren't just a small, technical invention. They required a whole new ecosystem to support the production, distribution, and showing of the films.

Big movie studios got people to write scripts with 3D in mind. They built new dual-camera setups to shoot 3D movies. They got cinematographers trained in how to film 3D movies and photo labs that could print film stock in this new format. The studios hired directors who were willing and able to work with all this new technology and created glasses that viewers had to wear to see the 3D images in these special films. Ultimately, they installed 3D projectors in movie theaters.

It was a vibrant, new experience that had people crowding back into theaters, donning red and green glasses that made images literally pop from the screen. Unfortunately, the product failed to meet one of the key requirements of any successful ecosystem innovation. It didn't have all the parts.

Instead of the standard approach to showing films in a theater—using a single projector—3D movies required two projectors that ran side by side—one for the viewer's left eye and one for the viewer's right eye. When the projectors were properly synchronized the effect was dramatic and people were dazzled by the medium. But if the projectors were off by even just one quarter of a frame, viewers often ended up with headaches, nausea, strained eyes—or all the above. The part of the new 3D ecosystem that the studios missed was consistently synchronizing the projectors.

Faulty synchronization of 3D movies ultimately became the medium's downfall. According to Polaroid, over 50 percent of movie theaters were showing 3D films that were out of sync in 1953. As a result, 3D film ticket sales began to plummet. In 1954, *Variety* declared on its front page that "3-D Looks Dead in the United States."[9] And those courageous studio executives helplessly watched as their whole venture was tripped up because they didn't deliver a complete working ecosystem.

But 3D wasn't dead. It just took another forty years before someone came up with a better 3D movie ecosystem, one where IMAX screens and digital projectors really did work together, and a movie like *Avatar* could be a top Oscar contender and be the first film to gross more than $2 billion worldwide.[10]

There are two big lessons for you in this story. The first is pretty inspirational. When the movie studios took on the disruptive threat of television, they didn't just try to make small improvements to their existing productions. They had the courage and vision to create a whole new ecosystem that would deliver a really different experience. The second lesson is a reminder that even if your new ecosystem is bold and innovative, all the parts must come together to work in the real world.

Step 4: Make Sure Everyone Gets a Pony

> We refuse unfair offers because people who meekly accepted unfair offers didn't survive in the Stone Age.
>
> **—Yuval Noah Harari**[11]

To be worthwhile your future ecosystem must work better than the current ecosystem. Ultimately you'll want to create positive impacts for those adopting the future ecosystem. You probably won't be surprised to learn that people don't adopt new innovations just because they work. They adopt them because they get value from them. So you have to ask: What value is created for each of the participants in my future ecosystem?

The reality is that every participant in the future ecosystem will be doing the math and asking, "Is this a good idea for me?" If you want people and organizations to participate in your ecosystem innovation they need to get rewards that are greater than their costs—things such as time, effort, expense, and lost opportunity.

The thing that is both powerful and tricky is that every actor, whether it's a person, government, or company, needs motivations that make sense to them. If you recall our bakery example from Chapter 2, the bakers are interested in practicing their craft in a good environment while getting a steady paycheck. Customers want fresh, tasty bread at a reasonable price. The suppliers want to sell more goods to the bakery.

When people are evaluating your change to their lives, they wrestle with new trade-offs. They listen to the value that is being promised and then consider the disruption, costs, and effort involved. Your job is to make sure that when costs and benefits are balanced out everyone gets a pony. You'll need to invest time in conversations with the diverse groups of people in your ecosystem so you can understand their motivations and interests. You can use these insights to make sure people get what they need, and that no one is overlooked or unfairly left shouldering the burden of our fast-changing world.

Don't expect people or organizations to do things that aren't in their interest, just because they should. That's just wishful thinking. For example, if a car buyer sees that EVs cost more than gasoline-powered cars, they are less likely to purchase an EV. Fortunately, you can do something about this; for example, adding government tax incentives for EV purchases, as shown in Figure 9.5. An ecosystem's flexibility—the ability to add Legos and change the way things fit together—is one of the things that will help you succeed.

It's particularly important to look for situations where someone is penalized while everyone else is getting a benefit from the ecosystem.

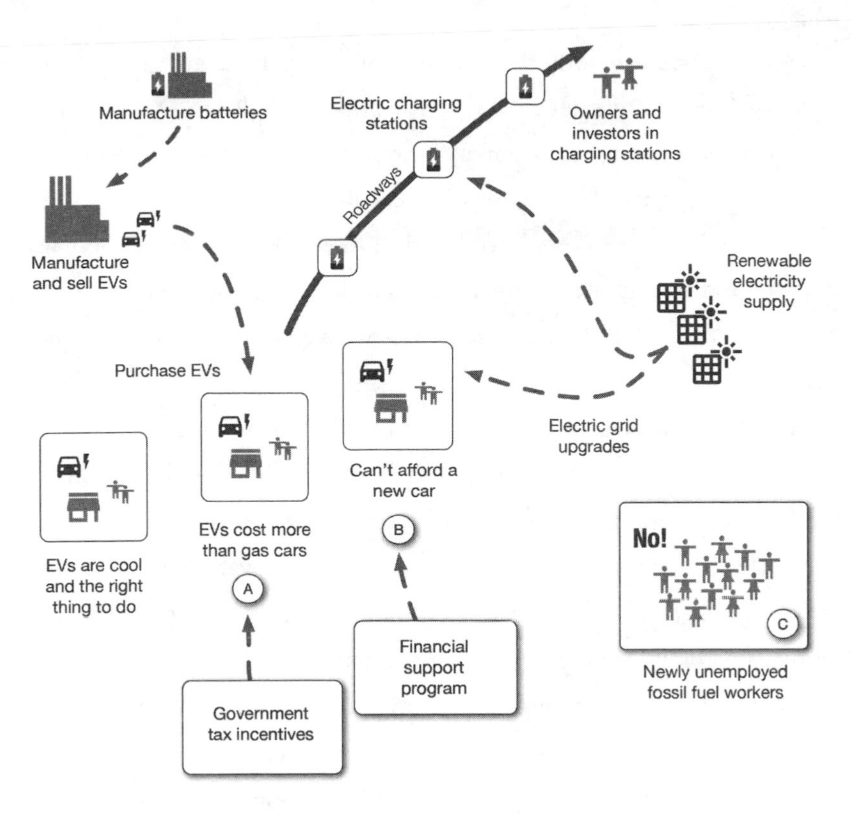

Figure 9.5. Future ecosystem for EV-based transportation

Costs and trade-offs don't mean your future ecosystem should automatically be tossed aside. No innovation has only positive impacts so you can't make everyone jump for joy or every cost go away. Instead, what you're trying to do is to be intentional about looking at and understanding those trade-offs and then dealing with them.

For example, in our transition to an EV future ecosystem, many people will not be able to afford to buy a new electric car. Over time they're going to be increasingly penalized for owning gas-powered cars—with fewer gas stations, lower car values, and more difficult repairs. For those with limited income, perhaps you could add a program that provides financial support to move from gas to electricity.

As you wrestle with these concerns, be careful to guard against demonizing or conveniently forgetting about people who for one reason or another can't gain easy entry to your future ecosystem. Be realistic about where you will see opposition coming from. Those future unemployed fossil fuel workers have legitimate concerns, even if their work contributed to climate change. You can count on vigorous opposition from any "ecosystem losers" if they are not accounted for in your future ecosystem.

Lastly, for those of you who are thinking, "This sounds hard!" think of it this way: All this complexity exists whether you deal with it or not. You can choose to ignore dissenters and focus on one or two groups, hoping that delivering a narrower win will make your innovation successful anyway. But over and over we have seen this tactic fail. You often only realize things are going sideways when it is too late.

Fortunately, you can build the motivations of many people into your innovation to make them supporters. Once you see what different participants need, you can intentionally remove barriers and create shared value.

TEN TESTS FOR A COMPLETE AND COMPELLING DESIGN

Here are ten ways you can make sure your future ecosystem is both complete and compelling. Complete ecosystems:

1. *Deliver value.* Make sure the future ecosystem is better than the current ecosystem.
2. *Stay inside the guardrails.* The ecosystem design should stay inside the "must do" and "must not do" guardrails.
3. *Have no gaps.* Are any pieces missing from the future ecosystem?
4. *Ensure capable parts.* Do all the parts work? Are they capable of fulfilling their roles?

5. *Are well connected.* Do all the parts work together? Are the needed connections in place?
6. *Are unicorn free.* Make sure the required skills, technology, and resources are actually available in the real world. Don't depend on unicorns that might only exist in the first year or far in the future.
7. *Have sustainable funding.* Is there a way to sustainably pay the bills over time? Are there ways to pay for future change and growth?
8. *Have sustainable leadership.* Is there a way to provide needed leadership and management over time? Does someone care enough to carry the work forward?
9. *Have compelling motivation.* Does everyone get a pony? Are there appropriate rewards for everyone?
10. *Minimize saboteurs.* There will always be someone who isn't a fan. However, can you minimize the groups positioned (or motivated) to actively undermine the ecosystem?

Step 5: Stretch the Innovation's Design

> Give me a place to stand and with a lever I will move the earth.
>
> —**Archimedes**[12]

Up until now you've been designing a future ecosystem that will work in the real world and be sufficiently compelling to be adopted. But you don't have to stop your imagining with the first thing that works. Once you have a foundation to work from you can explore bolder moves that stretch your vision and make it even better.

First Stretch Strategy: Add and Remove Legos

One way to fuel bigger possibilities is to add a new or unexpected piece to your ecosystem. This can unlock entirely different ways of approaching the problem—radically expanding your possibilities. You can also be creative by getting rid of Legos—setting aside existing parts of the current world—so that you don't have to be bound up in limitations of the way the world works now.

This is what Dollar Shave Club did. They got rid of traditional retail stores and distribution, throwing out those expensive and hard-to-access Legos. Instead, they added new pieces that the existing market leaders had ignored, tapping viral video advertising and delivery by mail to create an ecosystem they could rapidly set up and scale on a tight budget. Adding those new marketing technologies and approaches to distribution—a.k.a. new Legos—changed the kind of ecosystem they could create, unlocking all sorts of new possibilities.

What if we reimagine our future ecosystem of EVs to include self-driving autonomous cars that anyone could access anytime for on-demand ride services? By combining existing EV technology with the emerging self-driving vehicle technology, a driverless Uber-like rideshare service would be available, as depicted in Figure 9.6.

Looking at Figure 9.6, what could be different in *this* future ecosystem? First, people would no longer need to own cars to get where they want to go. They could request a car and it would show up at their front door anytime they wanted. Second, charging stations wouldn't have to be scattered all around communities. They could instead be centralized at one location and fleets of self-driving cars would automatically go home to get recharged when necessary.

Second Stretch Strategy: Tap Ecosystem Magic with Emergent Value and Win-Wins

There can be magic in a reimagined ecosystem. It's common to discover value that you weren't expecting or even looking for. Synergies in your ecosystem can create value seemingly out of thin air.

If you take the EV example one step further and imagine that many

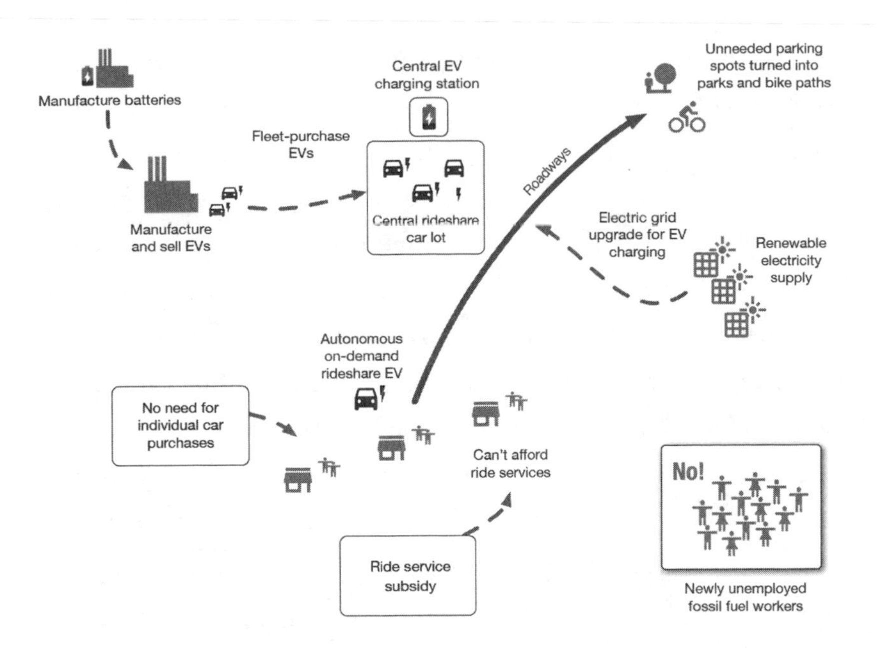

Figure 9.6. Reimaging the EV future ecosystem by adding self-driving cars

people are using autonomous, on-demand EV ride services, then cities wouldn't need nearly as many parking spots. This is potentially a huge benefit since in some US cities parking consumes as much as 14 percent of land space.[13] With less need for parking city leaders could expand roads so traffic moves more quickly or they could convert the parking areas into parks or they could build bike lanes or extra-wide sidewalks for people to enjoy. Parks and walkways weren't part of the original ecosystem vision but they could naturally emerge from the new thinking.

When you bring a future ecosystem together, there are often opportunities to create win-wins where you don't necessarily have to trade off the loss of one person against the win of another person. Instead, you set things up so there are benefits for both people. You avoid zero-sum games where everyone is fighting for a slice of pie and instead you make the pie bigger.

Third Stretch Strategy: Create Feedback Loops and Virtuous Cycles

Feedback loops are another way to leverage the power of your ecosystem. Positive feedback loops happen when one change or action grows because of other actions in a loop around it. Once the positive feedback loop gets going, the virtuous cycle of cost reduction continues to amplify the benefits. For example, the EV ecosystem can benefit from a classic type of manufacturing feedback loop; making something in high volumes is almost always cheaper than smaller quantities. So as people buy more electric vehicles the cost of producing each new car goes down. That lower cost can then result in a lower price, which makes even more people buy the cars, which lowers the price even further (see Figure 9.7).

Elon Musk had this in mind when he published his "secret" master plan for Tesla in 2006:

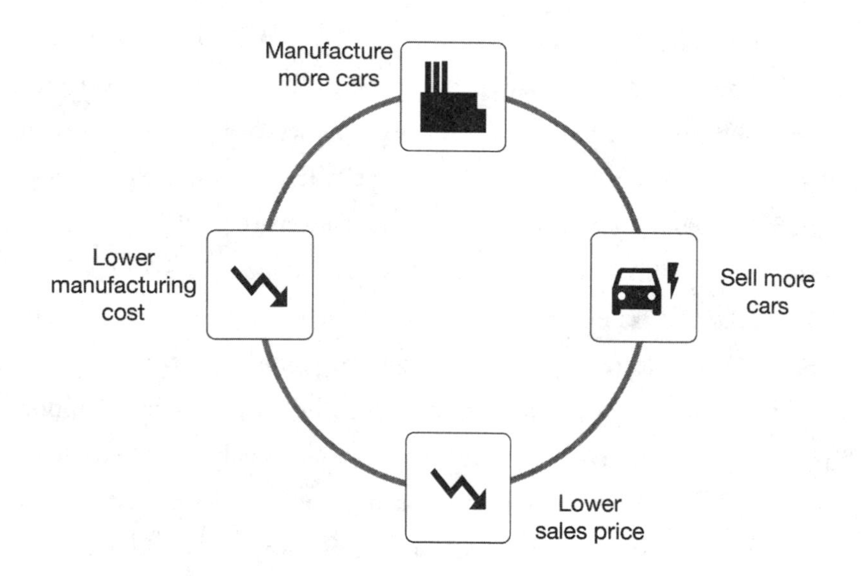

Figure 9.7. Feedback loop: more production drives cheaper EV cars, which drives more sales.

1. Build a sports car.
2. Use that money to build an affordable car.
3. Use that money to build an even more affordable car.
4. While doing above, also provide zero-emission electric power generation options.[14]

A good feedback loop can make your innovation naturally grow or get better over time without you having to do anything extra. And virtuous cycles exist in all sorts of ecosystems in our lives. When childhood mortality falls, for example, a community's population doesn't suddenly explode. Instead, parents choose to have smaller families, allowing for better care of each child, which further reduces childhood mortality.

NOT LIMITED BY THE DEMANDS OF MATHEMATICAL SYSTEMS ANALYSIS

If you have a computer system and a lot of data it is possible to really dive deeply into the way a proposed system design will perform. In fact, there is an entire field of systems analysis that offers very sophisticated ways to model how systems react under different conditions.

For example, supply chain experts often develop mathematical models to study how factory production, transportation, and stored inventories should be balanced. You might have heard this type of analysis described as a stock and flow model. It is just one of many formal ways of analyzing system behavior.

As you might imagine, these mathematical models aren't particularly easy to set up. They generally require a lot of detailed information about how the system is connected and how each part performs in it. For example, to analyze the simple feedback loop for EV car purchases, you would need data on how many more EVs people would buy if the price fell by a certain percentage and how much factory

continued

costs would fall if production increased. To be perfectly honest, you won't have that kind of information for many of the pieces of the future ecosystem that you're designing. Often the information isn't available, and even if it is, you may not have the resources or time required to do a detailed systems analysis.

But that's okay. You can still develop a useful future ecosystem design without all these details. At some point it may be useful to develop some more detailed mathematical models but you don't want to limit yourself only to future ecosystems that can be neatly put into a computer simulation.

IMPLEMENT YOUR (IMPERFECT) VISION OF THE FUTURE

> We seek excellence, not perfection.
>
> **—Stuart Kauffman**[15]

Now, with your innovation—a picture of the future ecosystem—in your hands, you can get people thinking about how to make bold changes in the real world. Your efforts have laid out a practical future where lots of moving parts could actually work together and where the participants see costs and rewards that work for them. It's a complete and compelling picture that allows you to step back and say, "This is the way the world could work; come join me in making it happen!"

The danger here is that it's naturally going to feel like you need to have everything defined and detailed *before* you can start taking action. That's not the case at all. In fact, *too much* detail is a problem so allow yourself some unknowns and space for a few miracles. Take this time to think big while still feeling that urgency to get started. That's your next job—taking action to transform today's challenges into tomorrow's success.

In the next chapter, we look at how you start taking action. It's hands-on work that involves a little bit of wandering, some great learning, and exciting discoveries along the way.

CHECKLIST FOR TASK 3: DESIGN THE FUTURE

- Step 1: Create a bold future.
- Step 2: Draw the future ecosystem.
- Step 3: Make sure the future ecosystem works.
- Step 4: Make sure everyone gets a pony.
- Step 5: Stretch the ecosystem's design.

PLAN TO IMPLEMENT THE FUTURE

You cannot cross San Francisco Bay with a long plank of wood. To bridge it you need to embark on a long evolutionary journey across many levels of innovation.

—Geoffrey West[1]

Years ago, Dan was part of a team that pioneered selling cars online in the United States. Their vision was pushing a lot of boundaries, and it turned out it was an incredibly messy thing. The team knew there would have to be a complete ecosystem that would eventually be able to handle the entire car purchase transaction digitally from start to finish. It just wouldn't do for people to order a car and then not be able to actually purchase it and have it delivered. But trying to get it designed and implemented up front was a fool's errand.

The team came up with a strategy that made it possible to pursue their big ground-breaking idea by moving fast, and still ensuring they could do the entire purchase to delivery process end to end. They decided not to put formal computer systems in place for every single function and they slimmed down the challenges by initially setting aside only a couple thousand cars of a single model in just two colors.

When the ordering system went live the website portal and online screens were set up but the entire backend process—the computer connections for handling an order after it was placed by a customer—was not. The project director happened to be an amateur athlete, a runner. Every time an online order was placed through the portal, he printed the order sheet and then dashed up the building's stairs with it, delivering the form to the people who typed the order information into their existing computer system for managing car orders. This guy was literally the connection (analog, not digital) that made this early online car ordering system work.

It was much the same in the early days of Amazon. There were no massive warehouses with robots pulling items off shelves, no fleet of delivery trucks and drivers roaming the countryside to drop off purchases on customers' front steps. There was just a small group of people working overtime taking the online orders for books and then running around like maniacs—grabbing books off the shelf and putting them in boxes to be shipped. In those early days, a bell rang every time someone placed an order on Amazon's website. It didn't take long for that bell to be turned off as orders skyrocketed.[2]

When you see completed ecosystems, it's easy to be impressed. "That must have required a huge master plan to implement!" you might think. But in the beginning, when a team created the first *thin slices* of a working ecosystem that did something, they didn't put all the pieces in place up front. Instead they focused on making something meaningful work. We would argue, in fact, that this is the best approach for testing and implementing ecosystem innovations in the real world, and in this chapter, we show you how to do just that.

PLANNING YOUR FUTURE ECOSYSTEM

In this chapter you will learn how to create a plan for testing and implementing your future ecosystem. This is important because it will help you deliver a big vision with lots of interconnected parts. Rather than testing individual bits one by one, only worrying about whether each part works in isolation, you use an approach that does multiple connected tests at once. You make sure the whole ecosystem can work together to deliver bigger, higher-value innovation.

Why Is This Important?

- *It allows you to act bigger, faster.* Thin slices allow you to build more of your innovation with each test. Because you're working with interconnected pieces of your innovation, rather than having to do a string of one-at-a-time tests, you can move faster toward strategic, sophisticated innovations.
- *It allows you to learn fast and reduce risk.* You intentionally identify questions and risks early so you can get answers. This avoids the risk of discovering big problems late in implementation.
- *It enables flexibility.* Because issues are identified early, it's possible to adjust the course before key choices are locked in stone. You can be creatively nimble and better utilize opportunities and value as you find them.
- *It delivers results and early wins.* You don't have to wait to get tangible results. It's not just about finishing tasks—you deliver measurable outcomes all along the way. This helps people buy in and stay engaged.
- *It uncovers and addresses hidden issues.* Problems and opportunities that come from messy challenges are exposed so they can be addressed. You can deal with failure points and challenges before they become critical.
- *It creates less waste.* Learning, flexibility, and wins don't require disposable prototypes where everything is thrown away with each test. Each piece of work you do builds a part of the ultimate innovation.

THE CHALLENGE: SUCCESSFULLY IMPLEMENTING MEANINGFUL INNOVATIONS

> The failure [of Three Mile Island] was not a freak occurrence, but a fundamental feature of the nuclear power plant as a system. The failure was driven by the connections between different parts, rather than the parts themselves.
>
> **—Chris Clearfield and András Tilcsik**[3]

In the previous two chapters, you created two really powerful views of how the world works. The first is a picture of how the world works today: the current ecosystem. The second is a picture of how you'd like to reshape the world: the future ecosystem. For this future vision you've probably imagined a number of changes, such as adding new players and new technologies, changing the ways people and organizations are connected, or shifting the rewards and trade-offs people get.

The question you must now answer is this: How do you get from the way the world looks today to the ecosystem you want to create for the future? Conventional innovators offer two very different approaches. One is highly structured. The other is more free-form. For your important work, neither of these methods will do the job alone, so we'll need to pursue a middle road that does both—a way to implement your ecosystem that provides structure but also gives you the power to learn and adapt.

When faced with a big project like this, many innovators fall back on their tried-and-true reductionist project-planning techniques. This is the highly structured engineering approach you see in Chapter 4. It's what organizations have been doing since the nineteenth century, and it's very comfortable for those who practice it because they have concrete plans and schedules to deliver projects.

Unfortunately, when you try to force such a highly structured approach onto messy challenges in the real world those detailed work plans are often little more than executive teddy bears, providing their owners a false sense of soft-and-cuddly reassurance and certainty. They might feel nice but in a fast-changing world with hidden issues and unexpected opportunities they aren't likely to succeed.

In reaction to this heavy reliance on planning, agile product designers and incremental innovators swing to the other extreme. They prioritize learning and adaptation, largely giving up on the pretense of futile planning and analysis, and just figure things out as they go. This approach works, but only because these innovators are exploring smaller ideas that serve specific needs. With smaller, simpler innovations, there is not that much risk if they wander around a bit on the way to coming up with a new product, service, or improvement.

As an ecosystem innovator, however, you can't be satisfied with either of these extreme choices. You can't plan everything out in advance when dealing with complex challenges—there are just too many unknowns and hidden challenges. But you also won't be able to just wander your way to the future. Asking organizational managers you are working with to simply trust that you will figure it out along the way isn't going to fly. They justifiably imagine how easy it would be for your innovation bus to drive off a cliff, with no one knowing until it crashes at the bottom of the canyon.

The solution is a middle path, a way to guide the implementation of your innovation that provides you flexibility to learn and adapt while also offering leaders, sponsors, investors, and others a way to evaluate progress and manage risk. Fortunately, you can apply a practice that does just that.

Welcome to innovating with thin slices.

THIN SLICES

It's pretty much impossible to create and implement an entire future ecosystem all in one fell swoop. Instead, you'll be far more successful if you take it on one thin slice at a time.

At the heart of this approach is the creation of a series of thin slices—portions of the future ecosystem—that let you get some real outcomes and see how things work in practice. For example, you could design a thin slice where you connect several different organizations and people to see if they will successfully work together. Or you could design a thin slice that puts some new technology in place and ask people to do a job with it. You could then evaluate real-world results to see if they get the value you expect or if they encounter unexpected problems.

The great thing about thin slices is they let you explore some pretty complex things without having to build out the entire innovation all at once. As you implement each thin slice, you can see how the innovation works and then make adjustments. These aren't just throwaway experiments. Each new thin slice creates something, building on the thin slices that came before. Your innovation adds more parts and connections, getting more and more sophisticated with what is developed in each thin slice, until you finally get the entire future ecosystem in place.

Each thin slice isn't just the execution of tasks in a project plan. You'll be doing much more—answering questions about how the innovation performs and uncovering risks and opportunities that you can use to make changes in your approach. In addition, you'll be able to keep people excited and engaged by delivering wins along the way to building your future ecosystem.

Step 1: Identify Your Big Questions and Challenges

> The quality of any answer is directly determined by the quality of the question. Ask the wrong question, get the wrong answer.
>
> —**Gary Keller**[4]

Ecosystems are filled with real-life people, organizations, and technology all working together on a variety of tasks. When you change how they work together unknowns are unavoidable. So the first step in implementing your innovation is to think about questions to work through what you don't know.

This step would be easier if your ecosystem were like a clock with fixed gears and springs that could each be analyzed and then built to specification. Every detail could be worked out in advance because you would know everything that mattered about every part. This is what most traditional project managers try to do.

But because you have all those unknowns of the real, messy world, there will be important questions you can't know the answer to now. So you'll need to figure out what these questions are and later create a plan to get answers. To see what this might be like let's consider the example of Irina's tutoring service.

Irina owns a tutoring service that serves students at a large, Canadian university. Business has been very good—Irina has a steady supply of customers—but there's trouble on the horizon. One day, a national tutoring chain opens an office within half a mile of Irina's business. With lower rates and more advertising than Irina's service, the new tutoring business quickly takes customers away from her business. Irina is forced to come up with a strategy to stem the bleeding—*fast*.

As she did more research on her competitor, Irina spotted an opportunity. The big chain tutoring company only teaches in English and French while many international students bring different native languages to the table. Could Irina offer a specialty tutoring service in each student's native language?

She thought the answer was yes.

Irina believed she could accomplish this business innovation by locating native-speaking tutors around the world and having them provide instruction to her customers via video call. Irina imagined a new, future ecosystem for her business using the potential to connect with expertise around the world using video (see Figure 10.1).

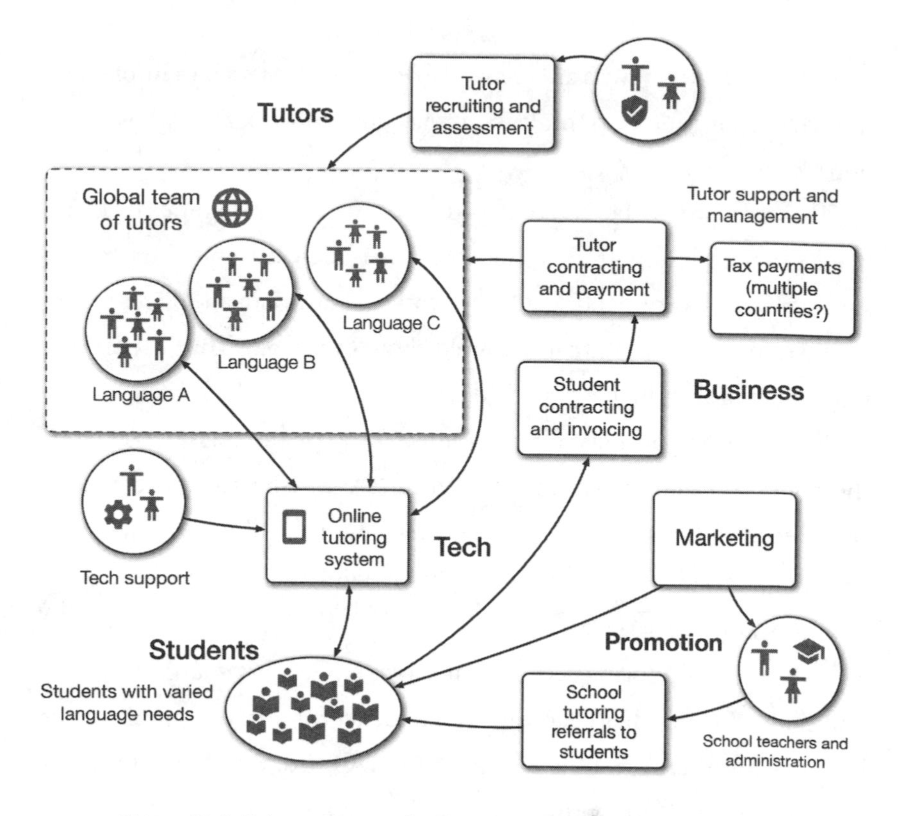

Figure 10.1. Future ecosystem for Irina's international tutoring innovation

So what are Irina's most important and urgent questions? Innovators tend to default to exploring the easiest and most obvious questions about their innovation and the things they are most interested in. Irina will need to avoid that temptation and seriously think about what big questions must be answered if her innovative idea is to be a success. She should prioritize questions that ask about:

- *Failure.* What things are most likely to derail this work?
- *Uncertainty.* What are the biggest areas of uncertainty?
- *Opportunity.* Where might there be unrecognized opportunities?

For example, Irina doesn't know if anyone will want tutoring in their native tongue or if there are tutors who will be available online for the different languages the students want. And will she be able to get support and referrals from the university?

A big list of questions and problems might seem scary, but it's worth thinking through. Ignoring messy challenges doesn't make them go away. In fact, it often leads to failure. For Irina, and you, seeing the questions that are most likely to affect success makes it possible to intentionally address them.

Identifying these questions isn't just an exercise to be ticked off as you begin the innovation implementation. They provide guideposts for where risks and opportunities lie in the journey ahead. By getting important questions spelled out and shared with others, you have a starting point for focusing implementation on the most important issues and biggest challenges. You get comfortable with exploring uncertainty and unknowns so they don't derail you later.

When compared to traditional project managers, this is a very different way of working. Traditional project managers want a project plan that squeezes out all the uncertainty and answers every question before work begins. As an ecosystem innovator, you can't do that and you shouldn't even try. Uncertainty and unknowns will be popping up throughout the implementation of your ecosystem. So you'll need to keep coming back to identify new questions that need to be answered based on what you've done.

QUESTIONS FOR IRINA'S INTERNATIONAL TUTORING

Like every ecosystem innovator, Irina will need to answer questions and solve problems to implement her innovation. Here is a list of potential questions whose answers could lead to her future ecosystem's success—or failure:

continued

- Will students want this service?
- Which subjects and languages will students want?
- Where will I find tutors?
- How will I pay the tutors?
- How will remote instruction work?
- Will the university support and recommend my new service?
- Will this new approach be profitable?
- If I'm successful, what barriers are there for expanding to other universities?

Step 2: Design a Thin Slice of the Ecosystem

> From a very early age, we are taught to break apart problems, to fragment the world. This apparently makes complex tasks and subjects more manageable, but we pay a hidden, enormous price. We can no longer see the consequences of our actions; we lose our intrinsic sense of connection to a larger whole.
>
> **—Peter Senge**[5]

So how does someone like Irina answer crucial questions about the future ecosystem they want to create? Irina could do some research or perhaps run a focus group, but many of her most important questions will only be answered by doing something in the real world and seeing what kind of choices people make.

For example, how will she know if students will pay to get a native-language tutoring course? And will tutors be willing to work overtime with students who are in a faraway time zone? Face it, people and organizations often don't know how they will act until they are faced with a real-life situation. To answer these kinds of questions, there's a good chance Irina will have to start up a working international tutoring service.

If you are working with people, organizations, and technologies, the best way to answer questions and solve hard problems is to put some pieces together in the form of thin slices and see how they work. These thin slices are your tools for gaining real-life experience and insights as you implement your future ecosystem.

Let's dive a little deeper into these thin slices. While each individual piece of a future ecosystem might have some value, the full impact comes when all the pieces are hooked together and they work in the real world. Ultimately your job is to create a future ecosystem where all the parts of your innovation work together.

Each thin slice has the same goal: combining different pieces and changes to create a working portion of your innovation that can be used to test your ideas and lay the foundation for further work. Early on, Irina will want to know if the heart of her new tutoring ecosystem will work. Can students and instructors come together to make this work? To find out as quickly as possible, she designs a thin slice, as shown in Figure 10.2, with a few students who all have the same language—say, Vietnamese. Irina then hires one or two international tutors who can instruct them in Vietnamese.

Irina's first thin slice quickly explores the viability of her future ecosystem. Figure 10.2 is a very small, but working, version of Irina's tutoring ecosystem. It's a slice that combines multiple parts of the ecosystem to accomplish something, in this case teach students with international tutors. Notice that she doesn't just check to see if each part works individually, like marketing to students or hiring an instructor. She needs those individual parts to work, but what really matters to her is whether, when she brings students and instructors together, her *slice* of the tutoring ecosystem works in practice.

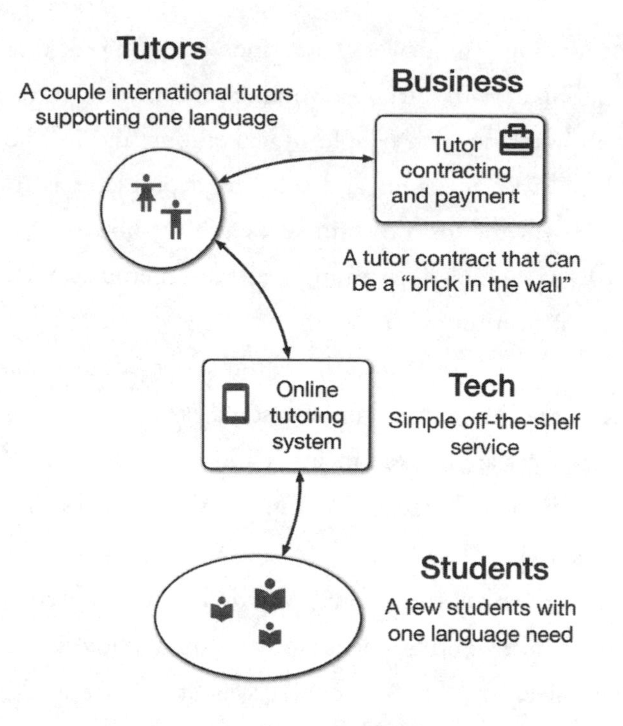

Figure 10.2. A thin slice to test ideas

While Irina is designing this thin slice, she'll ask herself, "How do we create a version of this ecosystem with people, organizations, and technology in a way that's fairly lightweight?" The emphasis is on *lightweight*—she won't build out an early thin slice with super-sophisticated technology, a large pool of professionals, or a big ad campaign. If her goal is to answer an important question about the value of her service, she won't want to weigh herself down with big demands on time and investment.

Thin slices are powerful because they allow you to accomplish three crucial tasks at the same time. She will want to:

1. Answer important questions.
2. Put bricks in the wall.
3. Deliver early wins.

Thin Slice Task 1: Answer Important Questions

As we've already said, one of the most important jobs of a thin slice is to chip away at the unknowns that are part of building an ecosystem in the real world. This is a job that doesn't end with early research and then simply settle into a fixed project plan. There will be some questions that can only be answered after a number of thin slices are in place. For example, it will be difficult for Irina to know whether other schools will use her tutoring service until she has it working in at least one school. The question is still really important, but it will have to wait to be explored in practice.

Irina is looking not only to answer questions with each thin slice but also to discover new questions about her ecosystem that she can explore. These might be unexpected challenges or they could be opportunities—possibilities that weren't on the radar when she originally designed the innovation. Irina might discover, for example, that her tutoring ecosystem is useful outside of colleges. This unexpected opportunity would still need to be explored by asking more questions but if it worked out, there could be an entirely new market.

Thin Slice Task 2: Put Bricks in the Wall

Thin slices aren't just about answering questions. They are also used to build your innovation, the future ecosystem. Each thin slice can "put bricks in the wall," creating the innovation slice by slice to move toward the future ecosystem.

If you have worked with other innovation practices, a thin slice might sound like a disposable prototype—an experiment that is built to answer a question and then just thrown away. Product innovators often do this. They test a hypothesis and then throw out their pilot or prototype and move on to the next one. When they're finally done learning, they plan to go back and build it from scratch.

When you're creating a future ecosystem, you can't afford to throw out your work. Doing work in the real world requires substantial time and effort, both for you and for all the other people and organizations that are part of your innovation. It's important that these investments eventually contribute toward your future innovation, building the ecosystem, bit by bit.

It's not necessary or helpful to try and make every piece of the thin slice a perfectly formed "brick" that can be used in the final ecosystem. But with a bit of thoughtfulness around this you can intentionally create opportunities to lay foundational bricks that can be used and built on later.

For example, Irina wouldn't set up a full-scale system for hiring and paying international tutors before she answered some important questions. But as part of her initial lightweight thin slice, she might work with a lawyer to write up a services contract that would ensure she was legally compliant now, and the contract could also be used later as more tutors join up. That would give her a valuable resource now to keep her out of early legal troubles, while providing a brick she could continue to use and build on in future thin slices.

Thin Slice Task 3: Deliver Early Wins

If you think of the effort and dedication needed to design and deliver a series of thin slices, you might wonder how you can manage to keep everyone engaged for the journey. There are going to be ups and downs and it's going to take time.

You will have already drawn a powerful picture of how the future ecosystem will create value and opportunity. But over time, people will naturally begin to feel fatigue and doubt. The final task of a thin slice is to combat this by continuously delivering wins and value. Each thin slice is a chance to demonstrate how the future ecosystem will work and some of the benefits that come with it.

One of the biggest faults and sources of failure in large, traditionally managed waterfall projects is that all the rewards are delayed until the conclusion of the work. Here project teams spend a lot of time *planning* to do something—say, build an entire new software product—and create the parts of it one at a time, with no product to deliver until all the parts come together at the end. These projects can go for years this way, while hope recedes and support fades.

Because a thin slice is a working part of an ecosystem, you don't have to wait years—or even months—to create value in the real world, and you shouldn't. You can create value and deliver wins early. Each subsequent slice can add to the overall results, delivering even more wins and creating even more value.

A win could be many things. It could be real value created from the solution—genuine benefits that are a first step toward even bigger value. But it doesn't have to be the final result you're delivering. A win could be a sign that the idea will work—an example of how all the parts come together and function in the real world. A win can even be a problem solved—an early thorn removed—even if the entire ecosystem isn't working yet.

Wins let you bring others along, which is incredibly important. For example, if Irina ended up with some satisfied Vietnamese students after her first thin slice, she might showcase that win with a press interview. Then her thin slice isn't just a chance to learn; it becomes an opportunity to demonstrate an early win. With evidence that her idea wasn't just some sort of lofty dream, she could be better positioned to get the local university interested in supporting her or even attract an investor or two.

If you design your thin slice well, you can get all three benefits—answering important questions, putting bricks in the wall, and delivering wins. Remember that the thin slice is actually a working piece of your future ecosystem. It isn't just a bunch of tasks that come from breaking a big project up into pieces. With each thin slice, you are making something that creates value in the real world. Something that you can use to test ideas and build on as you progressively make your future ecosystem a reality.

Step 3: Dance around Barriers

> You must learn how to become a deeply disciplined half ass. . . . Perfection is unattainable. It's a myth and a trap and a hamster wheel that will run you to death.
>
> **—Elizabeth Gilbert**[6]

You can creatively design your thin slice to move around barriers and limitations that might otherwise seem to limit your innovation. Think about the innovators who founded Dollar Shave Club, Airbnb, or even Amazon. None of them had the right, based on their size, to take on international leaders in their industry. But they danced around barriers others were stuck by and changed the rules of the game. There are several strategies to develop early thin slices that test ideas, put bricks in the wall, and create wins—all without huge budgets or taking too much time.

Improvise some Legos. One way to do more with less is to fill some of your gaps with improvised pieces that won't be part of the ultimate ecosystem. The team that was selling those first cars online couldn't hope to build a bunch of computer systems to automate the end-to-end process. Instead, they took advantage of the athletic ability of the project director to work around the barrier, running up and down stairs instead of writing software.

Leverage collaborations. Another powerful tool available to you is the ability to find collaborators who can fill in parts of the solution. In other words, let someone else provide a Lego block. For example, one of the challenges that Irina faced with her early thin slice was finding her first tutors, instructors who could teach subjects in Vietnamese. She could have put a lot of effort into finding and recruiting those tutors herself, but she could move much more quickly if she set up a relationship with a tutoring service in Vietnam that already had ready access to instructors. That partnership might, or might not, be a long-term solution to her recruiting challenges, but she could leverage it to quickly move forward with her first thin slice.

Design thinner slices. If you find that there are simply too many moving parts, too big a budget, or too many approvals to be put in place, that's a sign you're trying to do too much. If so, consider different creative options for designing a thinner slice, changing how you put the parts together, or trimming back the outcomes you are looking for in each thin slice. Then you can use the results of that more streamlined slice to set up the next slice.

Step 4: Plan a Journey of Thin Slices

> A man who sets out to achieve this adaptation in a single leap is not unlike the child who shakes his glass-topped puzzle fretfully, expecting at one shake to arrange the bits inside correctly. . . . His chances of success are small because the number of factors which must fall simultaneously into place is so enormous.
>
> —**Christopher Alexander**[7]

Obviously, you won't create your future ecosystem with just one thin slice (if so, your thin slice is way, way too big). Instead, you're going to need to do one thin slice, step back and see what you've learned, make some adjustments, and then do another. And another.

What you need to do is start with the current ecosystem and ultimately end up at the future ecosystem, as shown in Figure 10.3. Writing this out as a series of consecutive thin slices provides a high-level plan of how you

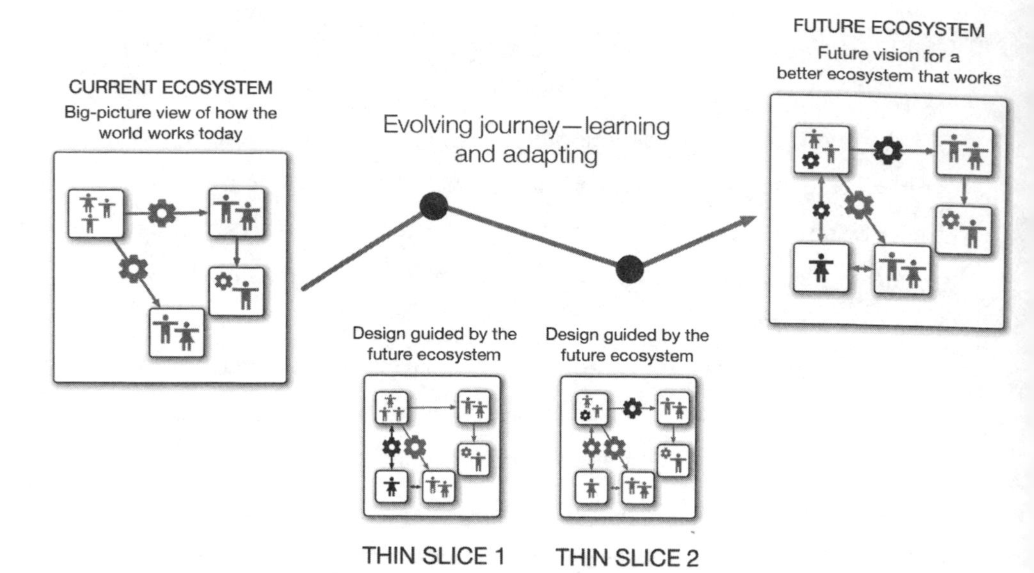

Figure 10.3. Evolving the future ecosystem with a series of thin slices

will actually create your future ecosystem. This isn't a rigorous project plan where each part of every thin slice is defined in detail. It's more like the road map for a trip where your destinations and accommodations are laid out but the specifics of activities are left until you actually implement the thin slice. And of course, your plans may change as you travel.

Even though you don't know everything that will be done in detail, you can still lay out outcomes for each thin slice. You can describe at a high level which parts of the ecosystem are being brought together and what they will be able to do. You can be clear about the key questions you want to answer, which bricks you hope to put in the wall, and the kinds of wins you expect to achieve for each thin slice as you plan and implement it.

The early thin slices—the ones you'll be starting work on soon—will have more detail. Later thin slices—the ones that are further in the future and are more uncertain—can be higher level since they are more likely to change as you go forward. When you bring this list of thin slices together you have a broad, flexible road map you can share with others.

This allows you to take a strategic path that leads to your future ecosystem rather than taking a stab in the dark at what parts should be done first. It also gives you the ability to show others you are working with that your innovation is practically achievable. And you can work with others to review and refine the approach. Are there ways to learn faster or more? Can an extra win be pulled out of an upcoming thin slice?

As you design your thin slices, avoid the temptation to immediately go for the obvious task or do the easiest parts first. One of the most important things you can do with your early thin slices is to understand and address the things that are most likely to derail your effort. Don't get drawn in by the natural tendency people have to focus on the parts of the innovation they find most exciting or that offer the greatest alignment with their skills.

At the same time as you're working on the challenging stuff, you'll also want to consider how to deliver some early wins. This requires you to do a balancing act, designing the thin slice to address important challenges, but also finding ways to keep everyone committed to the effort. Often the win you need won't have to be that impressive to be important. When one of our clients put together the first thin slice of their ecosystem their goal was to deliver exactly one dollar of revenue. You read that right: not $1 million, not $100,000, not even $1,000—just one dollar. "Why?" you might ask—they're not going to be able to run the company on a dollar of revenue. But that wasn't the point. The point was that if they could get a dollar of revenue through the first thin slice they built, that would be the proof they needed that the innovation could work from end to end. And it did.

This road map of thin slices isn't set in stone. You'll be creating it with the intention of changing it over and over again. It intentionally lacks the rigor and detail that make traditional project planners comfortable, but for you this kind of broad plan is still very useful. Laying out a journey of thin slices provides a tangible check of whether your vision can actually be done (perhaps with a little magic added here and there). You have the visibility to consider dependencies, evaluate the actual size of the change you're taking on, and lay out major milestones that will indicate success.

When Irina laid out her thin slices in broad brushstrokes, it was possible to see how the ecosystem she wanted to create would evolve and be progressively tested as shown in Table 10.1. Note that each stage of her journey tests key questions, generates wins, and puts bricks in the wall. Even though the evolution of the innovation will likely have detours and changes as she learns how things work in practice, her broad plan of thin slices provided a strategic road map of expected progress.

TABLE 10.1. IRINA'S TUTORING: MAJOR THIN SLICES

	Thin slice 1 Test the basics	Thin slice 2 Scale the parts	Thin slice 3 Get big
What's in the thin slice?	Find a few students Match with an international tutor Make the contracts and accounting work	Find more students and more languages Expand number and range of tutors Make contracts and payments work at scale Build relationships with the school	Marketing innovations/referral programs Expansion to additional schools Automated systems and management
What are the big questions?	Is there any interest at all? Can tutors be engaged? Is it profitable?	Is there enough total demand? Can operations scale profitably? Will the school endorse us?	Can this work at other schools? Can marketing keep growing demand? Can quality be maintained as scale grows?

	Thin slice 1 Test the basics	Thin slice 2 Scale the parts	Thin slice 3 Get big
What bricks are being added to the wall?	Basic sales pitch Contracting for tutors Basic accounting	Marketing to students Tutor recruiting and contracting Scaled-up accounting	Advanced marketing programs Business automation Transition to professional management
What wins are expected?	Some happy students—references Showcase the new approach—news articles	Lots of satisfied students Positive reviews from tutors Growing cash flow	Wide market visibility Significant business growth and profitability Sustainable operating structure
What outcomes can be measured?	Satisfaction of students and tutors Initial profitability	Satisfaction of students and tutors Revenue growth	Satisfaction of students and tutors Growth and profitability at scale Market awareness Dependence on the founder for ongoing operations

Step 5: Sell Others on Urgent Action

> Much of what needs to be done can be done by coalitions of the working—groups of influential citizens, companies, cities, or countries that get the issue, get the urgency, and by their coordinated actions generate momentum that pulls the laggards along.
>
> **—Ian Goldin and Chris Kutarna**[8]

Taking urgent action is essential since it's only by acting that you can really answer questions about how your ecosystem will work in a messy world. However, remember that choosing to act isn't something you do alone. You are laying out a great change so you'll need others' support and involvement. You will need to convince other people, and other organizations, to offer their power and resources and be part of realizing your innovation.

This can be difficult. Often you'll find that others are proposing to solve a hard problem with smaller, simpler ideas. Their projects will seem less challenging—either more precisely defined or smaller and easier to do.

Sometimes even proposals for big, traditionally managed projects might seem like a safer bet. If they have detailed project plans with "hard evidence" of returns, that may make them seem lower risk. They can be sold to sponsors by saying, "I've got hard data and detailed plans to prove that this will work"—even if they are likely to fail later when unexpected issues and changes invalidate their plans.

If you ever face this kind of opposition, you should avoid underselling your vision. You are doing big things and you have the opportunity to tell this kind of story. True, you don't have detailed plans and you are proposing a journey that requires real effort. By using your view of the current ecosystem and the future ecosystem, you can talk about the high value opportunity of your innovation.

You can show how you will manage the risks of implementing this future ecosystem—not by doing even more analysis, but by taking action, learning, and adapting as you go. You have a strong case that it's not possible to analyze the details of a fast-changing, messy world. That the only way to understand the future will ultimately come from building it, testing it, and seeing how it works. You sell a journey of progressive slices of change, using your road map of thin slices to show how you will learn and deliver outcomes along the way.

This is a story that you need to tell over and over again, as you will need many types of people to buy in. Some of the permissions you'll need will be formal—you're allowed to do it or you're provided access to scarce resources such as time, money, or priority in work queues. Other forms of support will be informal—such as getting people excited about participating or making sure the people with power and influence are on board—and sometimes permission means just getting someone to step back and not stand in your way.

PURPOSEFULLY IMPROVING THE FUTURE

You have a current ecosystem that shows where you are now, a future ecosystem of where you are going, and your thin slices providing a road map to get from one to the other. This plan isn't a fixed-and-rigid project plan. Almost from the moment you start you'll be discovering problems—and opportunities—that will make you rethink your design of the thin slices or even reimagine your vision of a future ecosystem.

This isn't a bad thing. In fact, the ability to learn and adapt is what makes it possible to deliver ambitious change in a messy, fast-changing world. You take advantage of having a big-picture plan while at the same time being flexible enough to adapt and make things work in practice. How you take that intentionally wandering journey is what we cover in the next chapter, the last of your five tasks.

CHECKLIST FOR TASK 4: PLAN TO IMPLEMENT THE FUTURE

- Step 1: Identify your big questions and challenges.
- Step 2: Design a thin slice of the ecosystem.
- Step 3: Dance around barriers.
- Step 4: Plan a journey of thin slices.
- Step 5: Sell others on urgent action.

11

BUILD THE FUTURE

Waiting until everything looks feasible is too long to wait.

—Rebecca Solnit[1]

Imagine you've arrived at a hotel in a city that's unfamiliar to you. You're excited by the experiences and rewards to be discovered, and in fact there's a great restaurant that a friend told you about. The internet on your phone isn't working, so the maps app you use can't help. Undaunted and wanting to experience this new metropolis on foot, you go and talk with the hotel concierge. They are briskly competent, with a neat desk, and studiously write out detailed directions to the restaurant which is located on the other side of town. They tell you every turn and every street you'll walk on your journey—left on this street, right at the fork in the road a few minutes on, and so forth. They promise that if you follow these instructions exactly, you're certain to get to the restaurant in time for your reservation.

Sadly, a few blocks into your walk, you find that there's construction, and several roads are closed or diverted. Your maps app still isn't working, so you make your best guess on which way to go. Bad choice. You make a wrong turn and end up lost in a part of town that wasn't even mentioned in your precise plan for getting to the restaurant. Once you're off the prescribed route, you have little ability to recover, and your arrival at the restaurant—much less in time for your reservation—is put in jeopardy.

Now imagine that in desperation you go into a different hotel, and their concierge gives you a *different* kind of direction. They point out the initial road to follow but tell you to keep aiming for the tall television broadcasting antenna with blinking red lights on top of the building next to your restaurant. You lack detailed directions, but when you encounter unexpected detours along the way, you quickly adapt—guided by the tall TV tower you can always see in the distance.

You have a less-detailed plan but ironically have more freedom and flexibility. You can choose to spontaneously follow the sound of music down a side street, where some local buskers are playing, or take a short diversion into a set of particularly interesting shops and still adapt your path to aim once again for the blinking red lights. The result might be a bit more of a wandering journey, but you are never lost. With each detour or distraction, you can still adjust your course and head to the destination.

Who gave you better directions?

The first concierge offered impressively detailed instructions and certainly inspired confidence in you with their precision and thoroughness. But in a messy and changing world (or a city with plenty of road work), isn't it likely that the more pragmatic and adaptive strategy of the second concierge has the greatest chance of getting you to the delicious food you desire?

We think so. And that's what we explore when we discuss the fifth task: build your future ecosystem.

BUILDING YOUR FUTURE ECOSYSTEM

In this chapter you will learn how to iteratively build your future ecosystem. This is important because it helps you succeed in a changing world.

It avoids fixed project plans that promise security and predictability but are too inflexible to work in a complex world.

Why Is This Important?

- *It solves problems early.* You learn about problems early and respond to them quickly, avoiding risks that would be impossible to correct later.
- *It responds to change.* You can adapt as the world changes around you. You aren't left hoping the solution will still work and be relevant when it's finally fully implemented.
- *It taps unexpected opportunities.* You can find and take advantage of unexpected and newly discovered opportunities as you go.
- *It provides confidence to others.* Evolving an ecosystem is flexible but still provides confidence to others that you're in control and heading in a clear direction toward success.
- *It lets you enjoy more flexibility.* You have the flexibility to dodge barriers and solve problems. You don't get locked on a fixed path that seems great today but leads to failure tomorrow.

THE CHALLENGE: BUILDING INNOVATIONS IN A MESSY, FAST-CHANGING WORLD

> The world is moving so fast these days that the man who says it can't be done is generally interrupted by someone doing it.
>
> —***Puck* magazine**[2]

You've learned a lot about creating your future ecosystem, now it's time to put your knowledge to work in the real world. You'll start by creating your future ecosystem thin slice by thin slice. As you do this exciting work, you will be dealing with a variety of risks, unknowns, and uncertainties. Many traditional project planners believe that detailed planning is the only way to manage these risks on important projects.

We beg to differ. When you're dealing with an ecosystem innovation in the real world, where there are lots of interconnected parts and a changing environment, detailed planning does not remove risk—it often creates it. It doesn't matter how diligent you are or how many numbers you run or spreadsheets you fill up. It is impossible to remove risk and uncertainty before work begins because it's impossible to fully analyze the challenge. As a result, traditional criteria that require detailed planning before beginning a project will almost always fall short for our innovations.

Paradoxically, the best way to deal with the risk of unknowns is not by doing more analysis but by taking action, learning, and adapting. Since you can't analyze the details of an exact future, the best way to understand how your future ecosystem will work is to build it, test it, and see it in action. Action in the real world uncovers how people and organizations react when they are brought together because it reveals unanticipated barriers and opportunities. This is how you will learn if they have the capabilities, resources, and motivations to participate.

We aren't saying you should ignore risks and charge over a cliff blindfolded. Instead, what you need is a methodology for managing risk that's appropriate to the nature of the challenge you're taking on. To build a future ecosystem where people, organizations, and technology all interact, you must balance two things:

1. First, you need the ability to intentionally aim toward a well-thought-out future. That's your future ecosystem.
2. Second, you will always encounter hidden challenges or discover unexpected opportunities along the way; you need to be able to learn and adapt as you go.

In this chapter, we discuss the approach for taking action that enables you to learn and adapt as you go. You want to be that visitor to the city who successfully makes their way through town, taking advantage of unplanned opportunities and dealing with unexpected challenges—all the while working your way toward the ultimate destination: a working future ecosystem, your successful innovation.

Step 1: Act, Learn, and Adapt

> Leaders should encourage experimentation and accept that there is nothing wrong with failure as long as it happens early and becomes a source of learning.
>
> **—Tim Brown**[3]

Act

The time to act is *now*. You'll need to convince sponsors and participants to begin work. You'll have to tell a convincing story of how by taking action now, you can actually better manage risks and ultimately succeed with your innovation.

We're not the first ones who have made this case. Over the last twenty years, innovators with roots in Silicon Valley have moved in the opposite direction of big project planners. Instead of planning everything up front, they have sold the idea that they can manage the risks of innovation by learning and adapting as they go. This is the foundation of *agile*—practices that use rapid, lightweight learning to creatively build new things. Agile practitioners pointed out that the detailed, up-front project plans embraced by most old, twentieth-century companies slowed them down, and that being fast and nimble was the best way to ensure success.

For smaller, lightweight product innovations, the pitch for agile has really taken hold. It's proven to work really well when exploring opportunities for incremental improvement or new digital applications, but there's been a lot of pushback when that freewheeling approach is proposed for bigger, more complex innovations. If you're working on something where there are lots of moving parts and substantial budgets involved, executives and investors often want greater discipline. They often feel drawn back to that comforting teddy bear where everything is planned out in detail and they feel they have contained their risk.

So when it comes time to build your future ecosystem, you have to explain how you're going to manage the risks. If you aren't going to create a detailed project plan (and we suggest you shouldn't), you need to make the case for why learning and adapting is actually a better way of succeeding by reducing risk.

At the heart of this approach is a cycle of acting, learning, and adapting (see Figure 11.1). As you implement a thin slice, you intentionally look at how that slice worked, learning about problems and discovering unexpected opportunities. With the new insights and knowledge that came from taking action, you adapt your approach.

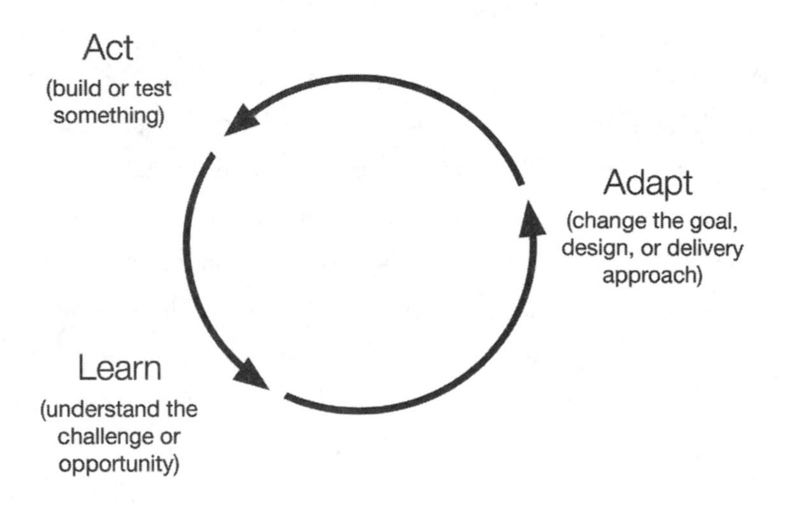

Figure 11.1. The act-learn-adapt cycle manages risk in messy environments.

Let's revisit Irina, who was planning a new international tutoring service. Imagine Irina met with a prospective investor over tea. The investor was intrigued by her vision, but worried there wasn't anything concrete in place yet. Based on their prior experience with entrepreneurial innovators, the investor wanted to see some detailed financial studies and multiyear plans before committing funds. That would help the investor feel like the risks are being adequately managed, even though both the investor and Irina knew those detailed plans were little more than wishful thinking.

So instead Irina offered the investor a diagram of her future ecosystem and her thin slice plan. She also made this promise: If they get to the end of the first thin slice, which requires only a small investment, and things aren't going well, she'll either pull the plug or she'll revamp her approach to account for the challenges she encounters. Irina pointed out that using the act-learn-adapt cycle should give the investor greater confidence, not less. By using this approach, either the project will end quickly or risks will be quickly identified and addressed. When Irina sees an unexpected challenge, she makes an adjustment. She figures out how to drive around the problem instead of just pushing forward. A fairy tale, three-year budget, and plan wouldn't help do either of those things.

This methodology for managing risk—where you combine a broad vision with flexible and smart adaptation—isn't just a theory. Increasingly, both large and small organizations are managing their most complex innovations by continually adapting their vision and plans as they go. In fact, some of the most successful innovators we have worked with make their case for a different and better future by taking a few strategic steps first.

Learn

Learning quickly so you can adapt is one of the most powerful skills you can develop. You want to be a master of generating knowledge that you can act on, and this requires intentional effort. Measure things that will highlight challenges, test success, and answer questions. Speed matters here. Early insights let you make early adjustments, more nimbly dodging around barriers. You will often have to be clever about this. Since your early thin slices won't have fully implemented the future ecosystem, you will often need to look for indirect or leading indicators of success.

For example, Irina's final measure of success will be lots of students signing up and then coming back again for more instruction. However, early in her ecosystem's implementation, there's no way for her to credibly know how many students she will ultimately attract. So she looks for a way to learn quickly. Instead of waiting for final results, Irina can interview a few students who are currently participating. If the first students through the door are happy, she has an early sign that other students might also want her tutoring.

Adapt

Learning is only valuable if you use it to adapt your approach. If you see a bus rushing down the road at you, you need to step out of the way before you are flattened. Standing without moving in front of a fast-moving bus is foolish, but this is exactly what many traditional project managers do. They see signs that things aren't going as expected and they flat out ignore them because it's too hard to deal with or because they would be penalized for changing plans.

The ability to adapt gives you incredible power. You can change the ecosystem to work better or take advantage of unexpected opportunities. It's even possible to pivot around people who act as barriers. As a result, many successful innovations end up in a much different place than originally expected.

So as you learn you should be adapting at all the levels of your innovation—the thin slices (implementation), future ecosystem design

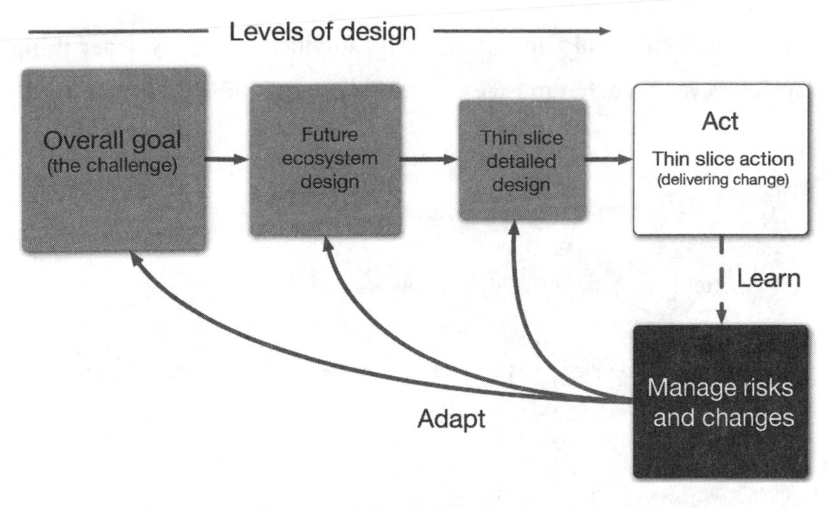

Figure 11.2. You can adapt everything from small details to the future ecosystem design.

(strategy), and the goal (vision), as shown in Figure 11.2. You don't want to casually make changes to your future ecosystem since it acts as the guiding light for your work. However, you may find this is the right thing to do when presented with information about a big challenge.

Imagine if Irina found that students were unwilling or unable to pay for one-on-one instruction with an international tutor. That would undermine her entire idea, that is, unless she made a deep pivot and redesigned the future ecosystem to offer prerecorded online courses at a lower price. This is not easy, as she would have new parts, such as video production and different contracts for instructors, but it would be more likely to work. Perhaps most importantly, Irina wouldn't just be standing there in the middle of the road waiting for a proverbial bus to run her over. Instead, she would actively adapt to the challenges.

While the brilliance of adapting is obvious, it can be challenging if you aren't used to it. Stepping back and making a change to a plan can be hard, as can taking a piece out of the innovation that you thought might work or going back to tell people that things have changed since you last talked. This is still really important work, and just like many other things, adapting is very much a muscle you can learn and build.

TED SAVES THE DAY: PIVOTING WITH ECOSYSTEMS

Being clever with the flexibility of ecosystems can help you escape dead ends. For example, Dan was working on an ambitious, forward-looking ecosystem innovation that brought together technology and business teams to reinvent the way education and careers fit together over someone's lifetime.

Several months into the program, much work had been done but there was a crisis. New insights gained from working with users revealed new needs that would require a deep strategic pivot. The technologists who had been building the different parts of the ecosystem looked at it in detail and shook their heads. The shift in direction would require them to start over, pretty much from scratch. Months of work would be wasted, which would be really expensive politically, not to mention all the lost time and money spent going the wrong direction.

Fortunately, Ted, an ecosystem innovator, had a big-picture view of the future ecosystem and the progression of thin slices. This big-picture view—of both what the team had done and where the team wanted to go—meant Ted could take the bricks the team had already built and adapt them to a new vision for the future ecosystem. Instead of throwing everything out, in a couple of weeks he had reoriented the design of the ecosystem and the team was off and running again.

Because Ted had the big-picture-thinking skills of a choreographer, he was able to problem-solve across the entire ecosystem—even changing key parts of the future vision. The project wasn't derailed. Instead the team was able to implement an elegant solution that embraced change and leveraged previous work on a difficult challenge, saving political capital, money, and time spent.

Step 2: Design for Flexibility

> Hustle and flexibility must become the norm. What has traditionally been seen as disruptive must now be seen as the chief source of opportunity.
>
> **—Tom Peters**[4]

To take full advantage of what you learn along the way you'll want to be as flexible as possible, so that when you discover something new, you can easily make the changes you need. You might think that being flexible is all about having the right attitude. You've probably read stories about how some great idea was blocked by an inflexible person. While it may be a story that resonates, be careful about blaming your barriers on someone else's defects. It's true that in a changing world embracing the need to adapt is important, but often the biggest challenges to flexibility are not personal; they are built into the way the world works.

Imagine if Irina sets up her first thin slice for the international tutoring service and decides to sign up her first instructors on long-term contracts. She might have some good reasons for taking this path. If Irina makes a long-term commitment to the tutors, they might agree to better rates, or Irina might find it easier to compete for good talent. But she'll also pay a flexibility tax for this choice. Those long-term contracts will limit the changes she can make later and they will limit how quickly she can make them. For example, Irina may want to alter the way she works with tutors or maybe move away from using tutors altogether. In these cases, modifying those fixed contracts may require a lot of added work and time. She's paying for advantages now, with a loss of flexibility later.

Flexibility is something you need to keep in mind with every choice you make as your innovation evolves. You should be asking, "How can I design this part, or make this choice, so that we keep options for change open tomorrow and the day after?" Fortunately, there are plenty of strategies for how to do this. The following are four of the most frequently used techniques for adding flexibility to your design.

Build reusable modular blocks. Legos are fun because you can build anything with them. Each block can be taken apart and put together in a myriad of combinations. In the language of design, the blocks are modular, and it's a strategy you can build into your work. For example, imagine Irina has a student onboarding package. Instead of making a new onboarding guide for each different class, she could create a set of modular units that she could mix and match for any number of different tutoring subjects. Modular blocks support flexibility because they allow you to assemble something quickly and still have the option to change and use that same block somewhere else.

Make it easy to connect. The other really powerful design feature of Lego blocks are the little bumps on the top. Those little bumps, and the holes on the other side, make it possible for even a child to easily plug one Lego into another. Your job isn't so easy because you're working with people, organizations, and technology, not plastic blocks, but you also want to easily make different connections. There are many different ways to do this. Software developers have techniques for building standard interfaces that allow one system to easily connect to another. In business, when working with organizations, standard contracts can provide the same benefit, allowing one business to plug into another. Irina might make it easier to connect with international tutors by adopting some standard practices, like those that universities use, so it's easier for tutors to join up and quickly get productive.

Use data for things that change. When you walk into your local restaurant, you might see daily specials written on a small whiteboard above the cash register. They don't reprint their regular menu each day to accommodate this daily change. Instead they write a few special items on the board, only to erase them at the end of the day. Similarly, instead of printing new brochures every time she makes a change to her tutoring offerings, Irina could make the change to her website and refer people there.

These are examples of putting things that change into data, rather than building them into something that requires a lot of effort to change, like a printed menu. Your mobile phone uses this strategy. The physical phone remains the same for everyone, but all your personal info—the stuff that makes it your phone—is kept in data (often stored in the cloud) that can easily be updated and changed. Capturing things that change in data, instead of building them into the innovation, creates the same kind of flexibility.

Delay choices that bind you. Eventually you will face some big choices that will be hard to undo. Some choices limit what's possible to do later. For example, Irina may need to decide where to legally set up her company. This is the kind of choice that once made will affect other choices far into the future. It's unlikely that you'll be able to build an ecosystem without making some of these big choices, but you'll be able to stay more flexible if you delay them until the last possible moment. You don't want to slow yourself down because you haven't made a key decision. But if you can wait a bit, you may learn more and be in a better position to make a choice that won't bind you later.

Step 3: Measure Success, Progress, and Performance

> As a human being you are motivated by progress. When you see concrete evidence of progress you are more likely to take further action.
>
> **—Scott Belsky**[5]

No one wants to hear someone say, "Just trust me." When people are buying into a big idea, they want to know how things are going and whether the future ecosystem you've sold them will work in practice.

There will be many people who have legitimate concerns about how the work is going. There are, for example, the people who give you money or resources, but that's only the beginning. Others who are partners in this change also have a deep interest in whether the future ecosystem is working and how well implementation is going. Therefore, to build continued support and to guide your own efforts, you should be ready to answer three questions relating to success, progress, and performance:

1. *Success.* Is the future ecosystem a success?
2. *Progress.* Is the work progressing as we hoped?
3. *Performance.* Are we performing efficiently?

These measures might all sound similar, but they are actually very different views on whether you are on track to succeed. Let's take a moment to explore each one.

Success. This first measure is the most important. You measure success through the outcomes and results you deliver. Your innovation is considered successful when it is working the way it should and creating value for all those involved. In her tutoring ecosystem, Irina would measure success based on the value everyone receives in her tutoring ecosystem. For example, do students learn? Are the tutors happy to participate? Is her organization making a profit on all the hard work? Remember: Everyone involved needs to get a pony for the ecosystem to be successful. It isn't just about Irina's business success. Everyone involved needs to see value and results.

Progress. Many traditionally managed projects stop asking questions about success once work begins. They assume that once a project is approved, the only real question is whether the work will get done. Instead of continuously asking questions about whether results are being created, they focus on whether the work is on track according to their detailed plan—closely monitoring the plan's activities or checking for outputs from the work.

Based on what we've talked about, you are probably questioning this approach. After all, if you are always making adjustments, you might be tempted to ask if all that effort invested in status reporting is just a wasted administrative task, one that misses what's most important in the long run—the value generated by the innovation.

Abandoning the measurement of progress would certainly be easier, but it would undermine your ability to bring others along on your creative journey. It's true, you could simply count the number of project tasks done, but that doesn't get you off the hook. You still need to show that you're making progress toward your future ecosystem.

Funding isn't infinite and people's patience is limited. To keep everyone engaged, you need to be able to tell a credible story of progress and have a way to back up the claims you make. In fact, this is a key part of your job. You should constantly be on the road, talking with people as each thin slice develops and your innovation evolves. When an innovation fails, it's often not because it costs too much. It's because it took too long or didn't create enough value along the way to convince people to continue supporting it.

This is where your thin slice plan can help. You may not have a detailed project plan, but your road map of thin slices gives you a broad vision of how your innovation is going to evolve and the questions you will answer along the way. For example, in addition to tracking how well her tutoring ecosystem is working (success), Irina can also evaluate whether she is moving through her thin slices as quickly and smoothly as she had hoped (progress). That way she can tell her partners and investors how the thin slices are progressing, show the important questions that are being answered, and talk about the worrisome barriers that are being overcome. It's more of a narrative than a spreadsheet (though numbers can help tell the story).

Performance. And last, we have our old friend performance. To measure performance, you need to be asking if the teams driving this work are as efficient and productive as they could be. There will always be opportunities to work more smoothly and productively together. For example, when agile software development teams are delivering big, high-concept technology systems, they also continuously try to increase their productivity by keeping track of how efficiently they move work through their development process.

BRINGING YOUR MEASUREMENTS TOGETHER

As an ecosystem innovator, you don't use just one of these forms of measurement. They work together, providing you a complete picture of how your adaptive journey of implementation is going. They make it possible to tell powerful stories and to make important changes as you go. Instead of being an administrative task—status reports that feel like an extra unneeded burden—using measurements to guide the creation of your ecosystem can help you become even more successful. Table 11.1 shows how all three forms of measurement work together.

TABLE 11.1. THE THREE TYPES OF ECOSYSTEM BUILDING MEASUREMENT

	Success	Progress	Performance
What do you measure?	Outcomes and value delivered	Assessment of where you are on the journey	Outputs produced versus time and cost expended
What's the big question?	Is the ecosystem working?	Are the ecosystem changes proceeding as hoped?	Are the teams as efficient and effective as possible?
Who's the audience?	Ecosystem designers, sponsors, and partners	Ecosystem implementers, sponsors, and partners	Teams working on the ecosystem

THE JOURNEY OF SUCCESS

> Nearly every man who develops an idea works it up to the point where it looks impossible, and then he gets discouraged. That's not the place to become discouraged, that's the place to get interested.
>
> **—Thomas Edison**[6]

The act-learn-adapt cycle lets you manage risks and challenges as you take action in a messy, unpredictable world. Yet one of the most powerful features of ecosystem innovation is something that comes as an extra bonus. If you can adapt, you're never really defeated as an ecosystem innovator. So long as you don't give up, you can just keep changing the future—adapting and taking advantage of opportunities—until the ecosystem finally comes together.

Of course, there may be a point where the right decision is to stop and step back from an innovation that won't succeed. There are times when ecosystems simply don't work. However, sometimes you may just need to figure out how to adapt your ecosystem to fit the new (or unexpected) circumstances. Global innovator Sam Altman affectionately names those he believes will succeed as *cockroaches*—tenacious people who never give up and keep adapting to succeed. Some of the greatest innovators of our time have this strong drive and persistence. And for good reason: If they don't give up, they get to make a positive dent in the world.

We began this book by talking about this unique and exciting moment in history. Our creative potential is unprecedented, and at the same time we all face bigger, more difficult challenges than ever before. Now, with a powerful practice in your hands, it's time to make the choice to act.

CHECKLIST FOR TASK 5: BUILD THE FUTURE

- Step 1: Act, learn, and adapt.
- Step 2: Design for flexibility.
- Step 3: Measure success, progress, and performance.

CONCLUSION: RISING TO THE CHALLENGE

If you embrace that the things that you can do are limitless, you can put your ding in the universe. You can change the world.

—Tim Cook[1]

Ecosystem innovation provides you with remarkable capabilities—allowing you to tap exceptionally powerful, creative strategies to solve hard problems. You don't have to scale down your ambitions or pretend that the challenges or opportunities you face are smaller than they are. You can, with the resources and capabilities you have, develop strategies that enable you to outstrip larger players and accomplish goals far more ambitious than others would think possible.

When you're looking at some big challenges or bold opportunity, it's natural to ask, "Can I do this?" You've no doubt read the stories of the elite club of innovators who seem to get all the accolades. So often the spotlight is shone on the brilliant entrepreneur who drops out of an Ivy League college to create world-changing businesses, such as Bill Gates, Mark Zuckerberg, or Steve Jobs. It's reasonable to wonder if those innovators aren't some rare species of unicorn, fundamentally different than everyone else.

In our experience the answer is a resounding no. Impactful innovators aren't just a few once-in-a-generation unicorns. The world is filled with courageous, big-picture thinkers—individuals and organizations who find ways to weave together connections, marshal diverse resources, and forge their own creative paths. For example, when she was twenty-seven years old, Sara Blakely took the leap to start a shapewear business with all $5,000 of her savings—writing her own patent application to conserve funds and launching the company out of her apartment. Over time she built an ecosystem to support and grow her innovative product, ultimately creating an entirely new category of clothing. She continued to put together the Lego blocks she needed for success, and her privately held company, Spanx, was recently valued at more than $1 billion.[2]

Blakely took advantage of an ecosystem innovator's ability to build and test her idea in thin slices. She didn't drop out of a fancy college, have special connections, or a lot of money. In fact, she sold fax machines for much of the time while developing Spanx. What she did do was to doggedly assemble all the pieces she needed to bring her idea to life, including product development, production, retail channels, and even promotion—Oprah Winfrey named Spanx one of her favorite things, kicking off a spike in growth.[3] She knew she had a fabulous product idea and she succeeded by building a powerful ecosystem to support it.

A WORLD FOR ECOSYSTEM INNOVATION

> In an age of discovery, the balance between risk and reward tips in favor of taking bold action.
>
> **—Ian Goldin and Chris Kutarna**[4]

It doesn't matter who you are, how old you are, or where you are. You can make important things happen. In fact, here are three reasons we believe you are so well positioned to make an impact in the world with ecosystems.

You can punch above your weight. Ecosystem innovation gives you the ability to do more and act faster than might seem possible with your organization's size or resources. You aren't limited to just your own knowledge, capabilities, connections, or money. Instead, by assembling your innovation from the resources of many different people and organizations, you can quickly create solutions that have an impact. And you can use those Lego blocks to adapt and respond to an ever-changing world.

Jenny's work with Response Innovation Labs (RIL) is a great example of how someone can access greater power in the real world. Jenny isn't a unicorn Harvard dropout with tons of connections and money. But she was still able to quickly make the vision for RIL come to life. Starting from zero, she brought together an ecosystem of NGOs, universities, international donors, and innovation specialists that made it possible for RIL to go from idea to launch in the span of just a few months and then be on the ground in five countries within two years.

There's a world of brilliance to draw on. One of the most exceptional features of our world today is its unprecedented global capacity to create. Talent, resources, and almost any capability you can imagine are all within your reach. There are billions of minds out there that are increasingly connecting online, creating a network of brilliance you can use to make remarkable things happen.

Consider the story of Hind Hobeika, who created an incredible innovation by piecing together the skills and capabilities of people she had never met from around the world. In 2010, Hind Hobeika was a college student and competitive swimmer. Hobeika won third place on a televised competition for young Arab innovators by creating swim goggles that could track heart rate, calories burned, and number of laps completed during workouts.[5] Later from her home in Lebanon, Hobeika assembled a network of global connections to fund, design, prototype, manufacture, and sell her swim monitor. Many pivots later, Instabeat's swim monitor went on sale globally for $250 each.[6]

Hobeika built her own ecosystem innovation by finding and working with collaborators around the world. She created an Indiegogo crowd-funding campaign to kick off her project,[7] built a team from global talent and production capabilities—finding engineers in Romania, technical support in Silicon Valley, and production in China—and then successfully leveraged international business collaboration to raise $6 million in investor funds.[8]

Technology offers new Legos every day. Many of the Legos you'll use to create an ecosystem will be drawn from people, organizations, and communities. This isn't the only source of creative power though. There is an ongoing technology revolution that is delivering truly jaw-dropping inventions every day and will continue to do so in the years ahead. Take the example of AI. In just three years, this tech went from an interesting lab project that could understand language half as well as a human, to suddenly being able to do a better job at it than the average person.[9] This is the kind of explosive growth that is going on in all sorts of technologies, which means that every morning when you wake up, there are new Lego blocks you can use to transform your innovations.

Each new technology Lego you draw on has the potential to open the door to a new and more powerful ecosystem. Consider the example of the Médecins Sans Frontières (MSF) Foundation—Doctors without Borders. The organization took the idea of being able to 3D print a prosthetic hand and wrapped an ecosystem around it. Previously, making a prosthetic limb required a doctor or skilled technician—essential players who were often not available in conflict areas—to measure and fit the limb. While digital printers could make the prosthetics, they weren't of any use without the skilled medical guidance for what was needed.

But when an additional piece of technology was added—a portable digital scanner—an entirely new treatment ecosystem emerged. The digital scanners connected patients with remotely located doctors providing the detailed measurements needed to design the prosthetic. The doctors, often in countries far away, could then send those designs back to the local area where a 3D digital printer could make the prosthetic. The result was high-quality, customized prosthetic limbs, delivered to individuals in conflict areas, expertly fitted in just days instead of the months it previously took—if patients in these war-torn areas could get them at all.[10]

THE WORLD NEEDS YOU

> Man's heart is restless unless he has found, and fulfilled, meaning and purpose in life.
>
> **—Viktor Frankl**[11]

The world is changing. It's getting more complicated and more complex with each passing day. There is an urgent need for people who can act in this age of exceptional opportunities and challenges—people who have the vision, determination, and skill to lead truly impactful innovations, rather than making small, incremental steps forward.

Sometimes it's hard not to feel that the problems you face are too big, or the organizations you work with are too difficult to change, or that meaningful solutions demand too much money or more support than you can provide. We understand these concerns. But in our years of experience with ecosystem innovation, we've found there are just two things that can stop your success dead in its tracks: not having the right tools and never trying.

Our goal with this book has been to provide you with practical, new tools you can use to do bigger things. This thinking and these practices aren't a magic wand that can be waved over a hard challenge, but they do open the door to taking action. So now it comes down to you taking the first step in your journey as an ecosystem innovator and giving it a try. As you do, ask yourself:

What world do you dream for?

What life do you dream of?

What do you want your legacy to be?

What you do now can potentially affect people's lives (and your own) for years and decades to come. The opportunities are waiting for you, and the practice exists. From our point of view, if you have unique talents and tools at your disposal, there is a particular responsibility—both to yourself and to the world around you—to step up and use those resources. Someone who arrives at the scene of a fire with a hose has a greater duty to act than the common bystander.

You can—right here, right now—choose something that matters, get started, and claim an exciting, important life. You have a chance to take the stage in history's most creative time. We're counting on you, as are the many people who will benefit from the bigger things you'll create.

We can't wait to hear what you do! Please send us your stories. We look forward to hearing about the learning and success that awaits.

> Every action you take is a vote for the type of person you wish to become.
>
> **—James Clear**[12]

NOTES

INTRODUCTION

1. "Stirred by Burnham, Democracy Champion," *Chicago Record-Herald*, October 15, 1910.
2. Agence France-Presse, "Mount Everest Moved Three Centimetres after Nepal Earthquake," *The Guardian*, June 16, 2015, https://www.theguardian.com/world/2015/jun/16/mount-everest-moved-three-centimetres-after-nepal-earthquake.
3. Twyla Tharp, *The Collaborative Habit: Life Lessons for Working Together* (New York: Simon and Schuster, 2013), 81.
4. Richard Florida, *The Rise of the Creative Class* (New York: Basic Books, 2019), 15.
5. Jim Taylor and Watts Wacker, *The Visionary's Handbook: Nine Paradoxes That Will Shape the Future of Your Business* (New York: HarperBusiness, 2001), 206.

CHAPTER 1

1. Quoted in Daniel Quinn, *Beyond Civilization: Humanity's Next Great Adventure* (New York: Three Rivers Press, 2000), 137.
2. Jordyn Imhoff, "We're Watching the World Go Blind," *Health Lab*, December 7, 2020, https://labblog.uofmhealth.org/lab-report/were-watching-world-go-blind.
3. Javed Farooqui, Umang Mathur, and Ashish Saksena, "Role of an Ophthalmologist after Patient Loses Vision—Are We Doing Enough?," *Indian Journal of Ophthalmology* 68, no. 8 (2020): 1715–1719.

4. Aravind Eye Care System, "Vision," accessed April 6, 2023, https://aravind.org/vision-mission/.

5. Ingrid Diep, "How McDonald's Inspired the Success of an Extraordinary Eye Hospital," *Insight*, March 5, 2017, https://www.insightnews.com.au/how-mcdonalds-inspired-the-success-of-an-extraordinary-eye-hospital/.

6. Aravind Krishnan, "Aravind Eye-Care System—McDonaldization of Eye-Care," Harvard Business School Digital Initiative, December 9, 2015, https://digital.hbs.edu/platform-rctom/submission/aravind-eye-care-system-mcdonaldization-of-eye-care/.

7. Aravind Eye Care System, "Genesis," accessed June 28, 2023, https://aravind.org/our-story/.

8. Susan Wolf Ditkoff and Abe Grindle, "Audacious Philanthropy: Lessons from 15 World-Changing Initiatives," *Harvard Business Review*, September–October 2017, https://hbr.org/2017/09/audacious-philanthropy.

9. Larry Downes and Paul Nunes, *Big Bang Disruption: Strategy in the Age of Devastating Innovation* (New York: Portfolio/Penguin, 2014), 25.

10. Subir Roy, "Gillette Marketing Strategy of Product Innovation," *Strategy Story*, August 2, 2021, https://thestrategystory.com/2021/08/02/gillette-marketing-strategy-innovation/.

11. Roy, "Gillette Marketing Strategy."

12. Clayton Christensen, Michael Raynor, and Rory McDonald, "What Is Disruptive Innovation?," *Harvard Business Review*, December 2015, https://hbr.org/2015/12/what-is-disruptive-innovation.

13. Darren Dahl, "Riding the Momentum Created by a Cheeky Video," *New York Times*, April 10, 2013, https://www.nytimes.com/2013/04/11/business/smallbusiness/dollar-shave-club-from-viral-video-to-real-business.html.

14. Check out Dubin's ninety-second video advertisement at https://www.youtube.com/watch?v=ZUG9qYTJMsI.

15. Tom Foster, "The Founders of Harry's Got a $1.37 Billion Offer to Sell, but the FTC Wasn't Sold," *Inc.*, Winter 2020–2021, https://www.inc.com/magazine/202102/tom-foster/harrys-jeff-raider-andy-katz-mayfield-edgewell-failed-acquisition-deal.html.

16. Myelle Lansat and Richard Feloni, "The CEO and Cofounder of a Shaving Company with 5 Million Customers Explains How He and His Co-CEO Stay on the Same Page at All Times," *Business Insider*, November 5, 2018, https://www.businessinsider.com/harrys-jeff-raider-stay-on-same-page-co-ceo-2018-11.

17. "Harry's," Crunchbase, accessed June 28, 2023, https://www.crunchbase.com/organization/harrys/company_financials.

18. Susan Caminiti, "Warby Parker Co-founder Takes on Gillette," CNBC, May 19, 2014, https://www.cnbc.com/2014/05/19/warby-parker-co-founder-takes-on-gillette.html.

19. Alexandria Olson, "Owner of Schick Razors Buying Upstart Rival Harry's for $1.4 billion," *Chicago Tribune*, May 9, 2019, https://www.chicagotribune.com/business/ct-biz-harrys-razor-schick-purchase-20190509-story.html.

20. "Profile: Gillette," *Forbes*, accessed August 4, 2023, https://www.forbes.com/companies/gillette/.

21. Nicholas Kristof, "This Has Been the Best Year Ever: For Humanity Overall, Life Just Keeps Getting Better," *New York Times*, December 18, 2019, https://www.nytimes.com/2019/12/28/opinion/sunday/2019-best-year-poverty.html.

22. Allwell Nwankwo, "Lighting Africa/Nigeria: Tackling Energy Poverty at Its Source," *Lighting Africa News*, July 13, 2020, https://www.lightingafrica.org/lighting-africa-nigeria-tackling-energy-poverty-at-its-source/.

23. United Nations, "Goals," accessed August 4, 2023, https://sdgs.un.org/goals/goal7.

24. World Bank, "Population, Female (% of Total Population)—Sub-Saharan Africa," 2022, https://data.worldbank.org/indicator/SP.POP.TOTL.FE.ZS?locations=ZG.

25. Climate Chance, "The Use of Clean Energy Products to Mitigate Deforestation in Northern Nigeria," accessed July 12, 2023, https://www.climate-chance.org/en/best-pratices/the-use-of-clean-energy-products-to-mitigate-deforestation-in-northern-nigeria/.

26. Solar Sister, "Hilaria," accessed July 12, 2023, https://solarsister.org/impact-story/hilaria/.

27. Solar Sister, "Hilaria."

28. Solar Sister, "What We Do: Our Impact," accessed July 12, 2023, https://solarsister.org/what-we-do/our-impact/.

29. Oliver Wendell Holmes Jr., *The Essential Holmes: Selections from the Letters, Speeches, Judicial Opinions and Other Writings* (Chicago: University of Chicago Press, 1992), 79.

CHAPTER 2

1. Mark Johnson, *Seizing the White Space: Business Model Innovation for Growth and Renewal* (Boston: Harvard Business Press, 2010), 15.

2. Michael C. Jackson, *Systems Thinking: Creative Holism for Managers* (Chichester, UK: Wiley, 2003), 3.

3. Ian Goldin and Chris Kutarna, *Age of Discovery: Navigating the Risks and Rewards of Our New Renaissance* (New York: Bloomsbury, 2016), 3.

4. Klaus Schwab, "The Fourth Industrial Revolution: What It Means and How to Respond," *Foreign Affairs*, December 12, 2015, www.foreignaffairs.com/articles/2015-12-12/fourth-industrial-revolution.

5. Intel, "A New Paradigm for Moore's Law," accessed July 12, 2023, https://www.intel.com/content/www/us/en/silicon-innovations/moores-law-technology.html.

6. Roy Furchgott, "Can Start-Ups Really Lower the Cost of Gene Sequencing?," *New York Times*, October 12, 2022, https://www.nytimes.com/2022/10/12/business/gene-sequencing-ultima-cheaper.html.

7. Intel, "A New Paradigm."

8. Scott Belsky, *Making Ideas Happen: Overcoming the Obstacles between Vision and Reality* (New York: Portfolio, 2010), 1.

9. Tom Huddleston Jr., "3 Things Oculus Co-founder Palmer Luckey Splurged on When Facebook Bought It for $2 Billion," CNBC, October 26, 2018, https://www.cnbc.com/2018/10/26/what-an-oculus-co-founder-splurged-on-after-2-billion-facebook-sale.html.

CHAPTER 3

1. Avery Hartmans, "Airbnb Now Has More Listings Worldwide Than the Top Five Hotel Brands Combined," *Business Insider*, August 10, 2017, https://www.businessinsider.com/airbnb-total-worldwide-listings-2017-8.

2. John Henry Holland, *Hidden Order: How Adaptation Builds Complexity* (New York: Helix Books, 1996), 62.

3. Rebecca Aydin, "How 3 Guys Turned Renting Air Mattresses in Their Apartment into a $31 Billion Company, Airbnb," *Business Insider*, September 20, 2019, https://www.businessinsider.com/how-airbnb-was-founded-a-visual-history-2016-2.

4. Airbnb, "About Us," accessed July 12, 2023, https://news.airbnb.com/about-us/.

5. Yahoo! Finance, "Airbnb, Inc. (ABNB)," accessed March 15, 2023, https://finance.yahoo.com/quote/ABNB/.

6. Michael Schrage, "Collaboration, from the Wright Brothers to Robots," *Harvard Business Review*, March 23, 2015, https://hbr.org/2015/03/collaboration-from-the-wright-brothers-to-robots.

7. Andrew S. Grove, *Only the Paranoid Survive: How to Exploit the Crisis Points That Challenge Every Company and Career* (New York: Doubleday Business, 1996), 28.

8. Airbnb, Form 10-K, fiscal year ended December 31, 2021, https://www.sec.gov/ix?doc=/Archives/edgar/data/1559720/000155972022000006/abnb-20211231.htm.

9. Steven Covey, *The 7 Habits of Highly Effective People* (New York: Simon and Schuster, 2020), 308.

10. Russell Lincoln Ackoff, *Redesigning the Future: A Systems Approach to Societal Problems* (New York: Wiley, 1974), 31.

11. Airbnb, "About Us."

12. Airbnb.org, "Airbnb.org Helps 100,000 People Fleeing Ukraine Find Places to Stay," September 2022, https://www.airbnb.org/about.

CHAPTER 4

1. Quoted in epigraph to David Epstein, *Range* (New York: Riverhead Books, 2019).
2. Eric Ries, *The Lean Startup* (New York: Penguin Books, 2020), 9.
3. Paul Kendall, "Angry Birds: The Story Behind iPhone's Gaming Phenomenon," *The Telegraph*, February 7, 2011, https://www.telegraph.co.uk/technology/video-games/8303173/Angry-Birds-the-story-behind-iPhones-gaming-phenomenon.html.
4. Mark Vaughn, "Tesla Roadster: Don't Worry about the Future of Transportation Being Fun," *Autoweek*, January 23, 2008, https://www.autoweek.com/news/green-cars/a2034736/tesla-roadster-dont-worry-about-future-transportation-being-fun/. See also Martin Eberhard, "Lotus Position," Tesla Motors, July 25, 2006, https://www.tesla.com/blog/lotus-position.
5. Russell Lincoln Ackoff, *Redesigning the Future: A Systems Approach to Societal Problems* (New York: Wiley, 1974), 21.
6. Pepe Escobar, "Dubai Lives the Post-Oil Arab Dream," *Asia Times*, June 7, 2006, https://asiatimes.com/2006/06/dubai-lives-the-post-oil-arab-dream/.
7. Ravi Panwar, "Burj Khalifa: Construction of the Tallest Structure in the World," *The Constructor*, accessed August 31, 2023, https://theconstructor.org/case-study/burj-khalifa-construction/62758/.
8. "Structural Details of Burj Khalifa: Concrete Grade and Foundations," *The Constructor*, accessed August 31, 2023, https://theconstructor.org/structures/structural-details-burj-khalifa-concrete-grade-foundations/20512/.
9. Council on Tall Buildings and Urban Habitat, "Samsung C&T Corporation," accessed August 31, 2023, https://www.skyscrapercenter.com/company/1701.
10. Gabrielle Desantis, "Build a Ford Model T in 84 Not-So-Simple Steps," *MotorBiscuit*, December 1, 2020, https://www.motorbiscuit.com/build-a-ford-model-t-in-84-not-so-simple-steps/.
11. "Frederick Winslow Taylor," *The Economist*, February 6, 2009, https://www.economist.com/news/2009/02/06/frederick-winslow-taylor.
12. "Ford's Assembly Line Starts Rolling," *History*, November 30, 2020, https://www.history.com/this-day-in-history/fords-assembly-line-starts-rolling.

13. Mark Johnson, *Seizing the White Space: Business Model Innovation for Growth and Renewal* (Boston: Harvard Business Press, 2010), 17.

14. Giles Slade, *Made to Break: Technology and Obsolescence in America* (Cambridge, MA: Harvard University Press, 2009), 45.

15. Alfred North Whitehead, *The Concept of Nature: Tarner Lectures Delivered in Trinity College, November 1919* (Cambridge: Cambridge University Press, 1920), 163.

PART II

1. Ben Woo, "Innovation Distinguishes between a Leader and a Follower," *Forbes*, February 14, 2013, https://www.forbes.com/sites/bwoo/2013/02/14/innovation-distinguishes-between-a-leader-and-a-follower/?sh=707e2a328447.

CHAPTER 5

1. "Jessica Chastain's Julliard [*sic*] Audition," *Off Camera with Sam Jones*, June 24, 2016, https://www.youtube.com/watch?v=kKNsRXTp_zY.

2. Scott Simon, "To Protect Their Texas City, Doctors Vaccinated the Sister City across the Border," NPR, April 30, 2022, https://www.npr.org/2022/04/30/1095750131/to-protect-their-texas-city-doctors -vaccinated-the-sister-city -across-the-border.

3. Karen Brooks Harper and Jason Garza, "In Laredo, a Bus Brigade Is Vaccinating Mexican Citizens with COVID-19 Shots That Texans Aren't Using," *Texas Tribune*, March 22, 2022, https://www.texastribune.org/2022/03/29/texas-mexico-coronavirus-vaccines-laredo/.

4. Simon, "To Protect Their Texas City."

5. Harper and Garza, "In Laredo, a Bus Brigade Is Vaccinating Mexican Citizens."

6. Cory Doctorow, *Makers* (New York: Tor Books, 2009), 45.

7. Ben Aston, "15 Statistics You Should Know about a Career in Product Management," *Product Manager*, accessed July 13, 2023, https://theproductmanager.com/general/statistics-career-product-management/.

8. Dale Leydon, "How Many UI UX Developers Are There in the US?," *WebsiteBuilderInsider*, September 24, 2022, https://www.websitebuilderinsider.com/how-many-ui-ux-designers-are-there-in-the-us/.

9. Nassim Nicholas Taleb, *Antifragile: Things That Gain from Disorder* (Harlow, UK: Penguin Books, 2013), 40.

10. Larry Downes and Paul Nunes, *Big Bang Disruption* (New York: Portfolio/Penguin, 2014), 115.

11. Richard Florida, *The Rise of the Creative Class: And How It's Transforming Work, Leisure, Community, and Everyday Life* (New York: Basic Books, 2002), 206.

12. Klaus Schwab, "The Fourth Industrial Revolution: What It Means and How to Respond," *Foreign Affairs*, December 12, 2015, www.foreignaffairs.com/articles/2015-12-12/fourth-industrial-revolution.

13. Seth Godin, "Tell a Better Story," *Seth's Blog*, November 13, 2019, https://seths.blog/2019/11/tell-a-better-story/.

14. Edward Hallowell and John Ratey, *Delivered from Distraction* (New York: Adfo Books, 2005), 13.

CHAPTER 6

1. Christopher Alexander, *Notes on the Synthesis of Form* (Cambridge, MA: Harvard University Press, 1964), 1.

2. Jane Jacobs, *The Death and Life of Great American Cities* (New York: Vintage, 1992), 29.

3. Jeffrey Young, "The Student Becomes the Teacher," *Slate*, April 23, 2014, https://slate.com/technology/2014/04/battushig-myanganbayar-aced-an-edx-mooc-then-gave-lessons-to-mit.html.

4. Laura Pappano, "The Boy Genius of Ulan Bator," *New York Times*, September 13, 2013, https://www.nytimes.com/2013/09/15/magazine/the-boy-genius-of-ulan-bator.html.

5. Justin Reich, "The Village of the Boy Genius of Ulan Bator," *Education Week*, September 15, 2013, https://www.edweek.org/education/opinion-the-village-of-the-boy-genius-of-ulan-bator/2013/09.

6. Reich, "The Village of the Boy Genius of Ulan Bator."

7. UNICEF, "Two Thirds of the World's School-Age Children Have No Internet Access at Home, New UNICEF-ITU Report Says," November 30, 2020, https://www.unicef.org/press-releases/two-thirds-worlds-school-age-children-have-no-internet-access-home-new-unicef-itu.

8. Loran Nordgren and David Schouthal, *The Human Element* (Hoboken, NJ: Wiley, 2021), 31.

9. Marcus Andrews, "42% of Companies Don't Listen to Their Customers. Yikes. [New Service Data]," HubSpot, June 15, 2021, https://blog.hubspot.com/service/state-of-service-2019-customer-first.

10. IDEOU, "Design Thinking," accessed July 25, 2023, https://www.ideou.com/pages/design-thinking.

11. Tim Harford, *Messy: How to Be Creative and Resilient in a Tidy-Minded World* (London: Little, Brown, 2016), 260.

12. "Revealed: Do Cats or Dogs Sell More Stuff in Ads?," *B&T Magazine*, March 7, 2022, https://www.bandt.com.au/revealed-are-cats-or-dogs-in-ads-better-for-selling-stuff/.

PART III

1. Scott Belsky, *Making Ideas Happen* (New York: Portfolio, 2010), 1.

CHAPTER 7

1. Armstrong said these words when the Apollo 11 spacecraft landed on the moon on July 20, 1969. See "Voice from Moon: The Eagle Has Landed," *Encyclopedia.com*, accessed August 4, 2023, https://www.encyclopedia.com/history/dictionaries-thesauruses-pictures-and-press-releases/voice-moon-eagle-has-landed-1969.

2. Elizabeth Hanes, "From Sputnik to Spacewalking: 7 Soviet Space Firsts," *History*, October 2, 2020, https://www.history.com/news/from-sputnik-to-spacewalking-7-soviet-space-firsts.

3. John F. Kennedy, "Address to Joint Session of Congress, May 25, 1961," John F. Kennedy Presidential Library and Museum, accessed August 4, 2023, https://www.jfklibrary.org/learn/about-jfk/historic-speeches/address-to-joint-session-of-congress-may-25-1961.

4. John F. Kennedy, "Address at Rice University on the Nation's Space Effort," Rice University, Houston, TX, September 12, 1962, https://www.rice.edu/jfk-speech.

5. Hanes, "From Sputnik to Spacewalking."

6. Chip Heath and Dan Heath, *Made to Stick* (New York: Arrow Books, 2008), 27.

7. Affelia Wibisono, "How Far Away Is the Moon?," Royal Museums Greenwich, January 6, 2018, https://www.rmg.co.uk/stories/topics/how-far-away-moon.

8. Jim Collins and Jerry Porras, *Built to Last: Successful Habits of Visionary Companies*, 3rd ed. (New York: HarperBusiness, 1994), 84.

9. For more information, see Arnold Levine, "NASA Manpower Policy," in *Managing NASA in the Apollo Era* (Washington, DC: n.p., 1979), https://history.nasa.gov/SP-4102/ch5.htm.

10. Matt Given, "Mark Zuckerberg's JFK Quote Is a Master Class on the Role of a Unified Purpose," *Inc.*, July 10, 2017, https://www.inc.com/matt-given/mark-zuckerbergs-jfk-quote-is-a-master-class-on-th.html.

11. Jim Collins, "BHAG," *Jim Collins*, accessed July 13, 2023, https://www.jimcollins.com/concepts/bhag.html.

12. For more information, see the organization's website, at https://elevatedchicago.org.

13. Bruce Horovitz, "Starbucks CEO on Digital Innovation," *USA Today*, April 24, 2013, https://www.usatoday.com/story/money/business/2013/04/24/starbucks-howard-schultz-innovators/2047655/.

14. ICRC, "Handbook on Data Protection in Humanitarian Action," accessed July 13, 2023, https://www.icrc.org/en/data-protection-humanitarian-action-handbook.

15. Watts Wacker and Jim Taylor, *Visionary's Handbook: Nine Paradoxes That Will Shape the Future of Your Business* (New York: Harper Paperbacks, 2001), 145.

16. Janet Tu, "Costco Gets Creative to Meet Shoppers' Huge Appetite for Organics," *Seattle Times*, April 1, 2016, https://www.seattletimes.com/business/retail/costco-gets-creative-to-meet-shoppers-huge-appetite-for-organics/.

17. Tu, "Costco Gets Creative."

18. Tu, "Costco Gets Creative."

19. Tu, "Costco Gets Creative."

CHAPTER 8

1. Hans Rosling, Ola Rosling, and Anna Rosling Rönnlund, *Factfulness: Ten Reasons We're Wrong about the World—and Why Things Are Better Than You Think* (London: Flatiron Books, 2020), 207.

2. Benjamin Mueller and Rebecca Robbins, "Where a Vast Global Vaccination Program Went Wrong," *New York Times*, October 7, 2021, https://www.nytimes.com/2021/08/02/world/europe/covax-covid-vaccine-problems-africa.html.

3. Kristen Jordan Shamus, "COVID-19's Deadly Domino Effect: It's Killing People with Other Health Problems, Too," *Detroit Free Press*, December 8, 2021, https://www.freep.com/story/news/health/2021/12/08/covid-19-deaths-university-michigan-hospital-surge-delays-treatment/6437205001/.

4. Apple+ promo for *The Problem with Jon Stewart*, September 30, 2021.

5. Rosling, Rosling, and Rönnlund, *Factfulness*, 193.

6. Alison Griswold, "Uber Won New York," *Slate*, November 18, 2015, https://slate.com/business/2015/11/uber-won-new-york-city-it-only-took-five-years.html.

7. Nick Sibilla, "Are Taxi Medallions Too Big to Fail, Too?," Fox News, August 16, 2016, https://www.foxnews.com/opinion/are-taxi-medallions-too-big-to-fail-too.

8. Sophia Waterfield, "Jimmy Carter 95th Birthday: Happy Birthday to the 39th President, Greatest Quotes from over the Years," *Newsweek*, October 1, 2019, https://www.newsweek.com/jimmy-carter-95th-birthday-happy-birthday-39th-president-greatest-quotes-over-years-1461817.

9. Horst W. J. Rittel and Melvin M. Webber, "Dilemmas in a General Theory of Planning," *Policy Sciences* 4, no. 2 (1973): 155–169.

10. Erin Morgenstern, *The Night Circus* (London: Vintage Books, 2012), 68.

11. Nadeem Aslam, *The Wasted Vigil* (New York: Vintage International, 2009), 319.

12. Quoted in Charles Moore, *Daniel H. Burnham: Architect, Planner of Cities* (Boston: Houghton Mifflin, 1921), 141.

CHAPTER 9

1. Daniel Pink, *A Whole New Mind: Why Right-Brainers Will Rule the Future* (New York: Riverhead Books, 2006), 1.

2. Elizabeth Palermo and Callum McKelvie, "Who Invented the Lightbulb?," *Live Science*, November 2, 2022, https://www.livescience.com/43424-who-invented-the-light-bulb.html.

3. Peter Senge, *The Fifth Discipline: The Art and Practice of the Learning Organization* (New York: Doubleday, 2006), 104.

4. Mark W. Johnson, *Seizing the White Space: Business Model Innovation for Growth and Renewal* (Boston: Harvard Business Review Press, 2010), 13.

5. Thomas L. Friedman, *The Lexus and the Olive Tree: Understanding Globalization* (New York: Farrar, Straus, Giroux, 2000), 13.

6. Christopher Alexander, *Notes on the Synthesis of Form* (Cambridge, MA: Harvard University Press, 1964), 8.

7. Thomas Kuhn, *The Structure of Scientific Revolutions*, 3rd ed. (Chicago: University of Chicago Press, 1996), 83.

8. "The History of Movies," in *Understanding Media and Culture: An Introduction to Mass Communication* (Minneapolis: University of Minnesota Libraries Publishing, 2016), https://open.lib.umn.edu/mediaandculture/chapter/8-2-the-history-of-movies/.

9. Jack Theakston, "What Killed 3-D?," 3-D Film Archive, accessed July 13, 2023, https://sites.google.com/site/3dfilmarchive/what-killed-3-d.

10. "'Avatar' Wins Box Office, Nears Domestic Record," *Today*, January 31, 2010, https://www.today.com/popculture/avatar-wins-box-office-nears-domestic-record-1C9398541.

11. Yuval Noah Harari, *Homo Deus: A Brief History of Tomorrow* (London: Vintage, 2018), 164.

12. Quoted in Pappus of Alexandria, *Synagoge*, bk. VIII, c. AD 340.

13. Jane Margolies, "Awash in Asphalt, Cities Rethink Their Parking Needs," *New York Times*, March 7, 2023, https://www.nytimes.com/2023/03/07/business/fewer-parking-spots.html.

14. Elon Musk, "The Secret Tesla Motors Master Plan (Just between You and Me)," Tesla, August 2, 2006, https://www.tesla.com/blog/secret-tesla-motors-master-plan-just-between-you-and-me.

15. Stuart Kauffman, *At Home in the Universe: The Search for Laws of Self-Organization and Complexity* (New York: Oxford University Press, 1996), 254.

CHAPTER 10

1. Geoffrey West, *Scale: The Universal Laws of Life, Growth, and Death in Organisms, Cities, and Companies* (New York: Penguin Books, 2018), 62.

2. Avery Hartmans, "Jeff Bezos Originally Wanted to Name Amazon 'Cadabra,' and 14 Other Little-Known Facts about the Early Days of the e-Commerce Giant," *Insider*, July 2, 2021, https://www.businessinsider.com/jeff-bezos-amazon-history-facts-2017-4.

3. Chris Clearfield and András Tilcsik, *Meltdown: What Plane Crashes, Oil Spills, and Dumb Business Decisions Can Teach Us about How to Succeed at Work and at Home* (London: Atlantic Books, 2019), 22.

4. Gary Keller with Jay Papasan, *The One Thing: The Surprisingly Simple Truth behind Extraordinary Results* (Austin, TX: Bard Press, 2013), 104.

5. Peter Senge, *The Fifth Discipline: The Art and Practice of the Learning Organization* (New York: Doubleday, 2006), 3.

6. Elizabeth Gilbert, *Big Magic* (London: Bloomsbury Books, 2015), 166.

7. Christopher Alexander, *Notes on the Synthesis of Form* (Cambridge, MA: Harvard University Press, 1964), 59.

8. Ian Goldin and Chris Kutarna, *Age of Discovery: Navigating the Risks and Rewards of Our New Renaissance*, rev. ed. (New York: Bloomsbury Business, 2017), 258.

CHAPTER 11

1. Rebecca Solnit, *Hope in the Dark: Untold Histories, Wild Possibilities* (Chicago: Haymarket Books, 2016), 13.

2. Untitled item, *Puck*, December 24, 1902, p. 2.

3. Tim Brown, *Change by Design: How Design Thinking Transforms Organizations and Inspires Innovation* (New York: HarperCollins, 2009), 230.

4. Tom Peters, *Thriving on Chaos* (New York: Harper Perennial, 1987), 146.

5. Scott Belsky, *Making Ideas Happen* (London: Portfolio, 2010), 91.

6. French Strother, "The Modern Profession of Inventing," *World's Work and Play* 6, no. 32 (July 1905): 186.

CONCLUSION

1. Rick Tetzeli, "Tim Cook on Apple's Future: Everything Can Change Except Values," *Fast Company*, March 18, 2015, https://www.fastcompany.com/3042435/steves-legacy-tim-looks-ahead.

2. Steve Dickson, "Oprah and Reese Witherspoon Invest in Spanx at $1.2 Billion Valuation," *Bloomberg*, November 18, 2021, https://www.bloomberg.com/news/articles/2021-11-18/oprah-witherspoon-invest-in-spanx-at-1-2-billion-valuation.

3. Clare O'Connor, "How Sara Blakely of Spanx Turned $5,000 into $1 billion," *Forbes*, March 14, 2012, https://www.forbes.com/global/2012/0326/billionaires-12-feature-united-states-spanx-sara-blakely-american-booty.html?sh=17ac13bd7ea0.

4. Ian Goldin and Chris Kutarna, *Age of Discovery: Navigating the Risks and Rewards of Our New Renaissance*, rev. ed. (New York: Bloomsbury Business, 2017), 239.

5. Qatar Foundation, "Story of Hind Hobeika," accessed July 13, 2023, https://www.starsofscience.com/alumni/hind-hobeika.

6. Jonah Comstock, "Swimtech Crowdfunding Sensation Instabeat Resurfaces with New, Mature Offering," *MobiHealthNews*, September 12, 2019, https://www.mobihealthnews.com/news/north-america/swimtech-crowdfunding-sensation-instabeat-resurfaces-new-mature-offering.

7. See her Indiegogo page, at https://www.indiegogo.com/projects/instabeat#/.

8. Tamara Pupic, "In the Pursuit of Greatness: Instabeat Founder Hind Hobeika," *Entrepreneur*, November 19, 2019, https://www.entrepreneur.com/en-ae/starting-a-business/in-the-pursuit-of-greatness-instabeat-founder-hind-hobeika/342524.

9. Max Roser, "The Brief History of Artificial Intelligence: The World Has Changed Fast—What Might Be Next?," *Our World in Data*, December 6, 2022, https://ourworldindata.org/brief-history-of-ai.

10. Ben Parker, "3D Printing Offers New Hope for War-Wounded," *New Humanitarian*, August 29, 2018, https://www.thenewhumanitarian.org/2018/08/29/3d-printing-offers-new-hope-war-wounded.

11. Viktor Frankl, *The Will to Meaning* (New York: Meridian/Penguin Books, 1991), 55.

12. James Clear, *Atomic Habits: Tiny Changes, Remarkable Results* (New York: Avery, 2018), 38.

ABOUT THE AUTHORS

Dan McClure has worked for more than forty years to empower bold innovators: global organizations facing threats of obsolescence, pioneering businesses in fast-changing markets, and passionate activists tackling hard challenges like climate change and humanitarian crisis response. He has been a hands-on thought leader, developing new tools and practices that make it possible for innovators to run into burning buildings looking for exceptional opportunities. His innovation methodologies and agile enterprise design have been applied across diverse fields including international aid, government, finance, retail, media, education, energy, and health.

Jennifer Wilde is an accomplished innovator working on the global stage. She built an international network of innovation labs, supported innovators from idea to scale, and shaped multimillion-dollar innovation programs. With more than fifteen years of experience in driving change in challenging, volatile contexts, Jennifer has a uniquely practical perspective on what it takes to identify, execute, and succeed with game-changing ideas.